LINCOLN &
THE POLITICS
OF SLAVERY

LINCOLN & THE POLITICS OF SLAVERY

By John S. Wright
University of Nevada Press **1970**
Reno, Nevada

University of Nevada Press, Reno, Nevada □ © 1970 by the University of Nevada Press □ Library of Congress Catalog Card Number 74-113811 □ Printed in the United States of America □ Designed by Ken Webster □ OSBN 87417-027-3

To L.W.W.

If the American experience in democratic, political processes has had a special and peculiar quality, it has been a tendency to state questions and issues in terms of right and wrong—to endow them with a moral quality. Right has ever been beleaguered by the forces of evil: Demon Rum, the Slavocracy, International Communism, Wall Street, even Do-gooders. Every movement for change has been a crusade. It is an interesting fact that the "Battle Hymn of the Republic" has served such diverse causes as abolitionism, progressivism, and Goldwaterism.

PREFACE

It is quite clear that to a large extent this has been an effective tactic, a way of stating an issue so that it will fire the zeal of political workers and voters. A splendid example of this occurred in the election of 1896 when the issues were economic but when William Jennings Bryan's moral outrage at the economic disadvantages under which some segments of the American society operated was expressed in terms of the highly moralistic concept of the "honest" dollar. Even in our relations with foreign nations, so critics have complained, the power and other "real" elements of the situation have been obscured by our tendency to express our ideas about these relationships in "legalistic-moralistic" terms.

Be that as it may, we have nevertheless had our share of genuine moral crusades in American politics—efforts to use the law of the state and/or nation to prevent immoral or wrong behavior on the part of individuals and institutions. In all but one of the permanently successful cases these crusades have captured the citadels of resistance—the state legislatures—one at a time, until many of the new moral standards have been incorporated into the laws of every state.

The political process in these cases, as well as in the earlier stages of the anti-slavery movement and the temperance crusade, was diffused in time and place by this state-by-state approach. For example, the feeling that dueling was morally wrong became national in scope but the legislatures responded to that feeling at different times over an extended generation. Since this was a matter constitutionally reserved for the states, the great national parties had nothing to do with the anti-dueling sentiment and it did not become a national party issue. This is the standard pattern for the functioning of a moral issue in politics under our federal system.

Two moral crusades have overleapt the constitutional and traditional bounds that reserved these matters to the states. In the cases of the anti-slavery movement (and by extension, the fight for Negro equality) and the prohibition movement, the crusaders sought to spill over the original boundaries of the constitution in order to place the power to legislate on these subjects in the hands of Congress when the state-by-state process seemed too slow or too unpromising. While both succeeded ultimately (temporarily in the case of the prohibition movement), three sharp distinctions may be drawn between the political aspects of the anti-slavery and the prohibition movements. The Eighteenth Amendment and the Volstead Act were achieved at the national level in the same manner as most moral reforms had been accomplished by the states—by pressures on the major parties whose main business was something else. On the other hand, anti-slavery reform was the main impulse that generated the Republican party. Secondly, the resistance to prohibition was scattered throughout the nation while the opposition to emancipation was regional. Finally, the anti-slavery reform led to a complete breakdown of the national political structure and to the Civil War.

The best documented career of a person at the heart of both the politics and the moral aspect of this unique experience in American political history is that of Abraham Lincoln. The following is an effort to glean—and glean is precisely the word for it—some insights into the interaction of a moral issue and the political process. The gleaning, of course, is from aspects of Lincoln's career: the kind of politician he was; the development of his understanding of the moral issue of slavery and its meshing with politics; and his politicianship in the movement that finally wedded a moral issue to a political party.

I am grateful to a number of friends upon whose knowledge and talents I have freely drawn at all stages of the progress of this manuscript. The kindnesses of librarians have been many, especially at the Library of Congress, the Illinois Historical Library, the libraries of the University of Chicago, the University of Illinois, the Illinois History Survey, the University of Nevada at Las Vegas, and the Chicago Historical Society. I am deeply in their debt.

John S. Wright
Las Vegas, Nevada
February, 1970

CONTENTS

1832 Lincoln was defeated for a seat in the Illinois legislature in his first run for public office. The parties—Whig and Democrat—were just jelling in this year in which Andrew Jackson, Democrat, was re-elected to the presidency, and the renewal of the charter of the Bank of the United States (the "monster" according to Jackson) was the most specific issue.

1834 Lincoln was elected to the lower house of the Illinois legislature to take his place among the Whig minority. State issues were improvement of the navigation of rivers, railroads, canals, and moving the state capital to Springfield.

1836 At the peak of a speculative land boom, Martin Van Buren, Jackson's hand-picked choice, was elected President. Lincoln was re-elected to the legislature and admitted to the practice of law.

1838 Lincoln was elected to the legislature again. The Panic of 1837 had hit the new states very hard for the immigration upon which they relied to help pay for internal improvements did not come. Banks failed.

1840 A nation prone to blame its presidents for depressions rejected Democrat Van Buren's bid for a second term. His Independent Treasury scheme was particularly assailed. The Whigs won the White House for an old Indian fighter and Western politician—William Henry Harrison—who failed to survive its rigors more than a month. John Tyler, the first vice-president to assume the presidential chair, believed in few of the Whig principles. The national program of the Whig party—a protective tariff, internal improvements at federal expense, and a new United States Bank—was not enacted into law in the main. The Liberty party, the political organization of the abolitionists who were not "above" politics,

appeared on the ballot for the first time and received a few votes. Lincoln was re-elected to the legislature.

1842 Lincoln was married. He did not run for any office.

1844 The issues between the national parties took a turn in the direction of expansion as the Democrats ran a dark horse candidate, James K. Polk, on the pledge to extend American sovereignty to all of Oregon and to Texas which had won its independence of Mexico in 1836. Whig Henry Clay came close to winning. The Northeastern section of the country was not enthusiastic for expansion and definitely was opposed to bringing into the Union the vast territory of Texas where slavery existed. Clay lost crucial New York by fewer votes than were cast for the Liberty party in that state. Texas was annexed before the Polk administration entered office in 1845. Lincoln sought the Whig nomination for Congress but failed to secure it.

1846 Lincoln was elected to Congress. War with Mexico had begun in May. The question as to whether the territories to be acquired from Mexico would be free or slave was raised by the Wilmot Proviso.

1848 The Wilmot Proviso proved to be such a divisive issue in the Thirtieth Congress of which Lincoln was a member that the Van Buren (anti-Polk) wing of the Democratic party, some antislavery Whigs, and the Liberty party combined into the Free Soil party which contested this one national election effectively. Congressman Abraham Lincoln worked for the nomination and election of war hero and slave owner Zachary Taylor, Whig. Taylor was sent to the White House by the American electorate. Lincoln was not a candidate for re-election to Congress.

1850 The issue of slavery in the territories reached a crisis in this year. Disunion was threatened before a compromise was passed by Congress. Lincoln resumed his law practice and handled some patronage matters.

1852 In an election in which the Whigs and Democrats contended over which was the more loyal to the Compromise of 1850, the former suffered a humiliating defeat. The Democrat, Franklin Pierce, was elected over General Winfield Scott, Whig.

1854 The Kansas-Nebraska Bill was debated and passed in Congress. Lincoln took an active part in the fall campaign against congressmen who had voted for the measure which had opened those territories to slavery. Lincoln's Peoria speech was made in support of a Whig candidate for Congress. The Democratic majority in the House of Representatives was overturned by Northern reaction against the bill. Fusion of diverse elements opposed to the Nebraska Bill not only defeated the Democrats but began to erode the Whig party. The Know-Nothing lodges with their anti-foreign and anti-Catholic bias appeared on the scene. Lincoln was elected to the legislature but promptly resigned. He began to campaign actively for the Senate seat held by Democrat James Shields.

1855 Lincoln failed to win the Senate seat in a legislature which was splintered politically—no longer Whig and Democrat.

1856 Sectional strife was intensified by violence in Kansas to which the decision as to slavery or no slavery had been transferred by the Kansas-Nebraska Act. The physical beating of Senator Sumner by a South Carolina congressman in the Senate Chamber augmented the trend. Democrat James Buchanan won the presidency over John C. Frémont, Republican, and Millard Fillmore, American party candidate. The Republican party had been organized in Illinois with Lincoln playing a leading role. Although Buchanan carried the state, the Republicans won the state offices.

1857 The Dred Scott decision at the beginning, and the Lecompton Constitution for Kansas at the end of the year, contributed to an increasingly sectional view of politics being taken by the American people.

1858 Abraham Lincoln, aided by the Buchanan administration Douglas had defied over the Lecompton Constitution, attempted to win the seat of the senior Senator from Illinois and came close to doing so. Lincoln began his campaign with the famous House Divided speech and then engaged in a series of debates with Douglas which attracted the attention of the country.

POLITICAL CALENDAR

1859 John Brown and followers attempted to establish a republic for escaped slaves at Harper's Ferry, Virginia. Lincoln addressed large groups of Republicans in several states. He also spoke at the Cooper Union in New York City.

1860 The Democratic party split over the question of a federal slave code for the territories. Douglas was nominated by one faction, Breckinridge, by the other. Lincoln's availability won the Republican nomination for him at Chicago. Bell and Everett were nominated by those who appealed to the unity of the past. Lincoln was elected President of the United States. South Carolina seceded.

The Whig Politician

Surrounding Abraham Lincoln's tomb in the Oak Ridge Cemetery in Springfield, Illinois, are the deep-shaded, moss-flecked monuments of many of Lincoln's contemporaries, the politicians and business people of Lincoln's generation. The observer is tempted to muse upon fate as he notes that the memorials of Lincoln's fellow lawyers and fellow politicians serve as mere backdrops to the grave of the martyred President in the minds of most who come here. Indeed, the memory **CHAPTER 1** of Lincoln's Springfield contemporaries lives in proportion to the degree to which their paths crossed his. What element of greatness or what chance of fortune set Lincoln apart from those beside whom he stood for most of his life as no more than an equal?

This question has been asked and answered in many (including some very odd) ways, but all fair-minded persons must agree that, whatever the nuances of character and mysteries of fate that enter the story, political achievement was the gross measure of the distance between the towering obelisk and the squat slabs of granite. Further, few successful careers in American politics have been identified so exclusively with one political question, in this case, slavery. If chance had struck Lincoln down before his involvement in the slavery issue, there is little doubt that his marker would now be indistinguishable from scores of other memorials in the beautiful old cemetery.

When the Kansas-Nebraska Bill was passed and Abraham Lincoln was challenged to rethink the slavery issue in politics, twenty-two years of political experience lay behind him, eleven seasons of campaigning, four terms of office in the state legislature, and one in Congress. He was an established political figure, mature, experienced in many ways, fixed in habits of political thought and activity, and adamantine in political character. The purpose of this chapter is to determine the political equipment with which Lincoln met the issue of the age—slavery—and to determine what kind of politician he was.

Had Lincoln's political career been terminated in 1854, it would have remained circumscribed by his association with the Whig party. Lincoln had identified himself with that crystallizing party when he had been elected to the state legislature in 1834. Twenty years later, when the old political order was crumbling in 1855, he still thought of himself as a Whig.[1] There is no record of Lincoln supporting a candidate of another party or of bolting the Whig party during these two decades of intimate association with it.

Why Abraham Lincoln, deeply in debt because of the failure of his country store and so poor that he had to borrow money to clothe himself decently for the legislative session, became a Whig, is one of the mysteries of his political career. The Whig party was the party which both nationally and in Illinois was the party of banks, business men, and the more "respectable" citizenry. The great majority of the people of southern origin, that vast, unsettled population which pioneered Illinois and much of the Northwest and Southwest, however, was Jacksonian. It adhered to the Democratic party as did most of Lincoln's New Salem neighbors and friends. Lincoln, merchant but briefly and unsuccessfully, may have identified himself with the "better element" of merchants, bankers, and real estate speculators which was Whig.

The Kentucky Whigs of the Prairie State were a contrast to most of Lincoln's neighbors at New Salem, but newly arrived with little and most soon to depart with little more. Followers of

Henry Clay, these men who brought their attachments and prejudices from the tense political atmosphere of Kentucky were the more prosperous farmers, the lawyers, the men of substance who had come to Illinois with means or prospects because of education or connections and meant to stay, to build up the country, to get ahead. Lincoln's later connection with men of this stripe may indicate that even at New Salem he had hitched the cart of his ambition to these men and their station in life.

Or was it his reading of strongly partisan newspapers at his all too quiet store and post office that fostered his Whig inclination? Did his Whig connection originate in some obscure personal relationship with some fellow citizen of new Salem or with John T. Stuart of Springfield? Or could it have been that the personal qualities of the headstrong, impulsive "King Andrew" Jackson repelled Lincoln because these were the opposite of Lincoln's own characteristics?[2]

There are no certain answers to these questions but we can be positive that Lincoln was a "good" Whig, with no doubts and no reservations recorded for posterity. He did not shape party doctrine: he received it ready-made. He supported all the principles of the national party and there were few Whig principles for state politics. Governor Thomas Ford, a Democrat who served his state ably in the critical years, 1842–46, commented that:

> By means of the convention system, and many exciting contests, the two parties of whigs and democrats were thoroughly organized and disciplined by the year 1840. No regular army could have excelled them in discipline. They were organized upon the principles of national politics only, and not in any degree upon those of the State.[3]

In four particulars, however, Lincoln's attitudes ran counter to current Whig prejudices. The typical "decided, sanguine" Whig leader was characterized by Democrat Ford as "an old federalist; he has no confidence in the people for self-government; he is in favor of a property qualification for electors. . . ." Lincoln, on the other hand, in a statement published in the Whig paper of Springfield to announce his candidacy for re-election to the state legislature in 1836, stated "I go for all sharing the privileges of government, who assist in bearing its burdens. Consequently I go for admitting all whites to the right of suffrage, who pay taxes or bear arms, (by no means excluding females.)"[4] At no point in the career out of which came the phrase "government of the people, by the people and for the people" was there any indication of the old Federalist viewpoint about the suffrage.

Secondly, while his party balked at accepting the new convention system of nomination in principle, Lincoln and the Springfield "junta" pressed for conventions to prevent division of the Whig vote.[5] The convention system had been introduced into the state by the Democrats, and Stephen A. Douglas had pushed for the fullest organization of the state by nomination conventions. Its effectiveness in mobilizing for campaigns recommended it to the more responsible Whig leaders who saw no reason to handicap themselves by splitting the often meagre Whig vote among any number of candidates who might happen to have the urge to run.

In the third place, the Whigs criticized the rotation-in-office dogma of the Jacksonians. But Lincoln's principle of "turn about is fair play," urged upon the Whigs in his quest for the nomination for representative in Congress, was scarcely distinguishable from the condemned Democratic rule.[6]

The Whigs had something of a bias against immigrants. On the other hand, the Democratic party was adept at wooing and winning the foreign-born voters. The Whigs, rather than compete for these voters by resorting to the methods used by the Democrats to attract the Irish and Germans to their camp, generally sponsored ways of delaying the granting of citizenship to immigrants. Lincoln and some of his friends took the opposite tack and obtained some favorable results. Lincoln succeeded in winning the support of a small German group in Cass County through his friendship with Francis Arenz who enjoyed a trip to his native land as a reward for his services to the party.[7] Lincoln's later career was to reveal a strong distaste for the nativist bias of his party.

In each case—with the exception of rotation in office, which died an early death at the hands of politicians of both parties who wanted to be re-elected—Lincoln aligned himself with the future and with the politically expedient viewpoint. If the Whig party had not modernized itself and adapted itself organizationally to fit the needs of Illinois politics, life in the Whig ranks would have been even more frustrating than it was.

Lincoln's removal from New Salem to Springfield and the shift of the state capitol from Vandalia to Springfield placed the young lawyer at the very center of Whig activity. The Sangamon country was the heart of Illinois Whiggery and formed part of the one congressional district which consistently elected Whigs to Congress. The state capitol, one of the land offices, and the courts drew the lawyers and politicians (usually one and the same) to Springfield. In both parties, those less in touch with things at Springfield and excluded from the inner circles of party activity charged a secret and sinister domination of the young state's political life by a Democratic "clique" and a Whig "junta." In any event, Lincoln was from the beginning an insider in Whig politics.

Political friendships were the cornerstone of the edifice of political influence in Lincoln's Whig days. Whig lawyers of the circuits in which Lincoln practiced and Whig Legislators with whom he rubbed elbows and exchanged favors formed a network of loyal and influential supporters who were to contribute much to the success of Lincoln's Republican campaigns. While the record shows that some of them, in the late 1850's, drifted over to the Democratic side because they feared the breakup of the Union, in no case was the rift personal. Lincoln was aware that much of his strength lay in these ties. In 1855 when the Whig party was collapsing and many of his friends toyed with the Know-Nothing movement, Lincoln knew that he could not make a political move until their illusions about that political alternative had been shattered.[8] Without these men he counted for little.

Lincoln's personal and political integrity was not a mere legend. The absence of acrimonious personal disputes with which the records of so many of his contemporaries abound indicates that those with whom he came in contact did not question the honesty of Lincoln's motives. The choice of Lincoln and B. S. Edwards to scrutinize certain data to exonerate a former U.S. Marshal of charges of partisan misuse of his office bespeaks a reputation for fairness for both men. On another occasion Lincoln served as one of the arbitrators appointed to determine the status of the accounts of his close political friend, A. G. Henry. Moreover, only a man with a remarkable reputation for objectivity and integrity could have escaped unscathed from the situation that developed in 1860 when Lincoln was a coy presidential aspirant. Each of the three candidates for the Republican gubernatorial nomination had claim to Lincoln's support. Lincoln had to write two public letters in refutation of false charges brought against two of the candidates by over-enthusiastic supporters of their rivals. In spite of this, Lincoln retained the loyalty of all three candidates.[9]

One of the prime requisites for political leadership was oratorical ability. This Lincoln developed fairly early in his career. In 1840 he observed that E. D. Baker and he, "whom they supposed necessary to make stump speeches," had been nominated for the legislature again. Stump speaking he did! As a Harrison elector, (electors being selected at that time for their campaigning abilities) Lincoln spoke in Jacksonville and Tremont and probably in several places on his home judicial circuit. But he also engaged in a broad swing through southern Illinois, the more Democratic and longer settled part of the state. This was a missionary effort for which the best oratorical talent of the party was enlisted.[10] The "speakings" on the judicial circuit were usual during campaigns and took the form of Whig lawyers debating Democratic lawyers in the evening after court business was finished. The southern tour was something out of the ordinary and meant a special effort and some pecuniary sacrifice for the speaker.

Illinois audiences would listen "at length" and Illinois orators harangued to taste—two hours being the usual length of one speech. Especially in the rural areas speeches were the main source of political information and were largely attended. The present-day politician rarely has the opportunity to make converts in personal appearances because the Democratic speaker attracts a Democratic audience, and a Democrat is a rarity at a Republican meeting. In Lincoln's experience, on the contrary, one's audience might well be hostile. This was probably the case when the crowds in the counties on the Ohio River and in the interior of Egypt (southern Illinois) came to hear their local heroes such as John McClernand "demolish" the opposition. One had to be sure of his facts and logical in his interpretation of them for he was sure to be answered, either that day or the next, and before much the same audience. It is obvious from his standing as a stump speaker that Lincoln had mastered the techniques of this sort of face-to-face encounter. In every subsequent presidential campaign during the life of the Whig party Lincoln presented its case to thousands of his fellow citizens from the speaker's platform.

Something of Lincoln's character is revealed by the fact that his oratory avoided one of the common pitfalls of this kind of presentation, the unfortunate tendency to be personal and vindictive. Only twice did Lincoln overstep his self-imposed bounds in this respect. An attack on James Shields (later General and Senator Shields) by means of anonymous, satirical letters brought the men to the verge of an illegal duel. The second instance occurred in the national House of Representatives when Lincoln impishly compared the military experience of General Cass, the Democratic nominee for the presidency, with his own in the Blackhawk War.[11] In neither case was the intent malicious. Each was an instance of Lincoln's good-humored sense of the ridiculous getting out of hand.

The tendency to emphasize the Lincoln-Douglas rivalry has all but obscured an important fact in Lincoln's political background as a Whig. Illinois was the "Banner State" of the Democracy: its electoral vote was never cast for a Whig. Furthermore no Whig candidate for the governorship was elected. Lincoln's party could count on winning only the Springfield congressional district, making a seat in Congress the highest public office to which a Whig might reasonably aspire. Whigs also dominated the county offices in some areas, especially around Springfield. But in the state as a whole failure was pretty much a foregone conclusion so that the party sometimes had trouble in finding someone to accept the dubious honor of running for state office.

The nature of the leadership of the two parties reflected the dominant role of the Democrats and the minority role of the Whigs. Stephen A. Douglas had a great political future in part because he led the Democratic party in a Democratic and rapidly growing state and section. The minor politicians and hopeful postmasters were attracted to his coattails because his prospects were their prospects.[12] But this was not without its drawbacks as we shall see.

The role of the leader (actually leaders) among the Whigs was quite different. His standing in the party depended largely on his ability to contribute to the party, his willingness to make sacrifices for the party. The most that realistic Whigs could hope for (most politicians of minority parties seem not to be realistic and expect miracles) was that a vigorous state campaign would help them win a few more local offices and assembly seats. The relationship of the local Democratic politician to Douglas involved both gratitude for past favors and expectations of favors to be received as Douglas ascended the political ladder. The relationship of the local Whig politician to Lincoln involved gratitude but no reasonable expectations unless the miracle of a Whig presidency should come to pass.

One objective of the political process is to fill various political offices. Obviously, a political education is not complete without some experience of the responsibilities of office. Lincoln served in the lower house of the Illinois General Assembly for four terms. His partisan leadership qualities were recognized by his fellow Whigs who made him their minority leader. He proved a

8

strong champion of the local interests of his district. He had a hand in securing for it the state capital, the first railway built in the state, and a promise to improve the navigation of the San-gamon River. As legislator, Lincoln's experience with patronage was nil but federal offices were opened to the Whigs in the Har-rison administration and Lincoln used his influence to secure them for friends.[13]

So much for Lincoln's political education.

What of Lincoln's credentials as an opponent of slavery? He said of himself that he was "naturally anti-slavery. If slavery is not wrong, nothing is wrong. I cannot remember when I did not so think and feel."[14] This bit of autobiography was bared to a group of Kentucky Unionists *opposed* to enlisting Negroes into the Union army; it was not subtle propaganda to coax support from Radical Republicans, and thus it should be accepted as a reasonably accurate definition of Lincoln's anti-slavery position.

It must be clear that in the course of Lincoln's public life the degree of dislike of slavery ranged all the way from the vehe-mence of the most radical Garrisonians to the modest wish that the slaves had never been imported into this country in the first place. Only a lack of historical perspective could lead one to consider Lincoln's attitude to slavery ambivalent because in 1837 he included in his formal protest against a "proslavery" resolu-tion before the legislature of Illinois a statement indicating dis-approval of abolitionism.[15] The old biographers have properly emphasized that only one other legislator was prepared to go as far as Lincoln did at this time in voicing a protest against slavery at all. For it must be remembered that in 1837 the voters of Illinois were still largely settlers who had come from the South. Mixing with like-minded persons in the Colonization Society and cheering on the emancipationists in Kentucky was about as far as his central Illinois constituency would permit a man to go and remain in politics. While the Colonization Society's achievement in freeing slaves and relocating them in Africa was puny and the effort to bring about gradual emancipation in Kentucky was a failure, both stemmed from a belief that slavery was a wrong, an idea receding under attack in the South.

Lincoln's bill (offered in Congress in 1849) to abolish slavery in the District of Columbia has been questioned on the grounds that it was hedged about with conditions.[16] The significance does not lie in the conditions but in the fact that a Whig congressman from a district with but a handful of abolitionist votes should have submitted a bill for that purpose at all. By so doing he placed himself in the dangerous company of Joshua Giddings; yet, so far as can be determined, Lincoln's Kentucky-born constituents did not object to this as many of them did to his anti-patriotic stand on the Mexican War. It may be assumed that they could support a form of emancipation that would be gradual, compensated, and acceptable to the majority of the people. This was as far as they would go on the anti-slavery issue.

It is unnecessary to accept his cousin's recollection in 1865 that Lincoln was suddenly converted to hatred of slavery while still a youth.[17] Sudden conversions were typical of the abolitionist way but out of character for the Lincoln we know. The Lincoln his generation knew was consistently anti-slavery within the bounds that made it not the only question before the public nor even the most important. When Lincoln finally decided that slavery was the most important question, he acted effectively on it. But by that time the issue had increased in importance for his neighbors, too. That is what made it possible for Lincoln to act effectively.

The threat to extend slavery created political crises of the first magnitude on three occasions: the Missouri crisis in 1819–20; the crisis engendered by the Wilmot Proviso in 1846–50; and the final, longer crisis, triggered by the Nebraska Bill, which culminated in the Civil War. Abraham Lincoln's political experience embraced the latter two of these crises. A comparison of the roles he played in each of these suggests something of the evolution of his personal reaction to the deepening rift between the sections and even more about the shaping of his political stance vis-à-vis the moral issue of slavery.

The highest political office attained by Lincoln before he became President was that of Representative in the Thirtieth Congress. This Congress was confronted with the problem of slavery in several forms but the Wilmot Proviso overshadowed all of the others. The Proviso was an amendment tacked onto an appropriation of two million dollars voted by the House of Representatives (but not passed by the Senate and therefore not enacted into law) to be used by the President in concluding a peace with Mexico. This "mischievous & foolish amendment" as President Polk called it provided that any territory to be acquired from Mexico (and expectations in this matter were pretty extensive) should be free. It was a Northwest Ordinance provision for the new territory.

Whatever the disputed motives of David Wilmot of Pennsylvania, whose claim to fame rests on the attachment of his name to this bit of defeated legislation, the Proviso obtained immense popular as well as political support in the North. Whigs supported it, of course. New York Barnburners, Democrats still resentful of the shelving of Martin Van Buren in favor of dark horse James K. Polk by the Baltimore convention, joined representatives disappointed by the tariff reduction in support of it. Northwestern Democrats had suffered a double disenchantment with Polk. He had encouraged them (they believed) to rage for all of Oregon, having accepted the party slogan "Fifty-four forty or fight" quite literally. The Oregon issue had been compromised with Great Britain and some of the politicians felt that as a result they had been compromised with their constituencies. Polk had vetoed the annual River and Harbor Appropriation (pork barrel) Bill which the Lakes region politicians had been able to load conspicuously with items for their burgeoning area. Mingled with the purely moral opposition to the spread of slavery was a dross of political and sectional resentment.

The significance of the Wilmot Proviso lay in two facts. In the first place, it assimilated all northern grievances and resentments to itself, arraying North against South in spite of the fact that the basic issue of territorial expansion by all rules of previous experience should have divided the country into a pro-expansion West and an anti-expansion East. In the second place, and more important for our analysis, it provided a way in which the slavery question could become a most formidable political issue.

Up to now the abolitionists had been hamstrung because in making slavery a moral issue they found themselves blocked by the belief that the newly sacrosanct Constitution delegated jurisdiction over moral issues to the states. Thus the federal system posed a cruel dilemma: legislation on moral issues appeared to be reserved for the states, but the states that had slaves to be liberated seemed unwilling and unlikely to free them. The northern portion of the Union in which abolitionist sentiment was greatest was impotent to achieve the desired moral result except by a constitutional revolution which would place slavery on a national rather than a state level. Indeed, the immediate emancipation of slaves as suggested by the more radical abolitionists involved so direct an assault on the federal system as well as on property and the *status quo* that the term "abolitionist" acquired a connotation of the subversive about it.

The Wilmot Proviso, however, although perhaps not so intended, provided a way in which the most impeccable constitutionalist could enter the fray against the evil of slavery at the urging of his still, small voice. The prohibition of slavery in the territories, existing and potential, was perfectly in harmony with the Constitution as then understood, supported by the tradition of the Northwest Ordinance and the Missouri Compromise restriction. It had the important additional advantage of being popularized in defensive terms, i.e., defense against the spread of slavery. It would stop the expansion of an evil but it did not attack the citadels of the evil—the states, property, or the Constitution. However, one could not argue against the *spread* of an evil without proving or assuming that the condition to be spread was evil. Thus, the naked question of slavery bowed out as an unsuccessful political formula to be replaced by another in which the whole gamut of the moral argument against slavery might be spanned quite logically but entirely in a defensive, conservative, constitutional way.[18]

Neither the Mexican War nor the Wilmot Proviso played any part in Lincoln's election to Congress in 1846. His nomination, secured with some difficulty because one of his predecessors was anxious to return to Washington, came to Lincoln as a deserving Whig whose qualifications for the post were measured in terms of service to the party. The Mexican War was not an issue in the district at this time for Illinois was enthusiastic for expansion and for the war. The incumbent Whig congressman, E. D. Baker, pressed the President for a commission as a route to that military glory he so aggressively sought and found at Ball's Bluff. Colonel John J. Hardin, the disappointed rival for the nomination won by Lincoln, led one of the Illinois regiments under General Zachary Taylor and found death on the battlefield. Lincoln, among others, made "warm, thrilling, effective" speeches at Springfield at the conclusion of which "seventy men gave in their names for the campaign against Mexico."[19]

The Wilmot Proviso was not a national issue when Abraham Lincoln was elected on August 3, 1846, in early voting Illinois. It *was* a factor in later voting states. The one scant report of a Lincoln speech indicates that he employed the classic Whig doctrines against his Methodist Circuit Rider opponent, Peter Cartwright, and "closed with some general observations about the Mexican War, annexation of Texas, and the Oregon question."[20] Lincoln won by an increased majority in the district.

The issue of the territorial expansion of slavery had been raised by the negotiations for the annexation of Texas. On this point we have what seem to have been Lincoln's private views on the matter. Lincoln was writing to Williamson Durley of Putnam County, one of the abolitionists arriving in that section of the northern part of Lincoln's congressional district in sufficient numbers to warrant some concern. Two matters were elucidated, an opinion about political means and moral ends and a judgment of the importance of the slavery extension issue. Here are the relevant excerpts:[21]

> If the whig abolitionists of New York had voted with us last fall, Mr. Clay would now be president, whig principles in the ascendent, and Texas not annexed; whereas by the division, all that either had at stake in the contest, was lost. And, indeed, it was extremely probable, beforehand, that such would be the result. As I always understood, the Liberty-men deprecated the annexation of Texas extremely; and, this being so, why they should refuse to so cast their votes as to prevent it, even to me, seemed wonderful.
>
> I perhaps ought to say that individually I never was much interested in the Texas question. I never could see much good to come of annexation; inasmuch, as they were already a free republican people on our own model; on the other hand, I never could very clearly see how the annexation would augment the evil of slavery. It always seemed to me that slaves would be taken there in about equal numbers, with or without annexation. And if more *were* taken because of annexation, still there would be just so many the fewer left, where they were taken from. It is possibly true, to some extent, that with annexation, some slaves may be sent to Texas and continued in slavery, that otherwise might have been liberated. To whatever extent this may be true, I think annexation an evil. I hold it to be a paramount duty of us in the free states, due to the Union of the states, and perhaps to liberty itself (paradox though it may seem) to let the slavery of the other states alone; while, on the other hand, I hold it to be equally clear, that we should never knowingly lend ourselves directly or indirectly, to prevent that slavery from dying a natural death—to find new places for it to live in, when it can no longer exist in the old.

In the sixteen months between the election and the time Lincoln claimed his seat in Congress, events pushed new political issues and new aspects of old issues to the fore. The Mexican

War moved along toward victory but more slowly than had been expected. Whig criticism of the origin of the war was rising. The Wilmot Proviso was becoming crucial. The clash of Mississippi-Ohio River interests with Great Lakes interests in the matter of internal improvements was intensified by two conventions with strong political overtones. The older river system was represented at the earlier Memphis convention at which John C. Calhoun sought to strengthen the damaged South-West political alliance.[22]

The counterblast to the Memphis convention was a "gigantic" meeting at Chicago in which New York and Boston interests were especially actively represented. "Harbor" (also Wilmot Proviso) Democrats of the area participated as well but the proceedings, after two Polk vetoes of river-harbor bills, had a strong Whig flavor. Lincoln was one of the lesser Whig figures in attendance. The convention passed a series of resolutions asserting congressional power and obligation to provide for river and harbor improvement and protesting against the discrimination against this form of federal expenditure.[23]

On his return to Springfield, Lincoln fell in with a journalist from the East who looked down his nose at the droll Westerners as they travelled to Springfield together. The journalist penned a caricature of Lincoln:

> We are now in the district represented by our Whig Congressman, and he knew, or appeared to know, everybody we met, the name of the tenant of every farm-house, and the owner of every plat of ground. Such a shaking of hands—such a how-d'ye-do—such a greeting of different kins, as we saw, was never seen before; it seemed as if he knew everything, and had a kind word, a smile and a bow for every body on the road. . . .[24]

1. Roy P. Basler (ed.), *The Collected Works of Abraham Lincoln* (New Brunswick: Rutgers University Press, 1953), II, 320–23, Springfield, Aug. 24, 1855, Joshua F. Speed. This invaluable collection will be referred to hereinafter as *Collected Works*.

2. I am indebted to Paul M. Angle for this very plausible suggestion. Herndon's attempt to trace the origin of Lincoln's Whiggism produced no satisfactory result. In Indiana, which Lincoln left before attaining voting age, it was remembered that he had once been a Democrat but changed. His cousin, John

Hanks, remembered to the contrary that in 1831 Lincoln was a Whig and that he had always been a "Whig; so was his father before him." Perhaps the most that is warranted by these recollections extending back to a time when the term "Whig" was not yet used, is that Lincoln sometimes differed from his Jacksonian friends on political questions and was a Whig as soon as that party had emerged. See Emmanuel Hertz, *The Hidden Lincoln* (New York: Blue Ribbon Books, 1940), pp. 348 and 356.

3. Thomas Ford, *A History of Illinois* (Chicago: S. C. Griggs & Co., 1854), p. 207.

4. *Ibid.*, p. 290; *Collected Works*, I, 48.

5. *Ibid.*, pp. 307–8.

6. *Ibid.*, pp. 352–3.

7. *Ibid.*, II, 103, 337–8.

8. *Ibid.*, pp. 316–7, Springfield, Aug. 11, 1855, Owen Lovejoy.

9. *Ibid.*, I, 183–5, 258–9; see below, pp. 173–175.

10. *Collected Works*, I, 218; Harry E. Pratt, *Lincoln 1840–1846* (Springfield: Abraham Lincoln Association, 1939), pp. 34–43.

11. Benjamin P. Thomas, *Abraham Lincoln, A Biography* (New York: Alfred A. Knopf, 1952), pp. 81–85; see below, p. 37.

12. It is curious that Lincoln's only known observation on this matter came in 1958 when he, not Douglas, was less than three years away from the White House. See *Collected Works*, II, 506.

13. *Collected Works*, I, 221, 233, 253.

14. *Ibid.*, VII, 281, Washington, Apr. 4, 1864, A. G. Hodges.

15. Richard N. Current, *The Lincoln Nobody Knows* (New York: McGraw Hill Book Company, Inc., 1958), pp. 214–236.

16. See below, pp. 32–33.

17. Paul M. Angle (ed.), *Herndon's Life of Lincoln* (New York: Albert and Charles Boni, 1936), p. 64.

18. *Sangamo Journal* (Springfield), Jan. 3, 1847. The editor, a Whig and a supporter of the Proviso, noted with surprise the changed temper of the times with a remark about the *Chicago Democrat* (edited by a Democratic congressman) which, he wrote, "can talk as flippantly about 'slave breeders' as Garrison himself."

19. James K. Polk, *The Diary of James K. Polk*, edited by Milo Milton Quaife. (Chicago: A. C. McClurg & Co., 1910), I, 387–9; *Sangamo Journal*, June 4, 1846.

20. *Collected Works*, I, 381–2, quoting the *Illinois Gazette* (Lacon), July 25, 1846.

21. *Ibid.*, pp. 347–8, Oct. 3, 1845.

22. Charles M. Wiltse, *John C. Calhoun: Sectionalist, 1840–1850* (Indianapolis: The Bobbs-Merrill Company, Inc., 1951), pp. 236, 239, 250–262.

23. See *Weekly Chicago Democrat*, July 6 and 13, 1847; *Galena Gazette*, July 16, 1847; also Robert Fergus (ed.), "Chicago River-and-Harbor Convention," *Chicago Historical Series*, VI, No. 18, *passim*.

24. Harry E. Pratt (ed.), *Illinois as Lincoln Knew It. A Boston Reporter's Record of a Trip in 1847* (Springfield: Abraham Lincoln Association, 1938), pp. 33–4.

The Whig Congressman

At noon on Monday, December 6, 1847, the House of Representatives of the Thirtieth Congress was called to order by the clerk, who then droned through the 227 names of the voting members. The venerable John Quincy Adams, the sixth President of the United States, moved that the House proceed to the election of a Speaker. Robert C. Winthrop, who was chosen, was one of the 117 Whigs who constituted the majority of the House. Abraham Lincoln of Illinois was another.

CHAPTER 2

This House contained some impressive personalities. In Lincoln's party, besides the ex-President, were Alexander Stephens of Georgia, destined to become Vice-President of the Confederacy; Robert Toombs, first Secretary of State of the Confederacy; Joshua Giddings, Lincoln's mess-mate and dean of the abolition Whigs; Caleb B. Smith of Indiana, to have a place in Lincoln's cabinet; and, in the second session, Horace Greeley of the *New York Tribune.* On the Democratic side were Robert Barnwell Rhett of South Carolina, the secessionist; Howell Cobb of Georgia; Albert Gallatin Brown of Mississippi; David Wilmot of Proviso fame; and "Long John" Wentworth of Chicago. The Middle Atlantic and New England Whig delegations were the most numerous: the Connecticut and Massachusetts members were all Whigs. Delaware, Maryland, Kentucky, and North Carolina of the slave states had returned Whig majorities and the Georgia delegation was split evenly. The newer states, however, had resisted the Whig resurgence. Of the representatives of states admitted after 1800, 52 were Democrats and only 22 Whigs. Half of the latter were from Ohio. In the older slave states the division was quite even, 32 Whigs to 35 Democrats.[1]

While in many ways Lincoln felt at home in the House, the situation was unique for him in one way: of the five terms he served in legislative bodies, this was the only one in which his party commanded a majority. Still, the President was James K. Polk, Democrat, the Senate was strongly Democratic, and the Supreme Court, Jacksonian. The first session of the Thirtieth Congress opened as the political pot began to boil for the approaching presidential election. The Whigs of the House had to establish an impression of what their party stood for and against by their votes, their speeches, and their resolutions: they could do so in no other place. They could provide the more easily the documents, the stirring condemnations of "loco foco" blunders, the appeals to the sentiments of the voters back home because they were in the majority. Also, although it seemed quite remote at times, there was a war going on down in Mexico.

The Whigs had arrived in Washington radiating confidence. An overwhelming Democratic majority in the House had been overturned in the midterm election, a hopeful sign for the presidential contest in 1848. The Whigs had military heroes uncommitted on any of the controversial issues—especially Zachary Taylor. On the other hand, the Democratic party, especially in the crucial large states, was divided and dissatisfied with the administration on a number of issues: the tariff, the River and Harbor Bill vetoes, patronage, Oregon, and personalities. Moreover, in the closing moments of the last session the Wilmot Proviso had risen to plague the Democrats.

However, there was some dynamite in the slavery question for the Whigs as well as the Democrats. Lincoln's enthusiasm for Whig prospects must have received a mild shock on his first day in the House when he discovered that, although the Whigs had a clear majority, it required three ballots to elect the Speaker.

If the new congressman did not at first understand the situation, Joshua Giddings, long-time Whig representative from the Western Reserve of Ohio, cleared it up a few days later when he rose to address the House on a question of personal privilege. He read a letter to the *National Whig* which alluded to the failure of the abolition Whigs to support the party candidate for Speaker. He then castigated the editor for the benefit of the House. John G. Palfrey of Massachusetts, with more of a sense of humor than was common among the earnest abolitionists, referred to the same article in this wise:

> A gentleman has spoken of the abolitionists in this House as "execrescences," which should be lopped off. The Whig party, numbering a majority of but five in the House, lop off six of that number as "putrid execrescences!" A laugh. It would hardly leave a very good working majority. The chairman of the committee of Ways and Means would not tell them it was very good financiering.[2]

Control of the House, then, depended on the uncertain support of these Whig-hyphenates.

Lincoln may, however, have consoled himself with the fact that the Democrats were much more fragmented than the Whigs. Of 110 Democrats, no more than 82 votes had been mustered for Linn Boyd of Kentucky for Speaker. A firm little knot of 13 Northern Democrats had supported Robert McClelland of Michigan. Time would reveal that they had a common interest in Great Lakes navigation and a common, fervent adherence to the Wilmot Proviso. There was still another small group that had voted for John McClernand, leading Democrat of southern Illinois.[3]

The annual message of President Polk informed the House of the progress of the Mexican War; of negotiations that had been undertaken to bring it to a close; of financial needs increased by the war; and of a recommendation that the Oregon country be formed into a territory. The message closed with the solemn admonition, "how scrupulously should we avoid all agitating topics which may tend to distract and divide us into contending parties, separated by geographical lines. . . ."[4] If the Wilmot Proviso had made little impression in central Illinois, here was a warning that it loomed large in Washington.

There were substantive matters in which the West had a high stake. Public land was still plentiful in Illinois and the neighboring states. Westerners thought that it should be used to stimulate immigration and growth. Volunteer soldiers, for example, should be (and were) rewarded for their patriotism and sacrifice by gifts of land which the federal government possessed in abundance. Land warrants issued as a sort of soldiers' bonus permitted the selection of public lands out of certain areas of the public domain. They were sold at less than the federal government price of $1.25 per acre by recipients who preferred not to settle on the land in person. This provided a bargain counter sale which Westerners believed would speed up settlement. It was upon an amendment to perfect an act of the previous Congress for such a purpose that Lincoln rose to suggest wider and freer use of the bounty in land.[5]

The West was anxious to bring statehood to the western territories. Several of the Illinois delegation, including Lincoln, participated in the discussion which led to the act that admitted Wisconsin to the Union. Federal donations of land for state educational, eleemosynary, and transportation purposes were eagerly sought, not only for the stated objects of the grants but in order to secure the transfer of land to the states. It was believed that the latter would dispose of the land more rapidly than the federal government, thus promoting more rapid settlement and increased prosperity in the West. The Western Interest was opposed to the doubling of the price of federal lands in the vicinity of canals and other projects for this would slow down settlement. Lincoln spoke his mind on this question.[6]

Of the classic party issues, internal improvements was the one that proved of most service to the Whigs in this Congress. Not only were federally financed public works time-honored Clay doctrine but they also constituted that element of the Whig platform which was most attractive to the transportation-hungry

West. A tug-of-war between the Eastern Whigs and the Southern Democrats for the political affection of the booming Northwest had emerged in the previous Congress. Eastern interests conceded lavish outlays for the Great Lakes while Southern political leaders advocated improvement of the Mississippi-Ohio River system. The Lakes region had won out in the River-Harbor Bill of the previous Congress but doctrinaire Democrat Polk had vetoed it. Each side had whipped up the enthusiasm of its partisans and furnished the regional press with ammunition in support of its contention by means of conventions at Memphis and Chicago.[7]

The Whig House of Representatives was cancelled out by a Democratic Senate. President Polk had vetoed two such bills earlier. Thus, it was perfectly clear that the first session House action on rivers and harbors was designed to produce more Whig votes in the presidential election than buoys in East River and remove more Democratic congressmen than snags from the Mississippi. Indeed, if the bare record of the *Globe* accurately reflects the situation, debate on resolutions that had originated in the Chicago River and Harbor convention, at which Lincoln had been a minor speaker, was more eloquent and copious than debate on the bill before the House.

The President's message exhaustively explaining his reasons for the veto of an earlier River and Harbor Bill opened the floodgates of Whig oratory. On July 5, 1848, just as the presidential campaign was beginning in earnest, a report of the Committee on Commerce containing a series of five resolutions favorable to the Whig view of internal improvements and condemning the "reasons assigned" by President Polk in his veto message was taken off the table. These resolutions of the Committee on Commerce put the Northwestern Democrats who had supported the bill in an awkward predicament, for criticism of the Democratic President and support of internal improvement "principles" were intermixed. The Whigs voted for all of the resolutions while the Lakes region Democrats either skulked or voted "no" on the third and fourth resolutions—all, that is, save John Wentworth of Chicago who went all the way with the Whigs.[8]

The Whigs produced a somewhat more complicated effort to secure still another politically useful veto from President Polk. A rider to the Civil and Diplomatic Appropriation Bill made provision for funds to clear the Savannah River. A veto of the measure would leave the administration without funds for ordinary operating expenses. The rider remained in the bill by virtue of the Speaker's vote but the whole bill was then voted down. The debate was more concerned with the positions on internal improvements of General Taylor and Senator Cass, the presidential candidates, than with the presumably clogged Savannah River. Lincoln took no part in these running exchanges.[9]

It was very late in the first session when discussion on the River and Harbor Bill began. Amendments to the committee report called for additional work on Eastern and lake harbors, including $5,000 for Illinois to improve the harbor of Little Fort (Waukegan), the pet project of Representative John Wentworth. Work on the St. Louis Harbor, Ohio River, upper Mississippi, and Wabash River projects was voted down. A proposed "improvement of Salt river, above the falls, for the benefit of the Whig party" must have reminded Lincoln of some of the streams he had helped make navigable by legislative fiat in the Illinois Assembly.[10] The general bill died in the Senate.

Lincoln's contribution on this matter, aside from his votes, was a prepared speech delivered between two periods of the important debates on the subject. It was a reasoned, well-organized, straight-forward answer to the veto message of President Polk. It seems to have attracted little attention in Congress and Lincoln himself refers to it in his correspondence but once, if at all.[11]

Whereas the Democratic representatives from the Northwest were at war with their party leadership in the matter of internal improvements, Lincoln was in perfect harmony both with his party's local and national policy on this score. However, his effort in this instance won him no special credit at home, for his district did not stand to benefit directly from these appropriations. Moreover, as the campaign developed after the Van Buren nomination, the Wilmot Proviso tended to blot out the other issues.

Lincoln easily fell in step with Whig criticism of the manner in which the war with Mexico had begun. He had not been opposed to the war when he had been in Illinois: as a matter of fact (see page 13) he had made a speech to secure enlistments for the war. But the Whigs in Congress, mostly from the older, eastern section of the country, were with few exceptions united against wholesale annexation of Mexican territory and highly critical of Polk's actions leading up to the war. This seemed an area, like internal improvements, in which the Whigs, North and South, could stand together in criticism of the Democratic administration. It would have been better to have waited until the war was over, Lincoln thought, but since Polk and fellow Democrats were using the war for political purposes, he joined in the fun with a set of resolutions asking the President for information about the status of the region between the Nueces and the Rio Grande which had been in dispute between the United States and Mexico when Polk's orders had sent General Taylor into the area. This is where the opening skirmish of the war had been fought—the justification for the war which Polk had been on the verge of asking for anyhow. These "spot" resolutions, so often in his later career turned against their author, were part of the partisan warfare against a "Loco Foco" President. Lincoln's speech on the subject weighed the President's stated reasons for entering the war and found them wanting.[12]

But though this speech was in line with the Whigs' national policy, Lincoln soon found that it did not reflect the views of his constituents, among whom the war was popular and the Manifest Destiny spirit rampant. The people "back home" were following the battles and the casualty lists closely, for Illinois troops had taken part in most of the battles in which Taylor's army had fought. Lincoln's friends warned him of his mistake. He was severely criticized by the Democratic press. There was little newspaper support for Lincoln's position in central and lower Illinois, indeed the management of the Whig *Alton Telegraph* split as a result of mild criticism of the origin of the war along usual Whig lines.[13]

A study of the resolutions passed in conventions of the Whig party—county, congressional district, and in one case, a judicial district—admittedly far from complete, indicates that Lincoln was out of touch with his own area of the state but that northern Illinois Whigs echoed the national Whig line in their conventions. The seventh judicial circuit convention at Naperville resolved that the war with Mexico had been "unrighteously and unconstitutionally commenced . . . to keep up the preponderance of the South in the Senate. . . ." Cook County Whigs tempered their charge that the war had been commenced illegally with the statement that the party had supported the war after it had been commenced. Stephenson Whigs had criticized the attack on those who questioned the President's actions as cutting off free speech. In Springfield, Judge Stephen T. Logan, running for Lincoln's seat in Congress, was reported as saying that while the United States had good and sufficient cause for war against Mexico, the manner of beginning it was objectionable. Resolutions describing the beginning of the war in the orthodox Democratic manner acquired three Whig votes in the Illinois House of Representatives in addition to the votes of all of the Democrats.[14] Lincoln, in support of a national party viewpoint, had wandered far north in the geographic gradation of Illinois opinion. He was levered away from the prejudices of his constituents by the national policies of his party just as the Whigs hoped to separate the Northwestern Democrats from their voters by means of the River-Harbor Bill and the Wilmot Proviso.

Lincoln was not persuaded that he had been wrong. His letters to W. H. Herndon, to Usher Linder, and a gratuitous one to John Mason Peck, the famous Baptist minister who lived outside his district, all ring with Lincoln's conviction that he was right.[15]

He wanted his friends to share his conviction and the national Whig line.

⌒

Politics, in sum, involved a great deal more than the slavery question even in a Congress sitting during the intense Wilmot Proviso controversy. The slavery issue appeared in the Thirtieth Congress in several forms. By far the most important and controversial was the question of the status of slavery in the territories defined by the treaty with Great Britain in 1846 (Oregon) and acquired in 1848 from Mexico (California and the Southwest). Three other questions relating to slavery arose: slavery and the slave trade in the District of Columbia; the petitions of citizens for payment for slaves who had escaped while "impressed" by federal military forces (significant because payment by the federal government would tend to serve as a precedent implying federal recognition of slavery); and the reception of anti-slavery petitions.

It was the Proviso that overshadowed not only the other slavery matters but put all other political issues in the shade before it was compromised in 1850. The question of slavery or no slavery in the lands to be acquired from Mexico had been before the country since 1846 and had been well ventilated. It had influenced elections in the eastern states. The aura of morality thrown over the whole northern sectional position in connection with the slavery issue engendered an attitude of greater rigidity, of greater reluctance to compromise over the territorial question than at any time since the Missouri controversy. Northern moral rigidity was met and matched by Southern pride and constitutional dialectic. These were the conditions under which the Thirtieth Congress undertook to work out the territorial organization for the new western lands. Also important was the fact that 1848 was a presidential year.

Before the Committee on Territories had even framed a bill, Lincoln heard speeches that must have come as a shock to him. John Gayle, an Alabama Whig, whose name immediately preceded that of the famous abolitionist Giddings on most purely partisan divisions, argued at length that the territory acquired by the common sacrifice could not exclude slavery since that would constitute unequal treatment, indeed, would "degrade" the South. He had hoped that Northern Whigs would not disturb "the desired harmony between Whigs of the North and the Whigs of the South on a mere abstraction." The Wilmot Proviso principle was, in Gayle's estimation, "a direct proposition to dissolve the Union." Seizing on some figurative language of Representative Joseph M. Root of Ohio, Gayle warned against the North going on the "warpath" against the South for, he said, "they will find that every ten-year old boy will have the brawny and stalwart arm of a full-grown and gallant soldier, and that they will encounter none but Palmetto regiments."[16] This from a Southern Whig in answer to a Northern Whig in a presidential year!

Curiously enough, the one completed piece of legislation extending territorial organization to previously unorganized territory and with the Proviso attached concerned itself not with the Mexican Cession but with Oregon. Settled for some years, clearly American since the compromise with England in 1846, plagued with Indian troubles, Oregon obviously and urgently needed territorial government. The Oregon question was pressing while the matter of slavery in the Mexican Cession remained hypothetical until the Treaty of Guadelupe Hidalgo, by which Mexico ceded California and New Mexico to the United States. The signing was announced to the House in a presidential message of July 6, 1848, late in the session.[17]

The debate had followed different courses in the houses. The Senate was Democratic and, of course, equally divided between members from slave and from free states. It had joined the question of Oregon to that of the prospective Mexican Cession. It sought to minimize the issue of slavery in the territories by compromise. It was willing to exclude slavery from Oregon on the basis that the region fell wholly above the 36°30′ line—the line of the Missouri Compromise extended to the Pacific. It

eventually yielded to the House of Representatives in the closing days of the session in order to bring government to distracted
Oregon. Democratic senators from Texas and Missouri voted
to accept the House view as did a Whig from Delaware.[18]

The House of Representatives was Whig and a considerable
majority of the members were from the free states. Here debate
had begun early and had been restricted to the subject of Oregon
in the main. The House version of the territorial bill contained
the language of the Wilmot Proviso, making the territory free
without assigning a reason. This was understood to mean that
Oregon would be free, not as a matter of compromise involving
other territory to be acquired, but as a matter of principle. The
implication was clear that the House would insist on the application of the same principle to the Mexican Cession.

The President took the unusual step of signing the bill and
returning it to the House with his reasons for signing it. Alluding
again to the great danger of agitating the slavery question, he
pointed out that in the South slavery "does not embrace merely
the rights of property, however valuable; but it ascends far higher,
and involves the domestic peace and security of every family."
He explained his approval of the bill by the fact that Oregon
fell into the area in which slavery had been prohibited by the
Compromise of 1820.[19] The message was a call to sweet reasonableness and compromise with an attempt to evoke the "mystic
chords of memory" by repeating the warning of President Washington against geographic factions. It was an earnest appeal by
a political lame duck, scarcely noticed, for objection prevented
it being read on this last day of a bitterly partisan session. Congressmen were off to the hustings in no mood for sweet reasonableness.

The slender anti-slavery minority (more anti-slavery than
Whig or Democrat), the Northern Whigs and the anti-administration Democrats, were not content that freedom in Oregon
should rest on any ground other than the exercise of congressional power for that purpose. On this decisive vote the Illinois
delegation split: Lincoln and three Democrats voted for inclusion

of the express prohibition while three Democrats from central and southern Illinois joined Southern members in opposition.[20]

This result could be ascribed to political considerations of three sorts. The case of the few who might be described as abolitionists first is obvious. They were sharpening a weapon to use in the coming debate as to whether the Mexican Cession should become slave territory. Secondly, as a leading Whig member from Ohio said, "slavery . . . as it presents itself for our consideration and legislation here . . . becomes mainly a question of political power."[21] Slavery in the new states raised the question of the federal ratio which gave to the slave states representation in Congress for three-fifths of their slaves. It not only added to the weight of the South-West Democratic alliance, assuming that one operated, but also to the political power of the South if the sectional alignment of the country were to function on a North versus South basis. In this sense, Lincoln voted with three Illinois colleagues to repudiate the South-West alliance and to reframe the sectional contention toward a North versus South, free versus slave orientation. In the same sense, Richardson, McClernand, and Ficklin, Democrats from southern and central Illinois, were voting to preserve the traditional basis of the Western Interest, the working harmony between the low tariff, agricultural sections. The Proviso adherents were almost exactly the same persons who supported the Great Lakes internal improvements. Leaving the moral issue entirely aside, the Wilmot Proviso was, in the hands of the Eastern Whigs, a sharp weapon for the destruction of a political combination of South and West which threatened to consign the East to a seemingly degenerating minority position in the expanding country.

In the third place, much of the determination of the Northern Whigs not only that there should be no slavery in Oregon and the Mexican Cession but that this result should come from a positive assertion of the power of Congress, flowed from party politics. The Democratic Twenty-Ninth Congress had raised the embarrassing questions. The Thirty-First Congress reached the brink of disunion before solving these questions by compromise in 1850. The Thirtieth Congress was concerned chiefly with the use of these questions to influence the election of 1848 that occurred between its two sessions. The Whigs believed that they had lost the presidential election of 1844 because the anti-slavery people "defected."[22] Therefore it was the Whigs who pressed the slavery question in this acceptable form in the first session, but, with a Whig safely elected to the presidency between sessions, the initiative passed to the Democrats of the North to outbid the Whigs for the future as well as to attempt to pry the Northern and Southern wings of the party apart.

The Proviso, like every other segment of the slavery question, was a double bladed axe that cut both ways. The Whigs who pushed the Proviso in Congress hoped to make political capital for the national party by adding the old Liberty (abolitionist) party vote to the Whig vote in decisive states in the North. However, their successes in 1846 led them to believe that their assured harvest would be reaped in governors, senators, congressmen, and control of state legislatures in the North. They expected to gain only where the anti-slavery vote was strong enough to carry the balance of power. The other blade of the axe whittled away at the Whig party in the South but this was a risk that was minimized with the prospect of a Southern presidential candidate. The issue embarrassed the party in power. The Northern Democrat faced a hostile electorate if he failed to support the Proviso, a wrathful national administration from which all patronage might cease to flow if he voted for it. Before the election it was to the Northern Whig interest to get as many roll calls as possible on which the Northern Democrats might impale themselves.

On the other hand, both parties were more than state and local organizations. In 1848 both parties must nominate candidates for the presidency who would be running in both sections and must be acceptable in all sections to have a chance of winning. They must provide platforms that would not be too distasteful to large numbers of Whigs or Democrats, as the case might be. The national Whig would have preferred to have seen the Democrats divided and his own party united, and the Democrats would have preferred the opposite, of course. The Wilmot Proviso, in the normal course of events, was not likely to achieve such a result for the Whigs. Sectional issues were destructive not only of the Democratic but of all national parties. In the event, it was the Whig party that succumbed to the sectional issue. The Proviso was one of those issues, comparable to the segregation issue in the Democratic party today, over which the national and local tendencies of the party are at war with each other.

The Whig party squirmed out of the awkward position in which it found itself by nominating the Mexican War hero, General Zachary Taylor, who was a Southerner and a slaveholder, but whose political views were as unknown as his military triumphs were renowned. The Democrats were less fortunate. Their nominee, General Lewis Cass, had been in public life since the War of 1812 and his Nicholson letter had expressed views on the territorial question which anticipated the popular sovereignty idea of Douglas. This failed to satisfy the Northern Proviso and Lake-Harbor Democrats who nominated Martin Van Buren as a third party candidate and thereby assured a Whig victory. The sectional strategy of the Northern Whigs had given them a national victory.

What happens in the national forum of politics is assumed to be something of a reflection of what goes on at the lower levels of political activity in which the voter is fairly directly involved. An example from one Illinois congressional district indicates the degree to which the Proviso issue in the halls of Congress was based upon trends at home. "Long John" Wentworth, Chicago editor, politician, and congressman in the 1840's, had been attacked by the abolitionist journal for his votes for the 21st (Gag) rule and for his opposition to some proposed civil rights for free Negroes in the District of Columbia in 1844. He was characterized as an *"advocate of perpetual slavery"* and his course in the House summarized as having shown "a willingness to sacrifice his honor, (if he has any,) and his oath to support the Constitution, cringe and fawn upon the slave minions, and do their most dirty work, but to receive a smile and kick from his haughty masters. . . ." In 1846, his district polled 3,541 votes for Owen Lovejoy, the Liberty party candidate. In 1848, counties in northern Illinois saw fusions of Whig and abolition forces to support local candidates for circuit clerk and prosecuting attorney. The Whigs of the Seventh Judicial Circuit located mainly in Wentworth's district resolved against the extension of slavery and their candidate was advised to "make a Wilmot proviso Speech in one of our Abolition Precints [sic]."[23] The abolition vote had become the balance of power in Wentworth's district. Whatever might happen to the Democratic administration and the national party, Wentworth's political life was at stake. If he had supported the administration by opposing the Proviso, he would have invited defeat by a fusion of the abolitionists and the Whigs. The Great Lakes region, northern New York, and New England had many such districts and the Free Soilers of 1848 proved themselves the balance of power in entire states. They, as bolters from the national party on a section and a slavery issue—the Wilmot Proviso—were a measure of the appeal of moderate abolitionism in politics.

Until after the election of 1848 and the high excitement of the sectional struggle reached a more distinct climax, the Proviso was not so crucial in districts such as Lincoln's where the Liberty vote was small (249 in 1846) or in Ficklin's district in eastern Illinois where no abolition vote was recorded. Congressmen from such districts could be more national in outlook and be more concerned with promotion of national candidates and the support of national administrations.

Lincoln's votes on slavery issues in this Congress have a consistency only if the touchstone is the pattern of partisan politics, not anti-slavery zeal. He voted for the Proviso with his Northern Whig colleagues on every occasion. This he was bound to do by partisan considerations as well as his own inclination. He voted to receive anti-slavery petitions. He had expressed himself strongly on the right of petition many years before in the Illinois legislature.[24] On these two points, political expediency and personal conviction conveniently followed the same groove.

Less consistent was Lincoln's record in the matter of slavery and the slave trade in the federal district. In the second session, Lincoln voted three times against propositions to bring bills to eliminate either one or the other or both of these evils from the District of Columbia. This is understandable. Zachary Taylor had been elected President, not by anti-slavery support, but by the separate Free Soil nomination. The Whigs, cabinet-making and otherwise preparing to take over the administration, needed party unity. Not so the "Whig execrescences"—the abolition Whigs. They were exploring the length to which their leverage would extend. Lincoln joined other Whigs from "safe" districts in deserting the Wilmot Proviso majority to reject this new demand of the abolition elements in order to reassure the Southern members of the party and pave the way for an effective Whig administration. The shoe was now on the other foot. Northwestern Democrats, so harrassed and bedeviled by Whig sectional tactics in the first session, now joined with the abolitionists to split the Whigs.[25]

Under these circumstances, it is surprising that Lincoln should have asked leave to introduce a measure for emancipation in the District of Columbia. Lincoln's bill asked for a favorable vote of the people of the district, compensation for owners, and gradual emancipation.[26] The bill contained principles that he would stick to until the subject was closed out by emancipation. It was not voted on and not pressed.

One could be tempted to guess that Lincoln's bill was introduced to show the radicals how a politician would write a bill for the purpose. At least, the contrast is sharp. For example, one of the radical measures would have simply repealed all acts maintaining slavery and the slave trade in the District.[27] Such an act if passed would have eased tender consciences by removing the sin of slavery from the capital. What would have been the practical consequences for the slaves of the District? Would their masters not have moved them across the District boundary?

Southerners argued that the people of Washington were opposed to emancipation and they probably were correct in this. To counteract this argument, Giddings proposed a vote in the District on the question of emancipation, for and against. Asked who should vote in such an election, Giddings grandly replied

> that when he looked abroad upon the family of men, he knew no distinctions. He knew of no persons in this District that did not come from the same creating hand that formed himself, or the gentleman from Mississippi, [Mr. Tompkins]; and when he [Mr. G.] spoke of the people of this District, he meant precisely what he said.[28]

The contrast with the moderate approach to emancipation in the District of Lincoln's bill is overwhelming. Giddings was moving toward emancipation by way of Negro suffrage which commanded a great deal less support than emancipation. Lincoln moved toward emancipation by appeasing those whose interests were threatened. Very few of the representatives in the Thirtieth Congress were elected by a body of voters that included the colored. Giddings' rigidity in not accepting what was the law in his own state, his all-or-nothing attitude, killed such prospects as existed for the relief of slaves in Washington. He would not waive or postpone the question of equality to get some slaves freed. A disdainful unconcern about political means and process characterized the abolitionist. Some, like William Lloyd Garrison, carried this to the extreme of isolating themselves from politics entirely. Lincoln's proposal, on the other hand, was framed with an eye to the votes necessary for its passage.

Lincoln and his fellow legislators were confronted with the problem of the heirs of one Antonio Pacheco whose slave Lewis had been hired by the army during the Seminole War. Lewis was not returned to his owner, having made his escape to the

Indians and having been moved to Oklahoma with them. The heirs asked the government to pay them for the loss of a presumably valuable piece of property. Lincoln, as a lawyer, knew that the sense of equity and justice of the community, as formalized into the law, demanded that the borrower, in this case the government, make restitution. But the property involved was a slave, a species of property Giddings claimed had not been and should not be recognized as property under federal law. Slavery was immoral; therefore, the abolitionists claimed, restitution—otherwise demanded by a sense of right—should not be made.[29] The moral issue of slavery was regarded by the abolitionist part of the community as overriding and superior and not subject to the normal methods of adjustment among "rights." Slavery, then, was not as other moral questions which sometimes come into collision, but something of a different order of "rightness."

In most cases, then, even moral questions were and are resolved by ordinary political means, by the adjustment of different views to obtain a consensus that most could at least tolerate. But the moral issue of slavery (and in this age for smaller numbers of people, temperance and monogamy) was not of this kind. Slavery was a wrong and a sin which for many (and for more as time wore on) stood outside the ordinary give and take of politics. It may safely be assumed that Giddings was a kindly, well-intentioned man who would have gone a long way to have seen the wrong done Pacheco's heirs righted if the property involved had been horses or a house. But the thousand dollars for a slave would have involved "the people of the free States in the guilt of sustaining slavery . . ." as Giddings stated it. The abolitionist, in conscience, could not compromise or accept a partial remedy about slavery. As the Baptist editor said, "we would be afraid to lift our hand to God," if the concession of a jot or a tittle were made to this sin.[30]

Lincoln, in quite a different connection, explained the political way of arriving at decisions:

> The true rule, in determining to embrace or reject anything, is not whether it have *any* evil in it, but whether it have more of

evil than of good. There are few things *wholly* evil or *wholly* good. Almost everything, especially of governmental policy, is an inseparable compound of the two; so that our best judgment of the preponderance between them is continually demanded.[31]

The contrast between the abolitionist and the politician in the Thirtieth Congress was apparent in several areas—the rigidity, the all-or-nothing quality of the former, his tendency to mono-mania, his lack of interest in means. Characteristic also was the abolitionist's tendency to organize and subordinate a great many facts into a generalized hypothesis based upon one cause, slavery. We recognize this tendency in our contemporary radical left and radical right. We call it the conspiracy theory. Thus, when Lincoln confronted the moral issue in the Thirtieth Congress, he met also a shadowy supergovernment of slaveholders called variously "the Slave Power," "the Slavocracy," and the "Pro-slavery Conspiracy," which, in the minds of the abolitionists, manipulated everything that stood in the way of moral progress and freedom. These were terms he would have met infrequently in Springfield, without attending meetings of the Illinois Anti-Slavery Society or subscribing to abolition journals, until the Wilmot Proviso controversy made them usable terms in the realm of ordinary politics.

Lincoln knew and apparently respected several of his Southern colleagues. In his correspondence or speeches there is no disparagement of them or their motives—no suggestion that they were conspirators, or participants in a vast, secret movement to spread slavery. There was, in other words, not the least hint that he was an extreme anti-slavery man in this respect.

If the Wilmot Proviso had been supported only on moral grounds, it would have amounted to little indeed. The supposition that slavery would actually spread to the territories involved was not general. Most Southerners would have conceded the territories to freedom to have saved the principle of equality of treatment among the free and slave states. The Proviso was useful in both inter- and intra-party struggles and was therefore exploited. All other sectional conflicts of interest such as waterway development, the incidence of a proposed coffee and tea tax, and the tariff were assimilated into the Wilmot issue. The land policies desired by the West were not passed: the Slave Power prevented it. The tariff was lowered on Illinois and Wisconsin lead: the Slave Power did it. The harbor of Little Fort was not improved: the jealousy of the Slavocracy denied its due to Little Fort. Thus the rigidity, the all-or-nothing spirit and the easy acceptance of a conspiracy theory—typically associated with a moral issue—permeated all real sectional conflicts.

Lincoln's stance on all these matters in the Thirtieth Congress (in spite of the bill to liberate the slaves of the District of Columbia) was that of a politician, concerned mostly with politics, the offices, the tactics, the party, and the elections. There was nothing to indicate that he had been deeply attracted by any particular substantive issue. The Wilmot Proviso was of a piece with all other issues. He was an eager partisan whose voice and votes conformed to his party's needs.

Very high on the list of Lincoln's interests in this period was the Whig nomination for the presidency. Lincoln had become one of the early and active Taylor supporters, not because he thought that Taylor would be a better President than Henry Clay but because he thought that Taylor could be elected. Over a decade later when Republicans and Democrats were battling unceremoniously for the mantle of Henry Clay, Stephen A. Douglas, in the very last speech of the famous debates, charged that General James W. Singleton "testified that in 1847, when the constitutional convention of this state was in session, the Whig members were invited to a Whig caucus at the house of Mr. Lincoln's brother-in-law, where Mr. Lincoln proposed to throw Henry Clay overboard and take up Gen. Taylor in his place. . . ." Lincoln, so Douglas' accusation ran, had on that occasion said that "the Whigs had fought long enough for principle and ought to begin to fight for success."[32] The constitutional convention had been held after the time of his election and before Lincoln had started to Washington. Whatever the truth of these specifics, he did attend the Philadelphia convention and he did labor for the nomination of General Taylor.

Lincoln was free of any anxiety for his own election in 1848. He had committed himself against seeking a second term. The tradition of the district which he had helped establish was against it, and "to keep peace among our friends, and to keep the district from going to the enemy . . ." he would accept nomination only if "nobody else wishes to be elected."[33] As a matter of fact, Judge Stephen T. Logan did want to run, was nominated and defeated by a narrow margin in the August election. His opponent was Thomas L. Harris, a returned war hero who reaped the advantage of the criticism of the "unpatriotic" stand of Lincoln and the Whigs on the Mexican War. It was a blow to the Whigs to have lost their only safe congressional district, softened somewhat by the fact that E. D. Baker, a Whig recently of Springfield, was returned from the previously Democratic northernmost district of the state.

Lincoln's share in the campaign for Congress in his own district was confined to the sending of documents, for the session had not ended. The bulk of even this activity came in August and was intended to influence the district and state for General Taylor. His effort included a stump speech for Taylor on the floor of the House, in which he matched his own Blackhawk War heroics with the military achievements of General Cass in the War of 1812, no doubt to the great amusement of the Whig portion of his auditors. Lincoln's efforts were focused on the presidential race. Although he had been named a Whig Elector in Illinois, more than half of the campaigning time remaining after the adjournment of Congress was spent in the East. While working at getting documents in the mail at Washington, he improved his time by making appearances in the nearby area. In September, he made a tour of Massachusetts to stem the desertion from Whig ranks of the more strongly anti-slavery voters with whom the nomination of a slaveholder of unknown slavery views did not "take."[34]

Lincoln then returned to Illinois where he made speeches at several points. In Chicago, where he made his first speech, he found the situation the reverse of that in Massachusetts where the Taylor nomination had driven great numbers of Whigs to support Van Buren. Here in northern Illinois the bolters were Democrats. John Wentworth was counting up the lost and the saved among the Democrats. But the argument of the Whigs was the same in Illinois as in Massachusetts: the Whigs of the North had voted for the Proviso as a unit; their candidate would not veto it. A vote for Van Buren who could not win, so it was argued, was a vote lost as far as slavery extension was concerned. Cass was "weak" on the slavery issue. The Democrats argued that Taylor could not favor the Proviso. The extension of slavery to the Mexican Cession would profit the South about $600,000,000 and Taylor personally $52,000 in the rise of the value of slaves, all of which the Proviso would undo.[35]

The sum of the matter was that there were three parties in the field. Over large parts of the North, the abolitionists and their sympathizers were the sought-after balance of power. Hence, the issue of slavery in the territories and related sectional issues received the nearly exclusive attention of the politicians. General Taylor was elected but lost to Cass in Illinois by only 3,000 votes. General Cass trailed the Democratic candidate for governor by 13,000 votes. Van Buren's total of 15,804 votes was not only decisive but came largely from those who normally voted Democratic. Significant, too, was the heavy concentration of the Van Buren vote in the northern part of the state. He carried nine counties and was second in four others. The Van Buren vote was significant in only one county in Lincoln's district, Putnam, and of no importance in southern Illinois.[36]

What of the local basis of this minority element which both parties were courting? One Whig compared it to the followers of Joseph Smith. "The Barnburning party, so far as I know them," he averred, "are the most deluded & extravagant set of people that I have seen of late." They were different as voters. Some of them believed "that God requires every man to act in favor of freedom and against slavery. . . . For ourselves we would be afraid to lift our hand to God, if we willingly used it to give one more foot of free soil of this world to be cursed by the dominion of slavery." Before the nomination of Van Buren gave them an escape, "thousands in the free states will refuse to vote for either of the candidates" rather than contribute to this sinful end. It was all or nothing for the extreme abolitionists of the precinct as well as of Congress. Winning an election was not the most important consideration (a view which was and is heretical among politicians, at least until the returns were in) for "the principles involved in the issue will in the main ultimately triumph."[37] They were one-issue men and in 1848 the Wilmot Proviso was the one issue.

When Lincoln returned to Washington to find the slavery issues argued under the new conditions brought about by the Whig victory in the presidential election, the Illinois legislature produced a reflection of what had happened in Washington. The Whigs of Illinois had read the election returns and sought to embarrass and divide the Democrats of Illinois in order to win the Van Buren vote for themselves. A Whig from southeastern Illinois proposed a resolution of instruction to the United States senators which, if passed by both houses, would have bound them to vote for the non-extension of slavery over any new territory. On January 2, 1849, this was laid on the table, every Whig having voted for it. In spite of the strongest pressure from the *Register,* resolutions of instruction did pass the House on reconsideration, 5 Democratic members having changed their votes to the Proviso side. The motives of the members in voting these instructions were subject to different interpretations. One, emanating from a religious journal, proclaimed that "this is a new era in the moral history of the Illinois legislature." A more cynical suggestion was that the Democrats who joined the Whig minorities in passing the resolutions may have had another reason—to create a senatorial vacancy by instructing Douglas out of his seat.[38]

The intent of the Whigs became perfectly clear when the vote on resolutions favoring the abolition of slavery in the District of Columbia was taken. Seven Whigs, 6 from central Illinois, opposed this resolution. They followed the example set by Lincoln and Whig moderates in Washington. "Proviso" was the magic word which might split the Democratic party. For that great end, the prejudices of conservative Whig constituencies might be disregarded but unnecessary adventures into anti-slavery beyond that point were likely to be unprofitable, politically speaking.[39]

In 1848, when Illinois had been slow to warm up to the Wilmot Proviso and must have seemed far behind the feeling at the nation's capital, Lincoln had been in Washington where the fire was hottest. In 1850, when the capital was aware of the deadly serious threat to national unity and Union saving became the center of political interest, Illinois was just thoroughly awakening to the political possibilities of the Proviso in its party politics. Lincoln was at home in Springfield, catching up the loose threads of his law practice and winding up the patronage affairs which it had fallen to his lot to manage.

The defeat of Logan for Lincoln's seat in the heart of Illinois Whiggery had the effect of placing on Lincoln's shoulders a large share of the burden of dispensing Whig patronage in the Taylor administration. This, of course, came after the expiration of his term in Congress. Normally ex-congressmen found places for themselves as many of Lincoln's friends in the Thirtieth Congress did. An old friend made the assumption that Lincoln would do just that, to which Lincoln replied that "there is nothing about me which authorize me to think of a first class office;

40

and a second class one would not compensate me for being snarled at by others who want it for themselves." He went on to outline the nub of what turned out to be his most painful patronage experience until he became President-elect. "I believe that," he wrote, "so far as the Whigs in congress, are concerned, I could have the Genl. Land office almost by common consent; but then Sweet, and Don: Morrison, and Browning, and Cyrus Edwards all want it. And what is worse, while I think I could easily take it myself, I fear I shall have trouble to get it for any other man in Illinois." Lincoln did not get it, but an Illinois man whom Lincoln had disapproved of for that post did. Lincoln's irritation with this and other failures are reflected in his letters. To one applicant he wrote, "No one man recommended by me has yet been appointed to any thing, little or big, except a few who had no opposition. . . ." Finally, he wrote to the Secretary of State, John M. Clayton, protesting against the placing of responsibility for appointment in the departments:

> It is fixing for the President the unjust and ruinous character of being a man of straw. This must be arrested, or it will damn us inevitably.
>
> The appointments need be no better than they have been, but the public must be brought to understand that they are the *Presidents* appointments. He must occasionally say, or seem to say, "by the Eternal, I take the responsibility." Those phrases were the 'Samson's locks' of Gen. Jackson. . . .[40]

He did have his successes in placing friends but they were outweighed by failures in cases in which the applicant was someone to whom Lincoln was particularly obligated.

Not only was Jackson's assumption of personal responsibility admired by Lincoln but his reasons for appointments argue a Jacksonian approach to the patronage problem. Lincoln's supposed superiority over his rival did not arise from any greater capacity to perform the services required in the Land Office but rather his greater services to the Whig party and to President Taylor.[41]

Lincoln's commitments did not end with the original filling of

the posts by Whigs. As late as 1851 he was instrumental in securing for his old friend Francis Arenz a free trip to his native Germany as a bearer of dispatches.[42] In this one recommendation
were joined two Jacksonian attitudes about party which Lincoln
practiced: the cultivation of the foreign vote and the use of
patronage to secure party workers.

While Lincoln was thus engaged on party affairs in Illinois the
Thirty-First Congress assembled in Washington and the efforts
of Clay and Webster to save the Union began.

The *Quincy Whig* published 1848 election figures to show
that "If the Whigs bring out a candidate who can unite the vote
of the party throughout the district, and who is not personally or
politically objectionable to the 1,435 voters who cast their suf-
frages for Mr. Van Buren, it is quite clear that he will be
elected."[43] If the other Whig newspapers were not so frank, they
were just as calculating. The Whigs in the legislature just adjourned had laid the groundwork for the campaign. There was
no embarrassing Taylor nomination to cancel out congressional
Whig support of the Proviso and legislative support of the Proviso instructions.

The timing of the Illinois Whigs was unfortunate for the pen-
dulum already had begun to swing toward compromise in Washington. The venerated Whig leader, Henry Clay, introduced the
Omnibus Bill; revered Whig leader, Daniel Webster, seconded
it. This placed the *Whig* editors in an extremely awkward position. They were required by logic to choose between compromise
and vote-catching support of the Proviso. The editor of the *Whig*
attempted to carry water on both shoulders. In July he was writing of W. A. Richardson, the Democratic congressman up for
re-election, as a *"Southern Sympathizer"* and the Whigs as "on
the question in which the Free Soilers feel the deepest interest
more nearly assimilate with them than the loco-focos. . . ." As
late as October, he displayed the vote of Colonel Richardson for

the Fugitive Slave Law in heavy, black letters and expressed fears that the kidnapping of free Negroes would become a regular thing. On the other hand, he thought that the Proviso might well be dropped to save the Union especially since the territory involved would be free anyhow and the Proviso would serve only to provoke sectional irritation. After the election, the Fugitive Slave Law appeared in a better light:

> The perpetuity of our union depends upon this allegiance and the prompt and faithful administration of the laws. The path of duty is plain. The people of the free States are not compelled to be the instrument of the slave hunter . . . any more than they were under the old law; and for the safety and perpetuity of the Union, and to allay sectional feeling which has been aroused throughout the south under the influence of bad men, it is a part of the duty and patriotism of the people of the free States to yield a passive obedience to the law, looking to the future for its modification.[44]

In Lincoln's own district, the *Journal* faced the same dilemma with the same ambivalence. In spite of the pending compromise, the representative of the Springfield district should vote with the knowledge that "the feelings of our people are against extending slavery into free territory." Yet earlier, and more months before the election, the same journal had commented on a bipartisan compromise meeting at Jacksonville with this purple prose:[45]

> May not every such cheering evidence of fealty to the common interests of our beloved Union, as that afforded by the recent meeting at Jacksonville, and similar assemblages of the masses elsewhere, gladden the patriot with the holy hope that never will come a night, to our country, so frought with mournful destiny as to darken one star whose radiance now embathes our nation's banner.

As a matter of fact the ground was being cut from under the feet of the Proviso supporters. As early as January 24, there had been a grass-roots Union meeting at Belleville. A similar meeting held at Springfield was addressed by men of both parties, not including Lincoln, and it unanimously passed resolutions favorable to the Compromise measures.[46] Support for the Proviso meant opposition to compromise. Wooing the Free Soilers now presented the danger of losing Whigs.

The Whigs of central Illinois were ready for compromise. "Many of the Whigs here that was [sic] very noisey [sic] some time past in favor of the Wilmot proviso now say that they never was [sic] in favor of it but as the party had taken it up and made it a question they advocated it," it was reported to a Democratic congressman. A Whig, stepping aside to permit Richard Yates to run for Congress, wrote a letter which appealed to the Whigs to discountenance "by the enlightened and comprehensive patriotism . . . every form and combination of ultraism and sectional feeling."[47]

The Whig convention of Sangamon County resolved that Clay's proposals contained "the elements of a just and liberal adjustment" and asked that a candidate who would "sustain Mr. Clay and his worthy co-laborers in their noble efforts to save the country from the evils of the ultraism of the South and the fanaticisms of the North" be selected to run for Congress. The candidate selected, Richard Yates, was told that "Warren and Kentucky Whigs was [sic] against you unless you come out against the 'proviso!' "[48]

Northern Illinois exhibited a quite different reaction to the compromise proposals. "As pro-slavery in their tone and principles as they could well be made," was the verdict of John Wentworth. Meetings were called to pass resolutions against compromise in Chicago and Waukegan. The "caving in of the Northern Whigs," according to Wentworth, was the cause of the whole compromise movement. The religious and abolition press was more extreme with no time for the partisan aside. The appeal to compromise in a brotherly fashion was spurned:[49]

> Dear as this Union is and its Constitution, we owe an obligation to God and his constitution of eternal principles, which must be discharged, even at the sacrifice of the Union of these States.
>
> Compromises in respect to what is right, only serve to involve us in deeper ruin. . . . Firmness is the most successful remedy for threats.

If no compromise plan could be carried, it would be a noble triumph in the cause of humanity and righteousness.

The resistance to compromise was not confined to the abolitionists and to the Democrats. Of seven Whig conventions in northern Illinois reported in the *Chicago Journal,* none favored compromise, two were silent, and five were for the non-extension of slavery or the Proviso by name. The two last held condemned specifically the Fugitive Slave Law.[50]

The competition for anti-slavery support in northern Illinois was brought to the highest pitch by the Free Soil convention at Elgin on August 28. It nominated William B. Ogden for Congress over Owen Lovejoy and adopted a platform which excoriated northern members of Congress who disregarded free soil pledges to vote for the compromise resolutions. It demanded that there be no more slave states, no more slave territory, and no more compromises with slavery. The compromise in the making should be repealed if passed, they proclaimed. The slave trade and slavery should be abolished in the District of Columbia. But the Free Soil movement was everywhere in a state of collapse. There is some reason for believing that some of the leadership of this convention had expected to sell out to the highest bidder among the two established parties from the very outset. R. S. Molony, the Democratic candidate, virtually accepted the Free Soil platform and Ogden withdrew. The old Liberty men resented the sell-out and held a new but inconclusive convention. Churchill Coffing, the Whig candidate, was permitted to speak at their meeting and was reported to favor the Proviso and oppose the Fugitive Slave Law. A Free Soil legislative candidate spoke at a Coffing meeting and his views were reported to coincide with those of the Whig congressional candidate.[51]

How much of an impression and what impression these events, pulling the two parts of the state in quite opposite directions on these slavery questions, made on Abraham Lincoln we do not know. The track of the development of his political ideas in these crucial months is lost. Someone remembered these matters in 1858 for Lincoln countered the radical Republican platform of 1854 brought up by Douglas, with the 1850 Democratic programs of the two northern districts which Molony and Thompson Campbell had accepted in order to compete for the Free Soil vote. Perhaps Lincoln was fortunate to have been neither a candidate nor a congressman in 1850. In 1852 when pronouncing a eulogy on Henry Clay, he said that there was "no disagreement among intelligent and patriotic Americans" about the "now recent compromise measure."[52]

Lincoln slipped back into the routine of local politics, but with a difference—he had been a congressman. He signed a call for a meeting in honor of Louis Kossuth, the Hungarian patriot who was visiting in this country. He was the orator at a memorial service in Chicago for President Taylor who had died suddenly, and subsequently delivered the memorial oration for Henry Clay on a similar sad occasion.[53]

Certainly the high point of the politically dull five years after his service in Washington was the presidential campaign of 1852. Yet it was one of the least colorful campaigns in our entire history. So dull was it that one of the Whig electors wrote his congressman that:

> The Convention appointed me one of the candidates for Elector and I think it will become my duty in that station to put forth some slight effort in favor of the Whig nominees. But I don't know where to begin. I have not been able to discover what are the issues to be tried.[54]

The *Alton Telegraph* carried an unusually frank appraisal of the Illinois parties of 1852. The state had always been Democratic, the Whig editor complained, with majorities "so overwhelming that the Whig party ceased almost entirely to make a show of resistance." But the Democrats were not the vigorous party they had once been for many Democrats "still hold to the name, but long since abandoned the spirit of the party."[55]

Free Soil men, with their conviction that slavery was the only important issue, thought that they knew why a Whig elector would not know what the issues were: there were none. The old parties, in the words of John F. Farnsworth, a Chicago Free Soil leader, had "merged into one and lost every distinctive principle." He believed that "no issue was now to be adjudged to these parties by the great jury of the American people." Owen Lovejoy "took the ground that the old party issues were abandoned, and that both were united on the one great question to be presented to American freemen at the ensuing Presidential election—the Finality of the compromise measures. . . ."[56]

Issues or no issues, candidates with color or without, the politician had to say something, the political editor had to write something. Democrat Franklin Pierce, Whig editors thought, would be unfavorable to the West, his loyalty to the compromise measures was challenged, and a mild play on the tariff issue made. Lincoln's one recorded speech of this dismal campaign was directed more at Douglas than at Pierce. Pierce was nominated, Lincoln suggested, to secure the Free Soil votes of New York, therefore, his fidelity to the Compromise was in question. His ability was unfavorably compared to that of John McClernand.[57] It is, altogether, one of Lincoln's poorest speeches.

In this presidential campaign Lincoln put forth the least effort since 1836. That he did speak many times in the campaign is more than likely. But there were no tours. Known speeches out of Springfield were made in conjunction with legal circuit-riding and the evidence of frequent attendance at court throughout the campaigning season makes it clear that he made no great sacrifices of time and energy in the Scott cause.[58]

The Illinois Whigs did very well in this election; they won four congressional seats. Certainly not on the national issues! The election of E. B. Washburne in the first district was explained in this wise: "Because he [Campbell—Washburne's Democratic opponent] would not, like the successful candidate, repudiate the platform of his party; because he would not get down on his belly and crawl into favor, he is made to feel the weight of anti-slavery wrath." The Whigs elected J. O. Norton in the third district because Zebina Eastman, the editor of the abolition journal in Chicago, wrote to the Free Soilers to go for Norton. Whatever the reason, a Democrat in the state capitol reported the Whigs to have been "almost in spasms" at their success.[59] The lever principle still worked for the abolition minority, even if quietly.

In this year and the next, Whig collaboration with abolitionists at the court-house level produced county offices and an important contribution to political strength, local men who had time and a reason to devote energy and intelligence to political organization.[60] But all of this took place in the northern part of the state.

1. *Congressional Globe,* 30th Congress, 1st Session, pp. 1–3.

2. *Ibid.,* pp. 2–3; pp. 23–4, Dec. 14, 1847; p. 246, Jan. 26, 1848.

3. *Ibid.,* p. 2, Dec. 6, 1847.

4. *Ibid.,* pp. 4–12, Dec. 7, 1847.

5. *Ibid.,* p. 550, Mar. 29, 1848.

6. *Ibid.,* p. 755, May 11, 1848.

7. See above, p. 15.

8. *Congressional Globe,* 30th Congress, 1st Session, pp. 30–8, 894, 896, 918.

9. *Ibid.,* pp. 946, 954–64, 965–82, 983–7.

10. *Ibid.,* pp. 1050, 1052–4.

11. *Collected Works,* I, 480–92, Washington, June 22, 1848, Wm. H. Herndon. If, as I doubt, Lincoln was referring to this speech rather than the one on the origin of the Mexican War, it was to complain that too few Whig papers carried it in their columns.

12. *Sangamo Journal,* June 4, 1846; *Collected Works,* I, 420–2; *Congressional Globe,* 30th Congress, 1st Session, 64; App. 93–95. The historian of the causes of the Mexican War is bound to ask the same questions and raise some of the same doubts that appeared in Lincoln's mind.

13. *Collected Works,* I, 451–2, Washington, Feb. 15, 1848, Wm. H. Herndon; 457–8, Washington, Mar. 22, 1848, Usher F. Linder; Donald W. Riddle, *Congressman Abraham Lincoln.* (Urbana: University of Illinois Press, 1957), pp. 35–41, Dec. 24, 1847.

14. *Alton Telegraph and Review,* May 5, 1848. The same resolve is reported somewhat differently but with no alteration in the sense in the *Chicago Daily Journal,* April 21, 1848; see also *Ibid.,* April 3, 1848; *Illinois Journal* (Springfield), Jan. 13, 1848; June 29, 1848; State of Illinois, *House Journal,* 15th General Assembly, p. 28, Dec. 10, 1846.

15. *Collected Works,* I, 472–3, Washington, May 21, 1848; also 451–2, 457–8.

16. *Congressional Globe,* 30th Congress, 1st Session, pp. 542–5, Mar. 28, 1848.

17. *Ibid.,* pp. 901–2.

18. *Ibid.,* p. 1080, Aug. 14, 1848.

19. *Ibid.,* pp. 1081–2.

20. *Ibid.,* p. 1027, Aug. 2, 1848.

21. *Ibid.,* p. 1022, Aug. 1, 1848.

22. See above, pp. 13–14.

23. *Western Citizen* (Chicago), July 25 and Aug. 15, 1844; John D. Caton MSS (Library of Congress), Joliet, Aug. 11, 1848, Wm. Smith; Oregon (Illinois), Aug. 25, 1848, E. F. Dutcher; *Alton Telegraph and Review,* May 5, 1848 (the resolutions of the seventh circuit Whig convention); Wallace-Dickey MSS (Illinois State Historical Library), Oregon, Aug. 19, 1848, J. M. Hinkle to T. L. Dickey.

24. See above, pp. 9–10; Thomas, *Abraham Lincoln,* pp. 61–4.

25. Thus it was a Democrat, C. E. Stuart of Michigan, who moved reconsideration of the Gott Resolution which would have required a committee report on the slave trade in the District of Columbia. See *Congressional Globe,* 30th Congress, 2nd Session, p. 107.

26. *Congressional Globe,* 30th Congress, 2nd Session, p. 212. See also, Riddle, *Congressman Abraham Lincoln,* pp. 172–4.

27. *Congressional Globe,* 30th Congress, 2nd Session, p. 39.

28. *Ibid.,* p. 55.

29. *Ibid.,* pp. 172–7.

30. *Ibid.; Watchman of the Prairies* (Chicago), May 30, 1848.

31. *Congressional Globe,* 30th Congress, 1st Session, App., p. 710.

32. *Collected Works,* I, 452, House of Representatives, Feb. 17, 1848, Thomas S. Flournoy; Paul M. Angle, *Created Equal? The Complete Lincoln-Douglas Debates of 1858.* (Chicago: University of Chicago Press, 1958), p. 398.

33. *Collected Works,* I, 430–1, Washington, Jan. 8, 1848, W. H. Herndon; Riddle, *Congressman Abraham Lincoln,* Chapter 10.

34. *Congressional Globe,* 30th Congress, 1st Session, App., pp. 1041–3; Benjamin P. Thomas, *Lincoln 1847–1853* (Springfield: Abraham Lincoln Association, 1936), pp. 89–92.

35. Sidney Breese MSS (Illinois State Historical Library), Chicago, Oct. 10, 1848, John Wentworth; *Alton Telegraph and Review,* Aug. 4 and Oct. 13, 1848; *Chicago Daily Democrat,* Nov. 2–4, 1848.

36. *State Register,* Dec. 1, 1848.

37. Wallace-Dickey MSS, Lee Center, Sept. 8, 1848, E. Ingalls to W. H. L. Wallace; *Watchman,* May 30, 1848; Aug. 29, 1848.

38. State of Illinois, *House Journal,* 16th General Assembly, pp. 18–9, 55; *Watchman,* Jan. 16, 1849; *Alton Telegraph,* Jan. 11, 1849. It will be remembered that senators often resigned rather than follow distasteful instructions.

39. *House Journal,* p. 314.

40. *Collected Works,* II, 28–9, Washington, Feb. 20, 1849, Joshua Speed; Riddle, *Congressman Abraham Lincoln,* Chapter 14; *Collected Works,* II, 46, Springfield, May 7, 1849, George W. Rives; 60, July 28, 1849.

41. *Ibid.,* p. 49, Springfield, May 16, 1849, W. B. Preston.

42. *Ibid.,* p. 103, Springfield, Mar. 11, 1851, The President.

43. June 18, 1850.

44. *Quincy Weekly Whig,* July 9 and 16, 1850; Oct. 1 and 29, 1850; Sept. 10, 1850; Dec. 31, 1850.

45. *Springfield Journal,* Sept. 4, 1850; Mar. 20, 1850.

46. *Alton Telegraph and Democratic Review,* Feb. 8, 1850; *Springfield Journal,* June 20, 1850.

47. John A. McClernand MSS (Illinois State Historical Library), Jacksonville, May 19, 1850, A. Dunlap; *Peoria Press,* July 10, 1850.

48. *Springfield Journal,* Aug. 2, 1850; Richard Yates MSS (Illinois State Historical Library), Washington, Sept. 5, 1850.

49. *Chicago Weekly Democrat,* Feb. 2, 1850; Feb. 23 and Mar. 16, 1850; Apr. 27, 1850; *Watchman,* Mar. 26, 1850.

50. *Chicago Daily Journal,* Aug. 13, 15, 16; Sept. 28; Oct. 21 and 25, 1850.

51. *Western Citizen,* Sept. 3, 1850; *Chicago Weekly Democrat,* Oct. 12, 1850; *Western Citizen,* Oct. 29, 1850; *Chicago Daily Journal,* Oct. 11 and 21, 1850.

52. Angle, *Created Equal,* pp. 211–3; *Collected Works,* II, 130.

53. *Ibid.,* pp. 115, 83–90, 121–32.

54. Yates MSS, Carlinville, July 16, 1852, I. A. Chestnut.

55. July 3, 1852.

56. *Chicago Daily Times,* Sept. 6, 1852; Aug. 9, 1852.

57. *Springfield Weekly Journal,* July 21, Aug. 18, and July 15, 1852; *Alton Telegraph,* June 28, June 30, Sept. 4, and Aug. 11, 1852; *Collected Works,* II, 135–57.

58. Thomas, *Lincoln 1847–1853,* pp. 287–305.

59. *Galena Jeffersonian,* quoted in the *Chicago Daily Times,* Nov. 20, 1850; *Ottawa Free Trader,* quoted in the *Chicago Daily Times,* Nov. 21, 1852; Mason Brayman MSS (Library of the Chicago Historical Society), Springfield, Nov. 10, 1852, John Moore.

60. *Chicago Democrat,* Nov. 9, 1852; Oct. 23 and Nov. 5, 1853.

The Politician Meets the Moral Issue

The opening days of the new year of 1854 brought the country news of a Nebraska Bill. This, of course, was no novelty. A bill for that purpose had failed in the last Congress. The vast territory lying to the north of 36°30′ (and therefore subject to the prohibition of slavery by virtue of the Missouri Compromise), west of the western boundaries of Missouri, Iowa, and Minnesota Territory, bounded on the north by Canada and the west by the new territories of Utah and Oregon, was Indian country, now eyed by prospective settlers. More important, perhaps, it lay athwart prospective railway lines which might link Chicago or St. Louis to the booming Pacific region. However, these were lines that would not be built until Indian title was extinguished, territorial organization completed, and some freight producing population settled in the area. New Orleans and Memphis, too, had hopes and plans for the first transcontinental railway and the business it would bring.

The Nebraska Bill was news because Senator Douglas had taken a calculated risk, as losing generals say, and added something to the earlier version of the bill to win the necessary votes to get the bill passed. The something added was first an equivocal, then—changed upon the demand of the necessary votes—a forthright repeal of the Missouri Compromise restriction of slavery in this region. Slaves might go to Kansas and Nebraska (the territory was divided to win the votes of the Iowans), hitherto free.

51

Looking at the events from some distance in time, one is struck by the fact that the first transcontinental railway did connect Chicago with San Francisco and that slavery found no permanent lodgment in this territory. This western link, added to the great rail highway into the South, the Illinois Central (which Douglas had secured for his state) made Chicago the railway hub of the nation. No statesman had done so much for the material interests of his state. Yet, reckoned by his own set of values, which placed sectional peace above every other good, the price was too high. The Nebraska Bill reopened the slavery question in national politics and this time a Civil War was required to settle it. The Nebraska Bill was even more potent than the Wilmot Proviso in reaching those whose feeling about slavery was minimal for it was a repeal of a sacred compact, a proof of a pro-slavery conspiracy, a perfidious aggression.

Douglas had miscalculated. One may guess only that he thought that the technical permission of slavery in a region to which slavery, in his judgment, would not extend, weighed but lightly in the balance against the alluring promise of material progress. It was dismissed as a "mere abstraction" in the language of that day. Projecting railways was the great business of the day. People, he perhaps believed, would understand that a little political maneuvering was necessary to obtain so great a prize. Opening the farther West always had been a prime concern of the West. But Douglas had underestimated three important considerations:

(1) The weakness of the political parties. The Whig party had been greatly weakened by the slavery controversy, by the loss of the great personalities that had dominated its life, and by the decline of public interest in the traditional issues. The Democrats had glossed over but not healed the breach of 1848. The Jacksonian revolution had been completed and the sense of mission of the early era had been dissipated.

(2) The intensity of the undercurrent of sectional animosity beneath the surface of the purely political compromise of 1850.

(3) The swelling moral sentiment that had made its last

uneasy compromise with slavery. New empires, vast railway projects and material advantage were as nothing compared with the sin of slavery.

Instead of the expected appreciation, Douglas received the curses of the majority of Northerners. His bill was not even argued in terms of sectional railroad advantage. The Kansas-Nebraska Bill was discussed in the North under the impression that it was intended to add to slave territory and people with slaves the vast area embraced in the act.

In two senses the Kansas-Nebraska Bill was the fuse which exploded a genuine revolution in politics. In the first place, it exposed and gave political leverage to—if, indeed, it did not create—a whole spectrum of possibilities on the slavery question. These possibilities ranged from the mere restoration of the Missouri Compromise to the total abolition of slavery everywhere. This wide scope of potential response is frequently a characteristic fatal to movements that seek to make significant alterations in the existing society, i.e., the failure of those who want change to agree on how much change there should be sometimes prevents any change at all.

In the second place, when a wave of revolutionary spirit begins to gather force, it releases the brakes on innovation in general. The demand for reform in one area encourages the demand for the repair of a myriad of other human and institutional flaws. Since the lid which had been holding down the slavery question had finally been lifted, reformers in other areas took heart. Thus the advocates of temperance were emboldened to press forward on their program for the betterment of mankind. Those who saw democracy most threatened by the unprecedented flood of foreigners and the growth of the Roman Catholic church felt that this must be the time to reverse that trend. If the interests of the West had been subordinated unjustly to the necessities of party alliances and outworn doctrine, now was the time to speak out firmly for sectional rights. If the way to political preferment for the young, the able, the ambitious, and the pure in heart was clogged by a compromising and an autocratically ruled machine, now was the time to cleanse the paths and remove the obstructions even if a thorough job meant the destruction of the machine. Thus, to the confusion of subsequent interpreters of these events, the conflict engendered by the Nebraska Bill was never one of pure anti-slavery versus slavery.

Finally, there was the question of the appropriate political means and organization to effect the objectives of the revolutionaries. The data upon which the historian must rely as he tries to find his way through the tangled issues of this period are complicated by the ramifications of the factors discussed above. Sorting out attitudes on slavery from attitudes and motives unrelated to slavery in the construction and reconstruction of the political parties during this era is difficult, but necessary, for the parties were the normal vehicle for reform movements as well as for the resistance to reform.

The situation in Illinois reflected these complications. The most universal ingredient of the compound reaction to the Kansas-Nebraska Bill among Illinoisans was regret shading into anger that the slavery question had been reopened at all. Lincoln's congressman and political friend, Richard Yates, received a letter from a constituent that expressed the apprehension and uncertainty that had been created:[1]

> I speak for myself and friends when I say that I hope you will find it to your feeling to oppose with all your power and Strength the Passage of the Nefarious Bill called [the] Douglass Nebraska Bill. I am convinced that our people are at least against the passage of it Believing that no good will come out of it other than making an agitation upon the vexed question and arousing a feeling throughout our Country that cannot easily be calmed. We have no Longer a Clay and Webster and that I am afraid

our people will find out to Late though if this thing is not stoped now. . . .

The Compromise of 1850 had postponed hard choices and difficult decisions: now these must be faced again.

Whig newspapers shared this attitude. The *Journal* warned its Springfield area readers that "if this measure of Mr. Douglas is insisted upon it will rouse up every sleeping energy of abolition fanaticism in the land." The *Quincy Whig* quoted a New York journal to the effect that slavery would not go to Kansas for reasons of climate and condemned the breaking of the peace between the sections for a mere abstraction.[2] The conservative reaction was regret that the dangerous subject of slavery had been reopened; its Whig character found expression in blaming Douglas, the old Nemesis, for this "attempt to repeal the sacred compact."

Perhaps the Brown County Whig who wrote that he and his friends were going to vote against the Nebraska Democrats deserves to be placed at absolute zero on the scale of opposition to slavery for he stated that

> thinking that it will create less agitation to allow it [the Kansas-Nebraska Act] to remain than to undertake to restore or re-enact the Missouri Compromise, yet we are anxious to show our condemnation of the course pursued by Douglas, Richardson & Co., in so recklessly getting up an agitation, by undertaking to repeal a compact which Douglas himself, said was canonized in the hearts of the American people, and which no ruthless hand would be reckless enough to disturb. . . .[3]

Putnam County, that New England enclave in the congressional district Lincoln had served, held an Anti-Nebraska convention that must be accorded the most extreme position on the anti-slavery scale. If he read them, the convention's resolutions must have horrified if not surprised Lincoln, for, among other things, it was asserted "that it is the duty of the North to demand of the South, the abolition of her slave system on condition of the continuance of the Union of these States. . . ." There was a feeling among those who had been strong "Proviso Men" that the repeal of the Missouri Compromise released them from any moral obligation to restrain their political and propagandist activity. The "sacred compact" had been broken by the South; the North was free to use its growing political ascendency to reform the country in respect to slavery. Furthermore, there was a tendency to assert that in view of this proof of Southern infidelity, no more compromises with slavery would be made. The North "had the power & if unable to effect our purpose otherwise we will do it by force; in other words let the South understand that the North are now the aggressive party moving forward for good. . . ."[4]

There was an organization and a core of interested people which found the means to approach the people of the northern part of the state in ways not open to the political parties. There was the abolition and religious press. There were mass meetings and conventions more like revival meetings than Whig speakings. The Putnam County Anti-Nebraska convention mentioned above was managed by Ichabod Codding, the abolitionist leader, and by ministers. In some cases the resolutions at the conclusion took the form of a pledge in the manner of the then currently popular Maine Law covenant:[5]

> This assembly therefore, pledge themselves to each other and to the world, to disregard party ties, to revolutionize the State and Nation, voting for no man who will not earnestly oppose every aggressive measure of the slave power.

It would be amiss to leave any impression that all of this was managed and artificial. The diary of Orville Hickman Browning records the extreme interest in the Nebraska question, not just the meetings arranged by the politicians of both sides but the spontaneous affairs at which the lawyers, at the conclusion of the business of the day in circuit court, debated far into the night for the edification of the county seat population.[6]

To say that other issues intruded upon this major one in the political revolution of 1854 would give an impression of precedence and order. But chaos and confusion would be a more accurate description of the times. One of the confusing issues was that of the Maine Law, a prohibitory liquor law then in force in distant Maine and strongly supported in the northern part of the Northwest. Even in the autumn of 1853 it occurred to one editor (he favored the Maine Law and jumped the traces of the Democratic party in 1854) that "the temperance question is everywhere tending to verge into party politics."[7] The Whigs, as the party of the "better" people, were more generally pro-temperance. The Democrats with their German and Irish minorities were in the main opposed to the prohibitory enactment.

It was among the radicals that the intertwining of the issues of slavery and the Maine Law was the most thorough. Many of them did not clearly distinguish between the two moral reforms. Anti-Nebraska and anti-whiskey were teamed in the radical mind. Several of the northern county People's (Anti-Nebraska) conventions pledged the fused party to the support of the Maine Law.[8]

Although this issue was more prominent in the northern part of the state, it also played a role in the old Whig centers. George T. Allen, elected to the legislature from Madison County and destined to play a vital role in the defeat of Lincoln's ambition to represent the state in the Senate, announced that he thought the Maine law would be the most important subject to appear in the coming session of the General Assembly. John M. Palmer, another dissident Democrat whose defection was of considerable concern to both Lincoln and Douglas, was willing to submit the question to a popular vote. A Whig abolitionist of Jacksonville wrote him to "inscribe on your banner 'an exterminating war against intemperance & restoration of the Missouri Compromise.' "[9]

In the cities of the nation, where the impact of increasing Irish and German immigration was first felt, a tide of anti-immigrant and anti-Catholic feeling rose toward a crest in 1854. It first found political expression in the Native American Party but was soon swept up in a broader, more successful movement using the formula of ritual and secrecy—the Know-Nothings. This secret lodge capitalized on the decline of the Whig party and reached its peak in 1854–55. It was reorganized into an open party and lingered on the political stage as the American party.

There had been for some time an anti-foreign undertone in the Whig party of Illinois, at least partly a result of the adherence of the foreign-born—the English excepted—to the Democratic party. In April, 1854, a Western counterpart of the Eastern Native American party appeared, quite unsuccessfully, in the municipal election at Quincy.[10] In 1854, the secret lodge of Know-Nothings reached Illinois and complicated the already involved situation. The secret nature of the organization added yet another uncertainty to an already long list of political imponderables.

Its greatest impact was in the Chicago area. The machinations of the Know-Nothing lodge were one of the important ingredients in the fusion party of the second Illinois congressional district. The most active members of the lodge had been Whigs who were ready to fuse or reorganize. The Whig *Chicago Journal* claimed that the congressional nominee, James H. Woodworth, and the *Chicago Tribune* management were Know-Nothing. Know-Nothing politicians, campaigning for a Maine Law enactment, won control of the Chicago city government in 1855.[11]

The three congressional districts across Illinois from Quincy to the Wabash were the scenes of important Know-Nothing movements. W. A. Richardson feared that he had been defeated by them in the Quincy district. In the Springfield district, Richard Yates was supported by this lodge to which he either belonged, or with which he enjoyed the closest *rapport*. Lincoln credited Yates' defeat to the reaction of the English-born Whigs of Morgan County to the rumor that Yates was a member of the secret organization. Democrat James C. Allen, who was re-elected by but one vote in the usually safe Wabash district, believed that the loss of Democratic votes in his district was the work of this order.[12] That the organization was composed largely of perplexed Whigs and constituted more of a threat to that party than to the Democratic party became more apparent after the election than before.

1854 was a trying year for Stephen A. Douglas. As a national politician who hoped to be the standard-bearer of his party in 1856, his energies were devoted to resolving the problems that divided his party sectionally. His position required him to take a more panoramic view than that of the local politician whose myopic vision welcomed the advantage a sectional issue might give his party in county, congressional district, or state. Thus Douglas offered what he may have considered to be a pair of comprehensive measures designed to heal the rifts that had threatened to pull the loosely knit Democratic party apart. Popular sovereignty, at least after its initial acceptance, seemed an appropriate way to terminate the threat of the slavery question in the territories. This formula would fend off any more Wilmot Proviso controversies, either with existing, unorganized regions or with new acquisitions. In this age of Manifest Destiny, of Cuba, Canada, and parts of Mexico—indeed, everything from Aurora Borealis to the Straits of Darien—ripening on the tree and ready to fall into the ample and receptive lap of Brother Jonathan (to be Uncle Sam when he grew), a formula that would eliminate the slavery question in Congress would smooth the path ahead.

Douglas at almost the same time proposed another nostrum to heal yet another running sore in the Democratic party—the internal improvement question. The newer regions of the Northwest especially hungered for improved transportation. They were "held back" by the failure of the federal government to clear obstacles to navigation of rivers, to improve lake and river harbors, and to build roads. On the other hand, the older democracy still considered Jackson's Maysville veto the law and the gospel. Men of the older and more southern part of the Northwest were more self-sufficient, producing less for market and buying less, more doctrinaire Jacksonian. The events of 1846 recalled the potential threat to the statesman of the Northwest implicit in this problem.

Douglas' "trial balloon" in this matter was contained in a letter to Governor Joel Matteson of Illinois, published in January, 1854.[13] He proposed that such improvements as were by their local nature excluded by the doctrine of the Maysville veto— even though interstate shipments might be involved—should be paid for by tonnage duties levied on the users. In this way, the Northwest would get its improvements without the annual battle for federal funds.

Some of the Whig editors, with a background favorable to internal improvements, found themselves in the position of scarcely knowing with which hand to hit first, that aimed at the tonnage duty scheme or that cocked to strike the Nebraska Bill. They tended to equate the two measures as pro-Southern and accused Douglas of joining the South to prevent the North from getting "anything." Even the Chicago anti-slavery organ, the *Free West,* found space to condemn the proposal as "peculiarly adapted to tax western trade, and western agriculture."[14] The long congressional battle over the Nebraska Bill, however, tended to absorb the most attention until the fall campaign.

The two Democratic newspapers that immediately attacked the Nebraska Bill included the tonnage duty project in the scope of their attacks on Douglas. Two other Democratic papers which were slow to commit themselves on the Nebraska Bill but which eventually threw themselves into the revolt against Douglas, either favored the Matteson letter proposal or, for a while, remained non-committal.[15]

Thus, not only did the very division of northwestern and Illinois Democrats which the tonnage duty proposal was intended to prevent take place, but it did so at a time when the Democratic party was already rent by dissension over the Nebraska Bill. The perennial River and Harbor Appropriation Bill came up in Congress soon after the Nebraska Act had been passed. As usual, the Illinois delegation was split on the measure: the two Allens from the southeastern districts voted against it; the two representatives from the southwestern area were absent; and Douglas voted against it. Pierce's veto message was the last straw and pushed the *Democratic Press* and the Wentworth organ, the *Democrat,* into revolt. The former, after months of hesitation, threw off the last shred of restraint and hurled defiance at the administration, "if this is treason to democracy, Mr. Pierce and Mr. Douglas 'may make the most of it.' " It was at this point, apparently, that the political alliance between Wentworth and Douglas went on the rocks for the previously silent Wentworth exploded with a letter to the *National Era* attempting to square himself with his old allies, the abolitionists, for his seeming indifference to the fate of the Nebraska Bill. A few weeks later he was claiming that it was the influence of Douglas' vote against the River and Harbor Bill that had induced Pierce to veto it.[16]

The association between what was regarded as a defeat of the Western Interest and the repeal of the Missouri Compromise restriction on slavery in the Nebraska region in 1854 reinforced the memory of a similar configuration during another phase of the slavery question—the Wilmot Proviso—with a similar defeat of the Western Interest. On this new occasion there was no doubt that the Anti-Nebraska sentiment took precedence over the economic issue. Yet, it was an age characterized by concern for material progress of which the railroad was the prime symbol. Among the people of the northern part of the Northwest especially, material progress was wedded to moral reform while slavery and the South seemed the great enemy of both. For some, however, the rivers and harbors were more near and dear than reform. Regardless of which of these considerations took priority, both led people into the broad channel of opposition to the Democratic party and to Douglas.

The Nebraska Bill provided the Whigs with a weapon with which to attack Douglas. That many professional politicians would regard the Nebraska Bill in this light was not surprising. In addition, however, it must be understood that the revolution of 1854 was, in part, a revolution against the leadership of the Democratic party, and nowhere was this more true than in Illinois. The centers of the personal revolt against Douglas and the Democratic leadership were in Chicago and in the region opposite St. Louis.

Long John Wentworth was the person around whom Chicago Democratic political unity shattered. There was a strong element of opposition to Wentworth among the Democrats of Cook County, an important segment which believed that after the Democratic success of 1852, the Free-Soilers (and Wentworth whose behavior had just stopped short of treason in 1848 should be whipped into line by being deprived of patronage under Pierce. Douglas had taken the opposite tack and attempted to reunite the party by providing support to Wentworth for Congress in 1852 and jobs for Free-Soilers. Indeed, the office of U.S. District Attorney was given to Thomas Hoyne, a Van Buren elector in 1848. S. S. Hayes had been the disappointed candidate of the Peck faction that had remained loyal through the Wilmot controversy. Therefore it was not surprising that in 1854, Douglas lost all of the soldiers of the Free-Soilers of 1848, although he retained some of the captains. He lost Wentworth and his personal following, and also the Peck-Hayes faction of "old Hunker" Democrats.[17] There was not much left except the Irish.

The populous group of counties opposite St. Louis was the scene of a stubborn struggle for mastery of the party. Wm.

H. Bissell had been announced as opposing the Kansas-Nebraska Bill on the final roll call but there was some evidence to indicate that he had promised that he would vote for the bill when the membership had been polled earlier. Bissell, immensely popular in the Northwest because of his belligerent answer to Jefferson Davis in the House of Representatives in 1850, had joined with former Senator Sidney Breese in an effort to buy the *State Register* and possibly to oppose the re-election of Douglas in 1852.[18]

Consider the course of ex-Senator Breese in the Kansas-Nebraska matter. He voted for the resolutions commending the Nebraska Bill in the Illinois legislature. In March, the Nebraska Bill embraced principles he had held for years: therefore he could not oppose it in spite of strained relations with Douglas. In September, his son, who had been "a little inclined to be Anti-Nebraska" although his objection had not been "to the *principle* of the bill, but the originator of it," knew that Breese was working to defeat Shield's effort to be re-elected to the Senate. During the State Fair, Breese assailed his former colleague, Douglas, as a traitor to the party for his appointment of Hoyne and other Free-Soilers to office and a traitor to the Union for imperiling it by the repeal of the Missouri Compromise.[19]

Nowhere was the spirit of the revolt against Douglas better expressed than in a letter written by one of the more moderate rebels, State Senator John M. Palmer, to his wife at the conclusion of the election to the Senate which saw Lyman Trumbull elected and Lincoln defeated:

> [The] great aim we have in view is the reorganization of the Democratic party on the basis of the personal independence of its members. Shields goes now which will be a warning Douglas cannot disregard.

When the last chance for reunion had passed, one dissenter, George T. Allen, expressed the bitterness of the feelings toward the Douglas-led remainder of the party when he wrote: "I feel that I have made a happy escape from a den of thieves, drunkards, gamblers and blackguards, and I would rather die than be again caught in such company."[20]

＊

The last of Lincoln's three law partners, Wm. H. Herndon, recalled that the repeal of the Missouri Compromise excited a new interest in politics in Lincoln. A personal conviction that the slavery issue would not be settled until slavery was either abolished or extended to the whole nation had been formed by this time. The partners represented the diverse influences playing on Illinois at this time—the emigrant from Kentucky and the younger man removed too late from the New England and abolition influence of Illinois College. Yet Herndon left a picture of the two lawyers reading the *New York Tribune,* the *National Era,* and the *Emancipator,* none of which was quite respectable in most Springfield libraries. Finally, they talked out the slavery question and Lincoln's office talk, after the Nebraska Bill had been introduced, "grew bolder."[21]

There is little contemporary evidence to support Herndon's recollections but they are supported by what followed. So far as is known, Lincoln made no Anti-Nebraska speeches on the spring circuit of the central Illinois courts of the kind Browning described as being made in the Military Tract (western Illinois). Although Lincoln became a candidate for the legislature, his law business seemed to have been interrupted but slightly.[22] His first speech was made to the Scott County Whig convention in Winchester on August 16, 1854. Several of his trips for other speeches outside Springfield were made in conjunction with his usual legal itinerary. None of this indicated any new fire, new zeal, or new patterns of political behavior. He had done as much or more for the Whig cause in other campaigns.

On the other hand, one point is clear: Lincoln displayed no interest at all in any matters that muddied the political waters of Illinois other than the repeal of the Missouri Compromise. His speeches made no reference to the temperance question. He seemed to have been singularly unaware (for a Whig) of the Know-Nothing movement and said nothing significant about it in public. For all his background in wangling internal improvements for Sangamon County, his interest in railways, and a Whig predilection for federally financed improvements, Lincoln left this issue to others. The one subject that seemed to interest him was the repeal of the Missouri Compromise.

Lincoln made but thirteen or fourteen speeches in the late summer and autumn of 1854. Most of them seem to have been the same speech, improved and enlarged, or cut and trimmed to suit the time and the audience. We know it as the Peoria speech because it was only in the form delivered at Peoria that we have a full report of it.[23] It was well prepared and beautifully organized. Indeed, it may have been the best of Lincoln's campaign speeches.

It was a good speech, in the main, because it represented a fusion of the political and the personal viewpoints to a degree that gave the speech a ring of integrity rarely present in campaign addresses. The circumstances required no exposition of the question of slavery itself. The public in 1854 did not find this branch of the argument necessary. Many argued a sectional competition in which the slavery issue was mainly symbolic. Abraham Lincoln, however, set the concrete problem before the country—slavery in Kansas and Nebraska—against the general problem of slavery, and sharply distinguished between the two.

The Peoria speech marked the beginning of Lincoln's record as an opponent of slavery. His exposition of the broader aspects of the question, reflective as it was of personal attitudes, included these well-known paragraphs:

This *declared* indifference, but as I must think, covert *real* zeal for the spread of slavery, I can not but hate. I hate it because of the monstrous injustice of slavery itself. I hate it because it deprives our republican example of its just influence in the world—enables the enemies of free institutions, with plausibility, to taunt us as hypocrites—causes the real friends of freedom to doubt our sincerity, and especially because it forces so many really good men amongst ourselves into an open war with the very fundamental principles of civil liberty—criticizing the Declaration of Independence, and insisting that there is no right principle of action but *self-interest*.

Before proceeding, let me say I think I have no prejudice against the Southern people. They are just what we would be in their situation. If slavery did not now exist amongst them, they would not introduce it. If it did now exist amongst us, we should not instantly give it up. This I believe of the masses north and south. Doubtless there are individuals, on both sides, who would not hold slaves under any circumstances; and others who would gladly introduce slavery anew, if it were out of existence. We know that some southern men do free their slaves, go north, and become tip-top abolitionists; while some northern ones go south, and become most cruel slave-masters.

When southern people tell us they are no more responsible for the origin of slavery than we; I acknowledge the fact. When it is said that the institution exists; and that it is very difficult to get rid of it, in any satisfactory way, I can understand and appreciate the saying. I surely will not blame them for not doing what I should not know how to do myself. If all earthly power were given me, I should not know what to do, as to the existing institution. My first impulse would be to free all the slaves, and send them to Liberia—to their own native land. But a moment's reflection would convince me, that whatever of high hope, (as I think there is) there may be in this, in the long run, its sudden execution is impossible. If they were all landed there in a day, they would all perish in the next ten days; and there are not surplus shipping and surplus money enough in the world to carry them there in many times ten days. What then? Free them all, and keep them among us as underlings? Is it quite certain that this betters their condition? I think I would not hold one in slavery, at any rate; yet the point is not clear enough for me to denounce people upon. What next? Free them, and make them politically and socially, our equals? My own feelings will not admit of this; and if mine would, we well know that those of the great mass of white people will not. Whether this feeling accords with justice and sound judgment, is not the sole question, if indeed, it is any part of it. A universal feeling, whether well or ill founded, can not be safely disregarded. We can not, then, make them equals. It does seem to me that systems of gradual emancipation might be adopted; but for their tardiness in this, I will not undertake to judge our brethren of the south.[24]

The main arguments against the Nebraska Bill were:

(1) That the repeal of the Missouri Compromise was unnecessary.

(2) That the repeal of the Missouri Compromise was a violation of a sectional compromise.

(3) That the repeal of the compromise might well extend slavery into Kansas and Nebraska.

(4) That slavery was different from the other, largely economic matters reserved to the states and to the people of new territories and therefore subject to the overall concepts of right and justice of the whole nation. The theory of popular sovereignty, on the contrary, "assumes that there *can* be *moral right*" in slavery.

(5) That the reduction of slavery to the level of other economic concerns was contrary to the spirit of the fathers of the country. "The spirit of seventy-six and the spirit of Nebraska, are utter antagonisms; and the former is being rapidly displaced by the latter."

(6) The only political issue out of the whole sweep of the slavery question was the repeal of the Missouri Compromise.

For the first time, Lincoln was compelled and perhaps wanted to face up to the most pressing problem of his time publicly. The dilemma of the moral issue and the constitutional problem was perfectly clear to him. Slavery was guaranteed to the states where it existed. A fugitive slave law was required by the Constitution. These facts must be respected. But an extension of the evil must be resisted and an awareness that it was an evil must be preserved if America was to be kept in the path of the fathers.

Lincoln provided small comfort for those who believed that all obligations to the South ceased with the breaking of the Missouri Compromise. On the other hand, he sought to combat the notion assiduously preached by Douglas and his followers that all who opposed the Nebraska Bill were abolitionists. "Stand *with* the abolitionists in restoring the Missouri Compromise,"

Lincoln urged his fellow Whigs, "and stand *against* him when he attempts to repeal the fugitive slave law."

The most remarkable feature of the Peoria speech was the way it foreshadowed almost every later Lincoln position. The need for moral alertness so much emphasized in 1858, the persistent flirtation with colonization, the suggestion of gradualism, these were constants. In an age of violent shifts and reversals by politicians, Lincoln's consistency was remarkable. One has to recall by way of contrast Prince John Van Buren, a bolter of 1848 and a regular of 1854; John Logan, the most pro-Southern of the Illinois Democrats before the war and the most radical of Republicans after the war; and, of course, Ben Butler, the Breckinridge Democrat of 1860 and the violent radical Republican later. Each may have had his own consistency. But the stability of Lincoln's views argues, as does Herndon, that Lincoln's fundamental concepts about the moral question in politics had been thought out before the campaign opened in 1854. One necessary ingredient of the full reorientation was still lacking at this stage—a realization of the revolution in party organization required to fit the moral issue into the political process.

What of the political "how?" How was the political process to be made to yield the desired result of putting the nation back on the track laid down by the fathers of the American Revolutionary Age? How well adapted to the end of securing such a policy was the party system of two great national parties? Were the usual techniques of compromise and adjustment sufficient to achieve the purpose? Were the usual practices of the parties, the usual incentives of offices and favors compatible with the high moral purpose of the anti-slavery movement? Lincoln would have a share in attempting to find answers to these questions.

For Lincoln, 1854 was a year of reversal of what might have been expected on the basis of his earlier experience. In the crisis of 1846–50, the evidence indicates that Lincoln was more concerned with process than policy, with party success than with the moral issue. In the year of the Nebraska Bill, on the contrary, it was Lincoln's views of policy that were of interest. A revolution in party organization was taking place all around him except in his home district in 1854, yet the hand of the master political manager was not set to the task of political reconstruction. When the Whig party was expiring, Lincoln was still a Whig.

The Whig party of the state and of the nation was literally, in the language of the time, "used up." The great national figures whose personalities had contributed to the party more of its uniqueness than its program had given it were missing from the stage. General Winfield Scott and Millard Fillmore were a far cry from Clay and Webster. The bright young man of the party, Wm. H. Seward, was a distinctly sectional rather than a national figure. The great national issues such as the tariff were still important in some areas but had always left the voters of Illinois cold. The prosperity of the fifties, too, had closed minds to the other historic economic issues that had distinguished Whig from Democrat in the 1830's and early 1840's, such as the United States Bank. The drubbing of 1852 was sufficient to persuade many that the Whig party had one foot in the grave. A recurrence of a slavery or sectional controversy tended to shove the very sketchy unity within the Whig party deeper into the background.

It must be remembered, too, that the Whig party had been a minority party in Illinois since its inception. There had been loaves and fishes for the faithful only in the national administrations whereas the Democrats had distributed the "pap" within the state steadily. If organization by modern standards was sketchy, there was yet a strong corps of interested persons to guide and do the "leg" work for the Democratic party. Not so the Whigs, except for a few counties in which they controlled the court house offices. They were an army without non-commissioned officers, strongly concentrated in certain areas where they enjoyed local success, cooperating in the well-nigh hopeless cause of the gubernatorial and presidential election "man to man" among the sectional leaders.

If the Whigs were divided from the Democrats on the national scene largely by hunger for office, there was even less to divide them within the state. The most serious controversial issues divided the state regionally, usually northern Illinois versus southern, as had been the case with the general incorporation law for banks, the Free Negro Act, etc. If there was any difference before 1854, it was in the greater ease with which the Whigs of the northern part of the state had cooperated with the radical anti-slavery people in local politics. Indeed, the one bright spot on the Whig horizon had been their success in the 1852 congressional elections when they won in four of nine districts: in three of the four cases abolitionist support had helped.

In the long run, the more pessimistic among the Whigs, the ones who gave up easily, were right. Illinois could only do as the nation did and reconstruct party politics to fit the state of the public mind. The more optimistic, viewing the shattering collapse of the Democratic party in the state with unrestrained glee, thought that the Whig strategy of 1846–50 might do the trick this time. The first reaction of a number of Whigs was to be grateful for an issue or issues that might vault them into the saddle at long last. The occasion seemed auspicious because Whigs could boast with truth that every northern Whig in Congress had voted against the Nebraska Bill. One party journal went so far as to regard the Nebraska Bill as "politically considered a source of gratification, for it raises up the WHIG PARTY from a season of depression and despondency and gloom to action and vigorous life."[25]

It was not to be. As Lincoln found out to his sorrow in the coming session of the legislature, Democrats had deserted the leadership of the party in such numbers that they did not automatically fall prize to the Whig opposition. Indeed, the distrust and dislike born of years of political battle proved an obstacle not easily surmounted and created an attitude not easily forgotten within the Republican party for many years. In the second place, a demand for fusion of the opposition, for party reconstruction was strong among the abolitionists and the more moderate ex-Van Burenites. Even some Whigs were ready to fuse and thought that the day of the politician was past. These were located in the northern part of the state and were probably influenced by Greeley. The *Chicago Tribune* plumped for fusion while the *Rock Island Advertiser* was urging statewide fusion for a time.[26]

The Whigs were handicapped by some desertion to the Democrats. Lincoln's old friend, General Usher P. Linder, quipped that "the Whig party is dead—and I am left a widower."[27] Another political friend of long standing, General James W. Singleton, bolted and the last Whig United States Marshal, Benjamin Bond, joined the trickle. These men, of southern origin all, had thought things out to the ultimate choice of Constitution and Union with slavery or abolition with war or a divided nation. They had decided for the former.

In faster growing northern Illinois, where in the absence of strong state organization the decisions were left to local leadership, the Whig party was to all intents and purposes liquidated. In the northernmost district, E. B. Washburne, who had won the Whig nomination in 1852 by a margin so narrow that a rump convention of his opposition had been threatened, faced a difficult time in the regular Whig convention. Pursuant to a call issued by leading Whigs and Free Democrats of Winnebago County, the Anti-Nebraska convention met at Rockford and renominated Washburne. These fusionists proclaimed themselves to be "Republicans" and their nominee made a speech in which he said that he gloried in going forth to battle under that name. The resolutions, typical of the northern counties, demanded repeal of the Fugitive Slave Law, no more slave states, non-extension of slavery, and the abolition of slavery in all federally controlled territory. A Whig convention met and endorsed the Washburne nomination over considerable opposition and feebly protested the establishment of a new party as unnecessary.[28]

In the second district, which ran across the state from Rock Island to Chicago and included both, county "Peoples" conventions elected delegates to the district convention at Aurora and passed radical resolutions. The Whig convention for the district met at the same place and date because a joint nomination scheme had been arranged through the Know-Nothings. But the plan fell through and the nomination went to a Democrat, possibly through superior connivance directed by Wentworth.[29] A separate nomination by the Whigs figured only slightly in the general election.

The third district saw a former Whig nominated by a hectic fusion convention. But in the old Whig area of the central part of the state, all nominations for Congress were made by regular Whig conventions meeting under their own name. One exception should be noted—the Alton district where the Whigs supported Lyman Trumbull against a "regular" Democratic nominee. Thus, of the nine congressional districts, three had fused and another presented no Whig nominee. In five of the districts of the state, the Whigs sought to move along their accustomed paths except for garnering in sheaths of dissatisfied Democratic voters or so they expected.

There was only one state office at stake in this off-year so that it was easy for the Whigs of the center to resist fusion at the state level. Fusion was repugnant to them not only because abolitionists were still distrusted among these Whigs of Southern origin but because the Whigs were at least "in the running" in this area. Fusion smacked of an effort to extort a share of the expected profits from the Whigs. A statement of this view in the *Illinois Journal* may have reflected Lincoln's opinion at this stage:[30]

> The Whig party, in our opinion, in this State, will not consent to the proposition to fuse into a single organization to effect the restoration of the Missouri Compromise. . . . They are a unit on the subject of the Nebraska outrage; and they see no necessity of breaking up their organization for the purpose of becoming a new political party, with a single object in view. . . . There have always been but two large permanent parties in the country; and when the Nebraska matter is disposed of, the members of the free soil party will fall into the ranks of one of the other parties. . . . What would the end be if the Whigs were to give

up their organization, and unite with the same men [Free Soilers] in the coming election?—They might carry the election in this State—but what would be the future of the Whigs?

All that passed in the northern end of the state was not hidden from Lincoln. He spoke in Chicago once and in Bloomington twice. These were in "fusion" country. The third district politicians and lawyers with whom he had travelled the circuit were his intimates. He had campaigned in Putnam which was as radical as any county. At his side was Herndon who had connections with the radical leaders. Lincoln found out about the Know-Nothings in the last stages of the campaign. He was invited to appear at a purported organization meeting of the Republican party in Springfield and declined with some awkwardness.[31]

It may have been that the Whig party to which Lincoln had adhered throughout his political career, set the limits of his thought about political organization at this time. An optimistic Whig might have misread the results of the northern Illinois fusion to mean that the Whig party was in the saddle. Things simply may have had a different cast viewed from where Lincoln sat at the heart of Whig strength. His candidacy for the United States Senate in 1855 certainly showed no appreciation of the fact that he was a leader of a defunct or fast falling party. While his own congressional district had been lost to the Democrats, there was a reasonable explanation requiring no loss of faith in Whiggery.[32] Certainly the results of the election were subject to the interpretation that the Democrats had lost one seat in Congress and carried a previously certain district by but one vote. Whig gain was the habitual reciprocal of Democratic loss.

Finally, it may have been that Lincoln's native caution prevented him from abandoning the Whig ship for want of any other likely prospect of political organization. There was no need, in the campaign of 1854, to offend or to embrace the Republicans (as the radicals called themselves), no necessity to commit himself one way or the other about the Know-Nothings. Certainly, after the prospects of the Whig party nationally and in Illinois became more dismal, this wait and see attitude was clearly defined. Just when it became clear to him that the beloved old party was shattered and gone is not certain.

If Lincoln was not entirely clear about the lay of the political land at the time of the election, his candidacy for the Senate seat to be filled when the newly elected legislature assembled in 1855 schooled him quickly. Exactly when it occurred to Lincoln to seek the post held by General Shields is unknown. Horace White, a Chicago newspaperman, urged Lincoln to make a speech in Chicago near the close of the campaign in order to make contacts which would be useful if he should become a candidate. If there had been any plan to run, it had been well concealed before the results of the election began to pour in with the news of an overwhelming Anti-Nebraska victory. His first letter of many soliciting votes in the legislature was dated November 10, 1854, after the election. It is difficult to believe that Lincoln would have allowed himself to have been elected to the House of Representatives had he been seriously considering running for United States Senator at the time his name was placed on the district ticket. The constitution of the state contained a provision that denied the legislature the right to choose one of its members for the post and Lincoln was compelled to resign his seat. This caused some embarrassment to Lincoln's candidacy, for the seat was lost through one of the oldest tricks in the business—the Democrats pretended to have no candidate, then trooped to the polls on election day in sufficient numbers to elect their man. Yet, if Lincoln had not been a pre-election candidate, it is difficult to understand how there could have been a deal by which the Chicago Whigs had run no legislative candidates in return for support for Lincoln in the legislature as Washburne believed.[33]

The nature of the political revolution became clearer to Lincoln as he encountered not the time-honored and clear-cut battle of Whig versus Democrat but pawns in the game who were "more whig than free soil," one a "secret nominee of the Know Nothings," and one who was "in reality for the man who will be of the most service to him," certainly no unique figure in the politics of any year. Winnebago (northern) members were distrustful of the old Springfield interest.[34] Besides people who had been one thing and were now another and legislators who were part one thing and part another, Lincoln was compelled to reckon with one open and avowed abolitionist, Owen Lovejoy, brother of the martyred publisher and just as radical.

Of the 28 Whigs and 14 Anti-Nebraska Democrats, Lincoln noted that many had "gone into the Republican organization."[35] It was the Anti-Nebraska Democrats who were the most uncertain element in the mixture. Few had been committed to any new organization. Many had ambitions. Most thought of themselves as returning to the Democratic fold at some future time when the party had been purged of Douglas and his henchmen. Indeed, genial James Shields, one-time challenger of Lincoln to settle a political quarrel on the field of honor, grievously wounded in the Mexican War and vaulted from a patronage office to the Senate as a protégé of Douglas, was not opposed either because of his personal qualifications or for his views on the slavery question but because he was regarded as a tool of Douglas.

The unmanageable aspect of the Anti-Nebraska Democrats at this stage of the political revolution was that they stood neither entirely within nor entirely outside the organization. A Northern editor surveyed the field of fellow bolters and listed 5 of the leading Anti-Nebraska Democrats in the legislature, each of whom had supported regular Democratic candidates for other offices or not actively opposed them. There was lots of talk of finding "grounds of reunion" and healing the breach in the party. Where they would be found when the final moment of decision would be reached was a very doubtful point. It was this particular uncertainty that led Lincoln to release his friends to vote for Trumbull lest the Democrats and Anti-Nebraska Democrats reunite on Governor Matteson who was more than willing.[36]

There probably was no way in which Lincoln's popularity

might have been enhanced sufficiently to have changed the out-come. The result was controlled by a handful of Democrats of an Anti-Nebraska turn who would not have supported a Whig. However, a move was suggested which at the time seemed to offer a chance for Lincoln to win—namely to commit himself to a more radical stance on the slavery question.[37] This raised questions that projected themselves far beyond the senatorial election into the realm of the future opposition party, which Lincoln at this time probably hoped would continue to be the Whig party. Would not the war be lost if, for the sake of the skirmish of the moment, the old and tried, regular troops, the central Illinois Whigs of origin not dissimilar to his own, were to be disregarded and tempted to follow their friends into the Know-Nothing morass or into the camp of the enemy? Whether restrained by his integrity, by a political prescience which saw the Whig strength of the central part of the state as the cornerstone of any new political alignment, or by a conservatism that made him stay where he was until he had a clearer view of what was to come, he went down to defeat without committing himself to any change of platform. He was still the Lincoln of the Peoria speech. Time—and a little politics—would bring the abolitionists and the politicians to him.

1. Yates MSS, Carlinville, Mar. 1, 1854, Joseph C. Howell.
2. *Illinois Journal,* Jan. 21, 1854; Jan. 23 and 30, Feb. 6, 1854.
3. *Quincy Whig,* Oct. 9, 1854.
4. *Free West* (Chicago), June 22, 1854; see resolutions of the Rock Island Anti-Nebraska convention in the *Rock Island Advertiser,* Sept. 13, 1854; Elihu B. Washburne MSS, (Library of Congress), Belvidere, Dec. 25, 1854 (Signature of writer illegible).
5. *Free West,* July 20, 1854. This particular covenant was adopted at Ottawa.
6. T. C. Pease and J. G. Randall, editors, *The Diary of Orville Hickman Browning* (Illinois Historical Collection), XX, I, 129–30.
7. *Alton Courier,* Nov. 18, 1853. He objected that the *State Register,* practically the official party newspaper, opposed the Maine Law and thus virtually committed the party to oppose it.
8. *AHMS MSS,* Nov. 20, 1854, Rev. S. W. Phelps. He interpreted the election returns "as an index of the temperance and anti-Nebraska feeling of Lee Center!" *Chicago Journal,* Oct. 24, 1854.

9. *Alton Telegraph,* Oct. 20, 1854; John M. Palmer MSS (Illinois State Historical Library), Sept. 18, 1854, David A. Smith.

10. *Quincy Whig,* Apr. 25, 1853.

11. Oct. 3, 1854. See also Washburne MSS, Chicago, Sept. 19, 1854, R. S. Wilson; *Chicago Times,* Feb. 19 and Mar. 8, 1855.

12. Stephen A. Douglas MSS (University of Chicago Library), Quincy, Nov. 5, 1854, W. A. Richardson. He reported "seventeen lodges in this District & the smallest no. of Dem. in either of them is twenty. . . ." He won re-election; Yates MSS, Springfield, July 5, 1855, J. M. Allen; *Collected Works,* II, 286–7, Springfield, Nov. 12, 1854, O. H. Browning; James C. Allen MS (Unpublished recollections of the former congressman in the hands of his descendants), p. 9.

13. The text of the Matteson Letter may be found in the *Democratic Press* (Chicago), Jan. 27, 1854. No suggestion is made that Douglas was an innovator in the case of either proposition. Popular sovereignty was developed in the Nicholson letter of Cass; the tonnage duty scheme was a suggestion made by Polk.

14. *Chicago Journal,* Jan. 21, 1854. Two long articles on the tonnage duty scheme found their way into the columns of the *Northwestern Gazette* (Galena), Jan. 31, 1854, compared to two paragraphs devoted to the Nebraska Bill; Feb. 9, 1854.

15. *Alton Telegraph,* Feb. 3 and 10, 1854, referring to the *Ottawa Free Trader* and the *Galena Jeffersonian; Alton Courier,* Feb. 7, 1854; *Democratic Press* (Chicago), Jan. 27, 1854.

16. *Congressional Globe,* 33rd Congress, 1st Session, p. 1712; Aug. 9, 1854; *Chicago Democrat,* Aug. 19, 1854; Sept. 23, 1854.

17. Douglas MSS, Dec. 29, 1852, J. Wentworth; Nov. 21, 1853, C. H. Lanphier; *Democratic Press* (Chicago), Mar. 18, 1853; *Chicago Journal,* Feb. 9, 1854.

18. George Fort Milton, *Eve of Conflict: Stephen A. Douglas and the Needless War* (Boston: Houghton Mifflin Co., 1934), p. 172; Brayman MSS, Jan. 8, 1852, Geo. W. Billings; Douglas MSS, Nov. 11, 1852, Maj. T. L. Harris.

19. Breese MSS, Mar. 20, 1854, unsigned and unaddressed draft of a letter; Sept. 26, 1854, H. L. Breese; *Quincy Whig,* Oct. 16, 1854.

20. Palmer MSS, Jan. 31, 1855; Lyman Trumbull MSS (Library of Congress), Jan. 19, 1856.

21. Paul M. Angle, (ed.), *Herndon's Life of Lincoln* (New York: Albert and Charles Boni, 1936), p. 292.

22. Paul M. Angle, *Lincoln 1854–1861* (Springfield: Abraham Lincoln Association, 1933), *passim.*

23. *Collected Works,* II, 247–83.

24. *Ibid.,* pp. 255–6.

25. *Alton Telegraph,* June 2, 1854; *Chicago Journal,* quoted in the *Chicago Democratic Press,* May 24, 1854.

26. *Chicago Journal,* Oct. 3, 1854; *Rock Island Advertiser,* Sept. 6, 1854.

27. *Peoria Press,* Aug. 30, 1854.

28. Washburne MSS, C. K. Williams (no date but ca. Sept., 1852); Sept. 17, 1854, B. G. Wheeler; *Galena Gazette,* Sept. 1, and Sept. 8, 1854; *Free West,* Aug. 10 and Sept. 7, 1854.

29. Washburne MSS, Sept. 19, 1854, R. S. Wilson; *Chicago Journal,* Oct. 2, 1854.

30. July 27, 1854.

31. Angle, *Herndon's Life of Lincoln,* pp. 299–300.

32. Angle, *Lincoln 1854–1861,* p. 44.

33. Robert Todd Lincoln Papers (microfilm), Nos. 506–7, Chicago, Oct. 25, 1854, Horace White. This title will be abbreviated to RTL hereinafter; *Collected Works,* II, 303–4, Springfield, [Jan.] 6, 1855, E. B. Washburne; RTL No. 632, Dec. 19, 1854, E. B. Washburne.

34. *Ibid.,* Nos. 585, 656, and 643; No. 594, Dec. 12, 1854, E. B. Washburne.

35. *Collected Works,* II, 296–8.

36. *Alton Telegraph,* Dec. 2, 1854, quoting the *Ottawa Free Trader;* Douglas MSS, Dec. 10, 1854, J. S. McConnell; *Collected Works,* II, 304–6, Feb. 9, 1854, E. B. Washburne.

37. Washburne MSS, Rockford, Dec. 18, 1854, Anson Miller.

Between Whig and Republican

1855, the year following his disappointment over not winning the Senate seat by a narrow margin, was unique in Lincoln's
political life—he was not a member of a party. His party had
dissolved around him. It was the end of a life-long, congenial,
political friendship. His political career and that of the Whig
party in Illinois had begun life almost together
and, except for his first election to the state
House of Representatives, his activity in public affairs had been channeled through the
Whig party. He found himself in a new, difficult, and unrelished
situation. Old and trusted political friends had gone over to the
Democrats. Other equally cherished friends were chasing the
will-o'-the-wisp of Know-Nothingism which Lincoln could not
abide. In a personal letter to a friend of earlier days, now living
in Kentucky, Lincoln wrote in his perplexity:

CHAPTER 4

> You inquire where I now stand. That is a disputed point. I
> think I am a Whig; but others say there are not Whigs, and that
> I am an Abolitionist. When I was at Washington, I voted for the
> Wilmot Proviso as good as forty times; and I never heard of any
> one attempting to unwhig me for that. I now do no more than
> oppose the extension of slavery. I am not a Know-Nothing; that
> is certain.[1]

In this dismal and uncertain year, Lincoln was very like the
blind man removed from the familiar certainties of his own home

into strange surroundings where every move could occasion a painful surprise.

Among the unfamiliar objects in his new political surroundings, and almost certain to become a permanent fixture with which he must come to some terms, were the abolitionists. These people, and there were more of them than Lincoln had believed existed, expected a sort of mass camp meeting reaction, a sudden dawning of the moral light, a conversion to the truth to which everyone but themselves had been blind until Kansas-Nebraska had opened their eyes. They reacted to the slavery issue in a different way than Sangamon County Whigs had reacted to the bank or tariff questions or even to the problem of where the state capital should be located. They were whole-hoggers with a contempt for the timeworn give and take of the partisan struggle. They were impatient of the slow processes of government, without the capacity to settle for less than complete victory, without respect for compromise or for politicians. What was wrong was wrong and should be eliminated forthwith.

Wait Talcott, one of the fusion representatives from Winnebago County, had come to Springfield with the intention of voting either for Owen Lovejoy or Ichabod Codding—both semi-professional abolitionists—for United States Senator from Illinois.[2] This was a sample of the abolitionist lack of political sense that a politician found so difficult to understand. Talcott was determined to vote for the most extreme person on the slavery question, the one least likely to attract the votes of other legislators. In a doubtful race, the politicians would run someone at the other end of the scale—a moderate who might win the votes of undecided legislators. In any case, politicians would know a hopeless political cause and would not throw away a vote when there was any chance to influence the outcome.

Not just party methods but the old parties, Whig and Democrat, were suspect among these people. Abolition journals had denounced them for years. Zebina Eastman, whose suspicious nose had wrinkled at every bit of political maneuvering in the fusion conventions of the past year, had written that the abolitionists "rejoice in the death of whiggery, and in the dying throes of the democracy. . . ." The old parties had condemned themselves by their failure to take "high ground" on the slavery issue. Lincoln himself had been dealt with unkindly by this grim, uncompromising editor when he had been campaigning for the Senate in words which emphasized how far apart he and Lincoln were: "he [Lincoln] is only a Whig and this people's movement is no Whig triumph."[3]

While Lincoln had not been without contacts with abolitionists before, this had been his first experience in having to deal with them as important building blocks of a political edifice. He had had the even more curious experience of being considered by the abolitionists as a potential block in their own projected edifice. In 1854, the abolitionists had attempted to organize a state committee of the "Republican" party at Springfield and had invited Lincoln to join them. Lincoln avoided committing himself. In November, in spite of his ambitions to be Senator, he had declined an invitation to attend a Chicago meeting of the central committee to which he had been named and the abolitionist press had remembered this against him.[4] It was this abortive effort of the abolitionists to set up state party machinery under the name "Republican" and under their control which delayed the use of this name for the party in Illinois until national elections made it necessary. In sum, here was a new and somewhat unpredictable element in Illinois politics.

How far these people wanted to go and how his Whig friends reacted to their demands was revealed in the same session of the legislature in which Lincoln's bid for the senatorship had been rejected. Resolutions introduced into the Assembly by Lovejoy would have instructed the Senators from Illinois to vote against any new slave states being admitted to the Union and to vote for the repeal or modification of the Fugitive Slave Law. The Whigs of the center had voted against these resolutions of instruction and Logan, Lincoln's second law partner, had lost his temper. He protested that:

he had been called upon from day to day to vote on proposition after proposition, introduced by the abolitionists of the north. . . . The Whigs had been rode, and rode, and rode to death, by this question; and for one he did not intend to submit to it any longer. He had consented to be rode, till the senatorial election was over, but it was now time to stop. The Whigs had been permitted to make a race for senator, just fast enough to lose money.[5]

In the autumn Joshua Giddings and Ichabod Codding stopped in Springfield on a speaking tour, the object of which was the revival of the abolitionist Republican party which had died out after the election of the previous fall.[6] Editorial comment in the *Journal* may have represented Lincoln's own thoughts at the time, or, at least, the thought of the kind of people he knew and understood—those who might support Lincoln in any political reconstruction that might take place in the future:

The Missouri faith-breakers led on by such men as Atchison and Douglas have done much to estrange the two great sections of the country from each other;—shall the conservative and Union-loving men of the great west go farther and be found battling with a party, which would only add fuel to the slavery excitement which now distracts the councils of the nation. We cannot but think our Whig friends—those, who opposed to the repeal of the Missouri Compromise, because it reopened a dangerous subject—will pause before they cut loose entirely from their old landmarks and yield up everything, even their name, to a party which is governed by but a single idea, and that of the most impracticable kind.

The new party that Codding and Giddings advocated

would have the north cut loose entirely from all political relations with the south, and form an organization of a purely geographical character. It would . . . create a sectional animosity between the two which would end,—in heaven only knows what. Its principles, as they are proclaimed by its leaders, know no mean, no point of compromise.[7]

To judge from the program of the eastern Republicans, the *Journal* commented, "this love for the Missouri Compromise on the part of such journals as the New York Tribune was a mere sham, intended only as bait to catch the unsuspecting, and to be cast aside as soon as it had answered its purpose."

If this bald rejection of the Republican radicalism was Lincoln's by authorship, by advice or by consent, it was far more emphatic and less tactful than the personal declination to assist in a fusion attempt that Lincoln had written to Lovejoy somewhat earlier. Reverend Owen Lovejoy, Princeton preacher and brother of the abolition martyr, had been a member of the Illinois legislature and was one of the leading abolitionists of the state. He apparently wrote identical or nearly identical letters to Lincoln and to Senator Trumbull suggesting steps to revive the coalition of 1854. Lincoln's reply was moderate enough, suggesting that the success of fusion attempts would be unlikely until the Know-Nothings had been deprived of hope of success under their own banner. Trumbull's reply was in the negative and curiously tactless for a politician in that he expressed hope that a convention of the Democracy "opposed equally to the spread of slavery, to abolition, & to Know Nothingism" would produce the best results. He expected much from Kansas as a means of "uniting the opponents of slavery propagandism. . . ."[8]

Sometime between his defeat for the Senate in January, 1855, and before the Springfield meeting of Anti-Nebraska lawyers that produced the first concrete steps toward the formation of a new party in December of the same year, Lincoln came to the most crucial decision of his political career, the slowly arrived at conclusion that the slavery issue would dominate American politics until a definite settlement—not a compromise—was reached. This decision represented no alteration of his long-held belief that slavery was immoral but, rather, an about-face on the political method for dealing with the problem. Until the doom of the Whig party was clear, Lincoln had clung to the prevailing notion that the national parties were agents for handling the general business of the country, in which all sectional viewpoints were trimmed down by compromise and adjustment so that each party, Whig and Democratic, would have appeal in the three major sections of the country.

The violence of the outcry against the Nebraska Bill convinced him that the anti-slavery feeling was too strong to be stilled. He accepted his own advice given in the Peoria speech in 1854. "The great mass of mankind . . . consider slavery a great moral wrong; and their feeling against it, is not evanescent, but eternal. . . . It is a great and durable element of popular action, and I think, no statesman can safely disregard it."[9]

Furthermore, Lincoln suspected that the one remaining national party, the Democratic, was not antiseptically neutral on the slavery question. Its "declared indifference" he feared was "covert real zeal for the spread of slavery."[10]

The art of the politician has something in common with the skill of the horse-trader. The skillful politician needs to know how anxious those with whom he is bargaining are, how far they will go. Here were straws in the wind. The Lovejoy letter and the Giddings-Codding mission were indicators that the abolitionists were anxious. Their hope of abolitionizing the country as a result of the Missouri Compromise repeal had faded. They were now jockeying for the most advanced position possible for the long fight, to get the "highest ground" on the slavery question. They were impatient. Something must be done to save Kansas, where the Emigrant Aid Society was operating to plant fighters for freedom. Financed by New England abolitionists, this Society provided support for emigrants willing to settle in Kansas and committed to keeping that state free. This was intended to offset the flow of slavery-minded Missourians into the Kansas prairies.

If the year following Trumbull's election had destroyed the Illinois abolitionists' illusions of a quick and complete victory, it also proved an uncomfortable year, a year of waiting to see, for the Anti-Nebraska Democrats. Indeed, they were out on a limb. They called themselves Democrats, yet the people who controlled the party machinery, the administration in Washington and Douglas in Illinois, repelled them. They were in that most embarrassing position—politicians without a party. Trumbull met Douglas at Salem in the autumn and a debate was arranged, but the former spent so much time proving himself a Democrat that Douglas cancelled the arrangement. John M. Palmer was not sure that he would not vote for James Buchanan for the presidency, if the Pennsylvanian succeeded in winning the nomination from Douglas. He spoke of uniting and discovering the strength of the anti-administration Democracy. Trumbull trusted "that a Democrat opposed to slavery extension and abolition" would run. Wm. H. Bissell asked Trumbull whom the Cincinnati convention would select "as our standard bearer."[11]

But the Democratic press, under orders from Douglas, carried a relentless "war on Trumbull," who "must no longer be considered a Democrat. . . ." The *Register* commanded the Democrats to "cut out this leprous spot from the Democratic party. Let 'NO TERMS WITH TRAITORS' be the watchword." By autumn, an impressive array of Anti-Nebraska Democrats of the Chicago region held a public meeting at which a set of resolutions was adopted which amounted to giving up all pretension of remaining in the same party with Douglas. Events in Kansas had some part in this proceeding.[12] With a national election just around the corner, here was a considerable body of politicians waiting for a political roof to get under.

What of Lincoln's own party—the Whigs? A considerable body of them had turned to the Know-Nothing movement which, however, had lost much of its glamour as the secrecy wore off. The Whigs, like the writers of the editorials in the *Journal,* were caught in a dilemma. The most outspoken critcism of their longtime opponents, the Democrats, came from the abolitionists. But the Whigs were the party of the Compromise of 1850, the conservatives, the Union-loving party. Their dilemma was so plain to see that it provided the Democrats with their line of attack. Douglas, who campaigned through the state in 1855 despite the fact that there was no state election, pleaded that it was "the duty of patriots, without distinction of party, to rally to a common standard for the maintenance of the constitution and the preservation of the Union." Just as Lincoln saw that the Know-Nothing movement was at best a temporary refuge for the Whigs, so did Douglas. He leveled his guns at this movement in order to force the Whigs to a final choice between the abolitionists and the Democrats. Whigs and abolitionists, "check by jowl, Whig colors under which they have fought so long and gallantly, with the black flag of abolitionism . . ."—this was the taunt intended to lever the Whigs away from their alliance with the radicals.[13] Democrats thought that it was working.

In the face of this attrition, how long could the Whigs last and still carry some weight into whatever successor organization would be created? Would the old party's strength be frittered away before a new structure could be created? Where would that leave Lincoln? Lincoln was a political general only because there was an army of Whigs. That is why Lincoln had been approached about fusion. But if his army melted away, so would his political future.

The Whigs, Southern in origin in many cases and with considerable seniority as citizens of Illinois, and the abolitionists, Yankee and more recent arrivals in the main, seemed poles apart at this stage. Suspicion characterized the relations among the Whigs, who salvaged very little out of the election of '54 with many votes, and the Anti-Nebraska Democrats, who reaped the rewards with fewer votes. Yet, Lincoln must have remembered the cooperation of 1854. He was also aware of another bond among the scattered foes of the Democracy—an implacable hatred of Douglas.

So, Lincoln waited and Trumbull delayed, each attempting to conceal his nervousness, his weakness, and trying to protect his bargaining position by waiting for the other to make the first move. There were several reasons why the move had to be made, important reasons why it couldn't wait too much longer. The first of these was that pressures from outside the circle of political leaders were beginning to tell. At Monmouth, a public meeting assembled to "harmonize and unite all and every citizen and voter on our liberal basis" and adjourned until Washington's birthday.[14] Things might proceed as in 1854 from the ground up, with no top echelon leadership at all.

Secondly, there was Kansas. As early as August, 1855, Trumbull had pointed out to Lovejoy that "Events now transpiring in Kansas will do much to unite the opponents of slavery propagandism. . . ." Matters there were deteriorating rapidly, moving inexorably toward the climax of the next May. Whatever constitutional views, whatever degree of opposition to slavery, friends of freedom were bound to cooperate to save this territory, this concrete case. A lot of Illinois folks were interested in Kansas. Some had emigrated to its wide-open spaces.[15] Some Democrats had secured political jobs there. The farther West had always been of concern to Illinois citizens. What happened there was their business.

Finally, there would be a national election in 1856. While it is a fact that the American political party is a bundle of state organizations, state politics also reflect national political trends. The flare-up of 1854 had occurred in the off-year. Anxious eyes turned to Washington to see what lead toward party reorganization the senators and representatives of the opposition (to the Democratic administration) would give. No clear signs had yet appeared. Men like Trumbull were still on the fence. But the necessity of nominating national tickets in opposition to the Democrats set a deadline to the waiting. Spring would be the last moment.

So much has the frontier condition of life in Lincoln's youth and young manhood been emphasized, and so skillfully was his frontier background exploited in his political campaigns that there is a tendency to forget that the drama of Lincoln and Douglas or even the impersonal drama of the politician and moral issue was played against a swiftly moving backdrop. The

Illinois of the 1850's was no longer a frontier, its people—even its newest people—were no longer pioneers. The state was forging forward in a great period of boom, of growth, of more settled and mature ways, of sprinting in the race of progress. The Illinois that voted for Abraham Lincoln for President in 1860 was the fourth state in the Union in population, having passed the venerable states of Virginia and Massachusetts and neighboring Indiana during the previous decade.[16]

The prairies which Lincoln had crossed in the not distant past on horseback, in solitude or in the rolicking company of fellow lawyers, were yielding to the plow. Land passed from the hands of the government into the hands of farmers, speculators, and railroads at the rate of twelve million acres in the seven years from 1849 to 1856, leaving only two million acres of public land in the latter year. The land offices, so much a part of the earlier political patronage landscape, were closed, save the one at Springfield where the remaining driblet of business was to be wound up. The land was being used. Illinois could boast (and most assuredly did) of being the first state in corn production, the first in wheat (having grown one eighth of the American crop), second in beef cattle and second in hogs.[17]

Railroads were beginning to criss-cross the state. With ten roads projected to every one completed, townsite speculation reached the proportions of the days when Lincoln had helped frame the ill-timed Internal Improvement scheme just as the Panic of 1837 was imminent. But towns were growing and Chicago had become a city of over a hundred thousand at the end of the decade. Amenities were added and life softened as the frontier receded into Kansas, Iowa, Minnesota, and into farther away places. The number of actors in the state increased from 2 to 66 (the census gives no indication of the regularity of work), bankers from a lonesome 3 to 216, music teachers from a dozen to 211, professors from 6 to 71, and teachers multiplied almost six-fold, while the population merely doubled.[18]

A new kind of people dominated the vast inflow—people from Ohio, New York, and Pennsylvania filled the prairie region while the earlier stream of Southern settlers which had furnished the mass of the population in the older Whig triangle had dried up to a trickle.[19] The older settlers, wedded to old ways, still dominated the southern part of the state. Lincoln knew these people— they were out of his own past. But the northern part, where population was trebling and wealth and ease accumulating, was the area of progress and promise.

It was also the area where the vote was or would be. In 1854, the Anti-Nebraska majority in the legislature had been largely Northern, the Nebraska minority largely Southern. People of the old Whig triangle lay between the past and the future of their state, between conservative Egypt with its many connections with the South and the newer, more radical, more Yankee North. There is no evidence that Lincoln's ultimate decision to ally himself with the North, to attempt to bridle its radicalism and ride the wave of the future was influenced by these facts. There is no evidence against it. But the facts were there. Lincoln lived with them. In 1855, Lincoln was pondering, weighing, considering. Could he have overlooked what was going on about him every day?

1. J. G. Nicolay and John Hay (eds.), *Abraham Lincoln Complete Works* (New York: The Century Co., 1894), I, 218. Springfield, Aug. 24, 1855, Lincoln to Joshua F. Speed.

2. RTL No. 605, Dec. 14, 1854, Thomas B. Talcott.

3. *Yates MSS*, Z. Eastman to Yates, Jan. 11, 1855; *Free West*, Nov. 30, 1854.

4. Angle, *Herndon's Life of Lincoln*, p. 299; *Free West*, Dec. 14, 1854.

5. State of Illinois, *House Journal*, 19th Gen. Ass., pp. 283, 306, 307–9; *State Register*, Feb. 15, 1855.

6. *Illinois Journal*, Oct. 3, 1855.

7. Oct. 10, 1855.

8. *Collected Works*, II, 316–7, Springfield, Aug. 11, 1855, Owen Lovejoy; *Trumbull Papers* (Illinois State Historical Library), Alton, Aug. 20, 1855, Trumbull to Lovejoy.

9. Basler, *Writings*, p. 322.

10. *Ibid.*, p. 291.

11. *Chicago Times*, Oct. 4, 1855; Trumbull MSS, Jan. 11, 1856, J. M. Palmer; George Thomas Palmer, "A Collection of Letters from Lyman Trumbull to

John M. Palmer, 1854–1858," *Journal of the Illinois State Historical Society,* XVI (April-July, 1923), 28–9; Trumbull MSS, Jan. 19, 1856.

12. Douglas MSS, Feb. 17, 1855, J. W. Sheehan; Feb. 15, 1855; *Chicago Times,* Oct. 25, 1855.

13. *State Register,* Feb. 14, and Oct. 25, 1855.

14. Trumbull MSS, Monmouth, Dec. 31, 1855, E. A. Payne.

15. See below, pp. 97, 116; Illinois stood fourth among the states furnishing population to Kansas to 1860. More Illinoisans were going to Missouri and Iowa but some were also going to Nebraska. *Eighth Census,* Population, *passim.*

16. U.S. Superintendent of the Census, *Eighth Census, 1860,* Preliminary Report (Washington: Government Printing Office, 1862), pp. 130–1.

17. P. W. Gates, *The Illinois Central Railroad and Its Colonization Work,* XLII of the Harvard Economic Series (Cambridge: Harvard University Press, 1934), 109; *Chicago Times,* May 15, 1856; *Eighth Census,* Agriculture, pp. xlix, xxix, lxxxvii, and cviii.

18. *Seventh Census, 1850,* pp. 727–8; *Eighth Census, 1860,* Population, pp. 104–5.

19. *Eighth Census,* Population, p. 104.

Politics — A Creative Art

The Anti-Nebraska party of Illinois—for this was its name until the use of the word "Republican" by the national party rendered this designation obsolete—held its convention at Bloomington, nominated its candidates, spelled out its platform, heard its favorite orators, and adjourned to start campaigning. Shortly thereafter, one of the vice-presidents of the convention, John H. Bryant of Bureau County, wrote to his better known brother William Cullen Bryant, editor of the *New York Evening Post,* a rhapsodic report of the convention:

CHAPTER 5

> It was indeed a glorious meeting. All parts of the state were represented, and all seem of one heart and one mind. There was no intriguing, no log-rolling, to secure votes for this or that candidate. The question, and the only question, seemed to be, who will best represent our principles, and at the same time secure the votes of the people.

> Happily on this point there was but one opinion, and the entire ticket was nominated and all the business of the convention executed without a difference of opinion worth naming.[1]

Mr. Bryant may have been somewhat more ecstatic than most but the great majority was highly pleased with the harmonious convention. It had provided an excellent beginning for a successful campaign.

Putting it quite another way, the professional politicians who had organized the convention had done a competent job. The highest tribute to their skill was the fact that their work had been done so unobtrusively that to this day it is impossible to trace in detail their extensive but quiet labors. A few facts are known.

In the autumn of 1855, the various elements of the opposition to the Democrats—the Whigs, the Anti-Nebraska Democrats, the Know-Nothings, the Germans, and the abolitionists—were at loose ends, the leaders of each group except the abolitionists waiting for the others to open negotiations for union. The waiting season ended in December when the outstanding lawyers of the state gathered in Springfield for the meeting of the Supreme Court. We know that the Anti-Nebraska lawyers held a caucus. We are certain that Gustave Koerner (a state official elected by the Democrats) was present, for it was his verbal report to Thomas Quick, relayed by the latter to Senator Trumbull that furnished the only direct statement that such a meeting took place. By one inference or another, it is fairly certain that Lincoln, Ebenezer Peck, and either Richard Yates or Paul Selby or someone acting for them were in on the discussions. Lincoln was involved for he was holding a pledge by someone, presumably a prospective candidate, a matter which concerned Yates.[2]

Quick's report stated that the caucus agreed that it would make no nominations. This statement must be taken in a literal sense: it would make no nominations in the final sense as caucuses had been wont to do. The group certainly engaged in—some probably considerable—slate-making. That Wm. H. Bissell was decided upon for governor was indicated by three mentions of Bissell by members of the caucus within a short time after it took place. Quick mentioned to Trumbull that Bissell was Koerner's choice for the highest state office. Ebenezer Peck, clerk of the Federal Court and leader of the "Old Hunker" Democrats of Chicago, made the same suggestion to Trumbull about the same time. Finally, Lincoln's seemingly off-hand mention of Bissell as a candidate for governor at the Decatur Editorial convention had all of the earmarks of a firm commitment of Whig support.³ The Selby letter mentioning a pledge was in itself a strong indication of slate-making.

The fact that of the three top offices in the state, one senatorship was held by a Democrat (Trumbull) and the governorship was offered to another Democratic rebel (Bissell) creates a strong impression that a Whig candidate must have received the support of the organizing party for the third major office— the U.S. Senate seat held by Douglas. Nothing is less probable than that the Whigs would have agreed to the part of the bargain which we know, i.e., the offer of the gubernatorial nomination to Bissell, without an equivalent. They had been cheated, as they thought, by not demanding surety for delivery of the Senate seat lost to Trumbull less than a year before. They had supported the Anti-Nebraska Democrats for officers of the legislature, thinking that the honors and crumbs of patronage would pave the way for the election of Lincoln to the Senate but the Anti-Nebraska Democrats had emerged with both the loaf and the crumbs. The events of 1858 strongly indicate that the choice of Lincoln to oppose Douglas had been determined earlier. Lincoln was pledged not to oppose Trumbull in 1860.⁴ When, other than 1856, was there a situation that called for pledges? What did Lincoln receive for his pledge?

There remains the letter promising something exacted in the interest of Yates. There were several possibilities but considering Yates' successful candidacy for governor in 1860, the most probable explanation is that Bissell was required to promise that he would not run again in 1860.

One further conjecture which seems a little less tentative than the above is that of the three basic elements of the fusion, Democrat, Whig, and abolitionist, the last-named part was neither a party to the bargain nor consulted in these preliminary stages. The abolitionists did not share in the offices but even more significantly, judging from the Bloomington platform, they did not share in the determination of policy. The other elements were in a very favorable position to disregard the abolitionists who had no satisfactory alternative. With the problem of Kansas becoming more urgent every day, the probability of the radicals rejecting a moderate program and the more professional leadership must have seemed quite remote. The Democratic party of Illinois was more and more the party of Douglas and he was still the *bete noir* of the abolitionists. The politicians must have calculated that the abolitionists would take no step that would jeopardize an opportunity to beat Douglas' party. Finally, in spite of the existence of evidence that great pains were taken to satisfy the Germans and the Know-Nothings and bring both into the fold, there is no evidence of any effort to negotiate with the abolitionists. Indeed, the evidence is to the contrary. Soon after the editorial convention there appeared in the *Quincy Whig* an editorial that bears all the earmarks of being an ultimatum of the old line politicians of both parties to the "ultras." The abolitionists were told that

> In view of the more exciting character of the coming Presidential contest, and in view of the character of the elements composing the anti-Nebraska party, the greatest wisdom is necessary in conducting this strife between the two greatest interests North and South, freedom on the one hand and slavery on the other. The true policy for the great National party in the coming election is, to elevate and keep first in importance the great question which awakened it into life and has given it strength. The ultra Northern measures must not be thrust in to the detriment of what we now deem the true Anti-Nebraska party. Ultra Northern measures can not be sustained, and if the Anti-Nebraska party is committed to them it will suffer inglorious defeat.

> The question which has given life to the anti-Nebraska party, as we understand it, is the Missouri Compromise and the attempt to wrest from the North the territory that has been consecrated to freedom. To restore this great principle, to give back to the North the territory which, by solemn compact, was once secured to freedom, is the ground upon which this party stands. Here is a national question, around which the true lovers of their country have rallied to resist . . . [aggression]. Let the question, in the coming contest, not be aggressions upon slavery; let it be the restoration of the country to the state it occupied before the passage of the infamous Kansas-Nebraska Bill. Let the ultra North meet the compromise men on this ground, if they wish to

retrieve the nation from the false step it has taken in the cause of freedom, through the treachery of Douglas and his agitators, otherwise they will gain no victory for freedom over slavery.[5]

Another warning came from a source which carried some weight with the abolitionists, namely, Wentworth. He specifically warned against bringing the Maine Law question and the Know-Nothing issues into the attempt to fuse. He wanted only pure opposition to slavery extension. He warned

The Ultra Republicans have heretofore been unwilling to admit that any man could be an honest opponent of slavery extension, unless he subscribed to all the isms advocated by the leader or founder of the party—Horace Greeley, who has as good right to his views as any other honest man; but they should be separated from slavery extension.[6]

Bearing in mind that the connected sequence which follows is subject to the limitations indicated above, it may be useful in understanding the campaign of 1856.

The leading lawyers of the Whig party (probably excluding those who had been lukewarm in 1854), and of the Anti-Nebraska Democrats, met in Springfield in December, whether by chance or prearrangement is not known. Lincoln, Koerner, and Peck were almost certainly among them and there were others. They decided:

(1) To combine forces in the formation of a new party.

(2) To provide a platform upon which they could all stand and which would be to the anti-slavery side of the Democratic party but not too radically so.

(3) To avoid every issue that might divide them. These issues were (a) the Maine Law (b) changes in the naturalization laws and other anti-foreign propositions advocated by the Know-Nothings and (c) the classic national issues that had divided Democrats from Whigs.

(4) To make no nominations but to work up a slate probably to be headed by Bissell, the lesser offices to be parcelled out in such a way as to give everybody but the abolitionists something. The awarding of the first two major posts to Democrats (Trum-

bull and Bissell) was balanced with a commitment to Lincoln that he would be the candidate for the Senate in 1858. Lincoln promised not to run for Trumbull's seat in 1860. Bissell was not to run for governor in 1860.

(5) To call the editorial convention to prepare for the convention at which the nominations would be made. The caucus would then fade into the background.

(6) To take a calculated risk that the radicals of the northern part of the state would join this effort without any concession of office or platform.

Between the caucus and the editorial convention called for Washington's birthday, much work was done. Leading members of each faction had to be contacted. If assurances were demanded, they had to be obtained. Participation of the "right" editors in the right places, and the "chance" appearance of Lincoln in the small assembly at Decatur seem not to have been left entirely to the accidents of the moment or so formalized as to destroy the invaluable impression of spontaneity. Dr. Charles H. Ray, the new editor of the *Chicago Tribune* was there early and, with Lincoln and George Schneider of the *Staats Zeitung* of Chicago, took the lead in framing the resolutions. Ray had opposed Lincoln's election to the Senate and had been characterized, perhaps uncharitably, by Washburne, as one who was *"for the man who will be of the most service to him."* He was a busy political "operator" who threw himself wholeheartedly into the fusion effort. After the editorial convention, he solicited the cooperation of two congressmen who leaned to the Know-Nothing side to not make demands for a change in the naturalization law in order "to save 20,000 German votes."[7]

The editorial convention went off smoothly enough. The resolutions offered something for everybody: restoration of the Missouri Compromise and the non-extension of slavery into free territories, which all could agree on; non-interference with slavery within the states, required by the more conservative; the formula that freedom was the rule and slavery the exception in national affairs, which would please the abolitionists; the maintenance of the public school system, a nod to the Know-Nothings; and a statement in favor of religious freedom, a bow to the Germans. A central committee was appointed and charged with organizing a state convention to be held in Bloomington in May. Speeches were made, the principal one by Lincoln.[8]

In the interval before the state convention, the editors had time to work up enthusiasm for it, warn off those who might drag embarrassing and divisive issues into the convention, take stock of local situations, and select delegations for the convention. All moved smoothly. The need for fusion received fresh impetus from the worsening situation in Kansas which was reflected in the resolutions of at least one of the county meetings. Only one of the principal characters in the drama to be enacted at Bloomington seemed unsure of his role: Bissell thought that the Democrats ought to be more forward in seizing control of the movement.[9]

Aside from the careful preparation for harmony in the weeks and months before the Bloomington convention, the harmonizers were aided by the fortuitous circumstance that timed its sitting with the most dramatic of the violent events in Kansas—the sack of abolitionist Lawrence by pro-slavery Missourians. Indeed, the meeting attained a second climax after adjournment when former Governor Andrew H. Reeder recently driven from Kansas spoke for over three hours to an audience of thousands, undoubtedly including many of the delegates.[10] Under the feeling of outrage and anger which prevailed, any tendency of individuals to quibble or to quarrel was too trivial to find expression.

The one day convention produced a platform which surpassed the resolutions of the Decatur meeting in timeliness in that it called for the immediate admission of Kansas under the Topeka Constitution. Perhaps just as appropriate and timely in this convention was a resolution submitted from the floor and adopted "amid deafening shouts, cheers and other manifestations of excited approbation." It read:

That STEPHEN A. DOUGLAS, having laid his 'ruthless hand' upon a sacred compact which had 'an origin akin to that of the constitution' and which had 'become canonized in the hearts of the American people,' has given the lie to his past history, proved himself recreant to the free principles of this government, violated the confidence of the people of Illinois, and now holds his seat in the senate while he misrepresents them.[11]

The unspoken bond of union that helped as much as anything in fusing the new party, hatred of Douglas, colored the feelings of triumph in the echoes of the convention. Congressman Knox, of Whig antecedents, reacted to reports of the harmonious convention by predicting that "we will redeem Illinois from the thralldom of Douglas." Jonathan Baldwin Turner, the abolitionist mentor of Yates, sent him notes on the convention which concluded with this abstract—"single issue: Treason & anti-treason; Douglas & anti-Douglas."[12]

Bissell was nominated and every other element of the party except the abolitionists received recognition on the slate—German, Know-Nothing, Democrat, and Whig. All were nominated without opposition. As at Decatur, the principal speaker was Abraham Lincoln. Crowded into a day of oratory, Lincoln's speech, which is now known only from some very general comments made in newspaper accounts, was the oratorical highlight.

The Kansas-Nebraska Bill had reopened the slavery question in such a way that a limited objective, the question of slavery in a given territory, fell quite properly within the scope of federal legislation, at least as it had been understood until the Dred Scott decision. The problem was an appropriate subject for legislation and a fitting reason for the choice of one candidate for congress over another, as, for example, slavery in Mississippi was not. Of course, some abolitionists had arrived at the notion that slavery itself was repugnant to the Constitution, an idea derived by deduction from certain phrases in the Declaration of Independence. Their forced logic, contradicted by practice since 1789, had few converts in Illinois. It was this disregard of the plain sense and common understanding of the compromises of the Constitution that earned for them the scorn of the plain man. To overcome this sense of being too radical to be trustworthy and make himself a slightly more comfortable associate in the great joint enterprise being set into motion, Owen Lovejoy repudiated this radical position and proclaimed himself a constitutional abolitionist at Bloomington.[18] One need not, as matters stood in 1856, do much violence to the Constitution or to logic to find a field to do battle on the Lord's side. Kansas and the vast territory of Nebraska was a prize worth the battle and the battle could be fought with ballots in the American way.

Parties were the normal channels of political activity, then as now. A party for preserving freedom in Kansas and Nebraska (Nebraska was lost sight of in the shadow of the exciting events in Kansas) was the one ingredient necessary to make the moral question digest in the bowels of politics. This important task, Lincoln and a little knot of politicians had accomplished exceedingly well and at exactly the right time. They had joined groups of Illinoisans not only of opinions spread across the spectrum of opposition to slavery but habituated to opposition to each other by earlier party connections and even by other moral issues such as the Maine Law. These "old pros" had welded a formidable political machine that would take the state government out of the hands of the Democrats who had held it since Lincoln's apprenticeship in politics. They had fused in around a moral issue but with a constitutional and practical objective.

They had found the least common denominator of opposition to slavery that would bring the scattered factions under one political roof. The denominator was in terms of moral crusade; the process of nicely calculating the fraction was a matter of the normal, everyday job of the politician. Each group had conceded something, the abolitionists unwittingly perhaps. Lincoln had known how to go about such a task since he had helped "bargain" a state capital for Springfield. This was the sort of thing a Lincoln could do but a professional abolitionist never.

Better yet, they had created an impression of spontaneity and unity that imparted the same zeal and intensity (and no small amount of the self-righteousness) of the abolitionist, of the pure, uncontaminated-by-politics zealot. It is only fair to add that in this matter they had had a bit of luck. They had fused, in Beveridge's words, "by putting aside every question which divided men, and centering their minds on the one and only issue upon which they agreed."[14] Under most circumstances, this would be a dull and negative way of achieving unity. Happily for those who organized the Republican party in Illinois the crisis of the slavery question, "the issue upon which they agreed," was Kansas. The very minimum program of the conservatives would be as effective for Kansas upon which all eyes were focused as the most radical abolition proposal.

There were skeptics, of course. An Anti-Nebraska Democratic editor evinced no enthusiasm when he wrote that "while I regret to be compelled to join in the ranks of *some* of the leaders of the Republican party, I can still see no escape from it with our principles whole." The alternative of setting up shop as an independent party, he rejected because "there is but one question which divides us from Douglas, Pierce & Co, & if *that* should be settled (as I hope it may) we then must go back to the old Democratic party. . . ." He hoped that holding the Republicans "to a respectable & commanding conservatism, we may be able to give their move a connexion with other principles, that will perpetuate the party."[15] Perhaps he was representative of the kind for whom the orating and cheering of the convention was designed—to make them forget their reservations and wax enthusiastic.

Mr. Bryant may have been taken in by appearances at the convention but that old war-horse of Illinois abolitionism, Ichabod Codding saw in it "a superficial policy of availability." The fusion on one issue left Codding with the prophetic hope, however, that with but two parties "the Republicans will be driven to take the whole Anti-Slavery issue before they are through with this controversy." Although left off the state ticket and out of the division of the prospective spoils of office so far as the organizers of the fusion were concerned, the abolitionists, to the surprise and chagrin of the Whigs who had controlled the district previously, nominated Owen Lovejoy in the Ottawa district fusion convention. This created the one breach in the unity of the fusion for, in the words of the man the bolters wished to nominate, "About ½ the delegates bolted the nomination and called another convention to nominate another candidate who would not only oppose the introduction of slavery into Kansas but would at the same time be true to the acknowledged rights of the South under the constitution." Judge David Davis wrote T. Lyle Dickey, the favorite of the dissidents, to persuade him not to run. He thought that the Kansas outrages and the administration "have made abolitionists of those who never dreamed they were drifting into it." Davis, the conservative Whig, felt that "We, the old Whig party, will be stricken down during this campaign. Had we not better bide our time & brush up our armor for future operations?"[16] There were some former Democrats, some abolitionists, and some ex-Whigs who thought of the Republican party as a temporary alliance. After the 1856 campaign and the Kansas issue were settled and in the past, it would be time to bend this new party—or what might flow from it—in the Democratic, abolitionist, or Whig direction.

That the American political party is a loose federation of state organizations is a truism beautifully demonstrated by the process of party disruption and formation in Illinois in 1854 and 1856. The absence of a national election in 1854 permitted the breaking up and reorganization of parties to proceed in each state almost as if each state were a political island unto itself. Only the great questions of national interest—notably the Nebraska Bill—set any limits of a national character to the events and movements within a state. Illinois, as has been pointed out, had lacked an exciting state contest in 1854. There had been no internal reason to hasten statewide reorganization in that year.

In other states, results had been quite different. Massachusetts, for example, had reorganized much more hastily and there the impact of the Know-Nothing movement had been much more keenly felt.

The organization of the Republican, née Anti-Nebraska, party at Bloomington in 1856 had been achieved almost wholly without reference to national politics except in the matter of timing. It has been directed by local men without the help of organizers, financial assistance, professional public relations consultants or advice from national headquarters. It could not have been otherwise for there was but one national organization—feeble by present day standards—the Democratic party. For the party in power, patronage provided a lively staff of party members whose work was, nevertheless, handicapped by informal and sometimes contradictory direction. For the party out of power in Washington, the wells of patronage dried up, and accordingly, the means of centralizing party activities. So it was with the Whigs. There was no national organization and not even a very influential national press to stem the decay and ruin of the Whig party. Nor was there a national Republican organization to influence the course of Illinoisans formulating their own special brand of Republicanism in May, 1856. The attempt of the radicals (Lovejoy had been among them) to nationalize their movement at the Pittsburgh convention had reckoned without the politicians, and it amounted to very little.

On the other hand, this did not mean that there were no influences promoting national uniformity and harmony. The foremost of these, as has been pointed out, was the fact that there was to be a national election in 1856 when a President would be chosen. For a state to be effective in electing a President—and what greater recommendation for the great places in the administration was there for a state political leader than carrying his state for the successful candidate—it must be organized to fight the electoral war. Its forces must be lined up in some way with the other state organizations. The national candidates would have some influence on the choices of voters for state and local offices. Even at that time, before presidential candidates stumped the country or monopolized television or radio time, the voter tended to lift his gaze from his feet to the horizon of national politics in the presidential years. The schedule of events arranged by Lincoln and his friends was intended to anticipate national developments.

The great national newspapers had some influence in setting some limits to the diversity of opinion. Greeley's *New York Tribune* was widely read in northern Illinois. The *National Era* at Washington carried a less personal and more consistent anti-slavery view of politics into Illinois. St. Louis papers were read in southern Illinois. Most local readers received the editorial bias of out-of-state editors in the columns of their home town papers either in the form of recast editorials or "clips" directly from the exchanges.

Members of Congress reported more directly to their smaller constituencies of that day. "Long John" Wentworth had published his own newspaper and represented his district in the national House of Representatives. The *Register* in Springfield and the *Times* in Chicago faithfully broadcast Douglas' views which were repeated by the Democratic newspapers in the smaller towns. The vast volume of the correspondence received by Lyman Trumbull, and the surviving correspondence written by Trumbull in this period, indicate at least the potential for tempering the parochial with the national at the service of the Senator. The party movements in Illinois were not made in a complete void as far as national politics were concerned.

The obverse of the coin was that state organizations sought to influence the national parties in such ways as would secure votes within that state. The most obvious example of this tendency occurred in 1860 when neither the Southern nor the Northern Democrats could accept a candidate or a platform that would be acceptable to the other. In 1856, the conservative Republicans of Illinois were anxious that the standard-bearer of the national party should be one who would contribute to the success of the fusion in their state. Congressman James Knox feared that "unless the Republicans nominate and unite in supporting a *conservative* man, I think we are beaten in the next campaign." Lincoln plead with Trumbull to work for the nomination of John McLean, pointing out that "nine tenths of the Anti-Nebraska votes have to come from old Whigs." Ebenezer Peck, ex-Democrat, urged that a conservative be nominated and that the platform be moderate.[17]

The case for a conservative nominee was made stronger by the fact that James Buchanan, the nominee of the Democrats, had not been associated with the Kansas-Nebraska measure. Lincoln was alarmed by the danger this nomination presented and wrote to Trumbull that the "news of Buchanan's nomination came yesterday; and a good many Whigs, of conservative feelings, and slight pro-slavery proclivities withal, are inclining to go for him, and will do it, unless the Anti-Nebraska nomination shall be such as to divert them. . . ."[18]

The members of the Illinois delegation to the Philadelphia convention were quite different from the "impracticables" of the abortive Pittsburgh meeting. John M. Palmer, N. B. Judd, George Schneider, and Wm. B. Archer, politicians all, represented the Republicans of Illinois and attempted in vain to balance the Democrat Frémont for President with the Whig Lincoln for Vice-President.[19] The platform was considerably broader than that of the Bloomington convention: it called for national river and harbor improvements, a railway to the Pacific, and condemned the Ostend Manifesto (an abortive administration effort to buy Cuba), besides adopting the more radical position that neither Congress nor the territorial legislatures had power to legalize slavery in a territory.

While it is true that some Whigs were wooed into the Democratic camp, the more serious problem, as it turned out, was the nomination of Millard Fillmore, the most recent, and destined to be the last Whig President, by the American party (Know-Nothing) and by an "Old Whig" convention. His candidacy served to focus Whig sentiment—unionism over sectionalism, nativism over ardent pursuit of the foreign vote, reconciling loyalty to an old party chief who had had a hand in the compromise measures with anti-administration, anti-Democratic and anti-Douglas feeling. When Fillmore's name was brought out at the American party convention, it created in the mind of one former Whig editor the hope that the Republicans might create a union of anti-administration forces by joining in the Fillmore nomination.[20] Nothing came of the suggestion, for the German vote was an important part of the Republican combination and any further concession to the Know-Nothing element would raise the risk of losing it. 1856 was to be the year of the dissident Democrats: Bissell in Illinois, and Frémont (the candidate of the Blairs) in the nation.

The seriousness of this Fillmore threat did not impress itself on the minds of Republican leaders early in the contest. Perhaps, they—including Lincoln—had been committed fully personally and failed to realize the difficulty others had in making up their minds. It may have been the Frémont nomination, that is, the nomination of a Democrat rather than some Whig, which threw the last weight in the balance in favor of Fillmore among ex-Whigs. In any case the Fillmore men were, in the main, friends and former party workers of Lincoln's. His own political following was split down the middle.

E. B. Webb, who had been the Whig's nominee for governor in 1852, illustrated the trend of thought with which Lincoln had to reckon. A friend and former co-worker in the Whig party wrote that Webb was *"really right, & wants to have Richardson & Douglass defeated,* but stands opposed to Abolitionism, & *is afraid of Separating the Union through any means & fancies the Republican movements* are likely to do it."[21]

B. S. Edwards, a Springfield Whig of some prominence, expressed the same dilemma:

I have not yet decided what course to adopt, nor what candidate to support. I am an antislavery man, though not sympathizing with abolitionists in their views or measures. Am also opposed to the extension of slavery. I furthermore deeply deplore the

105

present state of feeling existing between northern and southern men. . . . I am tired of the agitation of this slavery question, and perplexed as to the best mode of adjusting it.[22]

John T. Stuart, Lincoln's first law partner, supported Fillmore. He made his decision not to decide in 1856.

In the old Whig triangle, the rupture was more a trial separation than a divorce. In Sangamon County, for example, the former friends united to preserve their monopoly on the courthouse jobs by nominating a combined slate for county offices. One gains an impression of tentativeness in this Fillmore activity, namely, that the old Whigs were seizing an opportunity to postpone a hard decision, either choice going against the grain of their tradition. However, Fillmore was supported with a desperate enthusiasm. The Republican paper at Springfield grudgingly admitted that the Fillmore procession was the best in the county. On the other hand, there were negotiations with the Republicans aimed at presenting a common ticket but these failed, among other reasons, because of the predicted effect on the German vote. A Douglas man reporting on the situation around Springfield thought that the "rank and file of the opposition keeps the leaders in the Fillmore ranks from going over to Frémont."[23]

Lincoln, a Republican elector, campaigned vigorously. The turn of events described above tied Lincoln down to the effort to hold (or to win) the Whig vote. There is some indication that in his opening speech of June 10, 1856, at Springfield he may have expressed sentiments similar to those that were to mark his "House Divided" speech in 1858. The *Register* reported that "He boldly avowed, in one of his many escapings, that there could be no Union with slavery, that agitation would be ceaseless until it shall be swept away."[24] But the aggressive mood of the ratification meeting was soon overtaken by the stubborn and unexpected reluctance of Lincoln's Whig following to follow. The tone changed to one of emphasis on the conservatism of the Republican party in answer to the objections of the Fillmore supporters.

The main points of Lincoln's arguments as can be reconstructed from snatches and highly condensed versions of his speeches in the newspapers were:

(1) The Republican party was no more sectional than the Democratic. The Republicans took one side of an issue over which the country was divided sectionally. The Democrats took the other but appeared less sectional only because Democrats put support of their party and party leaders above their convictions.

(2) Fillmore had no chance of winning. To give one's vote to a candidate who could not win was merely increasing the chances of victory for the "pro-slavery" Democrats.

This latter argument was printed up as a letter and mailed over Lincoln's signature to many of his old Whig friends and former constituents.[25]

In July, Lincoln filled engagements in a broad sweep of the northern part of the state, the sort of campaigning that would have helped Abraham Lincoln were he to be a candidate for the United States Senate in 1858, as well as making a contribution to the success of the national and state tickets.[26] Trouble with the Whigs altered whatever plans he may have had for extensive out-of-state and northern Illinois touring. He made one trip to Kalamazoo, Michigan, where he spoke before a large audience, and made just three more speeches in northern Illinois during the remainder of the campaign. His work was concentrated in the Whig middle of the state from Paris and Lawrenceville on the Indiana border to Belleville, Pittsfield, and Peoria—for this was where the trouble was. He spoke four times in Urbana and West Urbana (Champaign) and seven times in Springfield. He was at the service of the party and was used where he could do the most good.

The newspapers and campaigners dwelt lengthily and feelingly on the war in Kansas. In the northern part of the state, the Kansas Emigrant Aid movement was practically fused to the Republican political activities. A Chicago meeting to ratify the work of the Bloomington convention raised $15,000 for Kansas aid. At a Kansas Emigrant Aid mass meeting in the same city "at the mention of the name of Frémont the crowd broke into cheers prolonged and loud." In the opinion of Judge David Davis, the Kansas and Sumner "outrages" had "made abolitionists of those who had never dreamed they were drifting into it." Even in the southern part of the state, the excitement over Kansas and the caning of Charles Sumner, Republican Senator from Massachusetts and anti-slavery orator, by a Representative from South Carolina in the Senate Chamber, contributed to "a deep seated feeling of hatred against the South which until recently was almost entirely unknown."[27]

It was said of Judge William P. Kellogg that "he delights to dwell on a few 'horrible scenes' said to have occurred in Kansas."[28] This was not Lincoln's meat. His task, more congenial to his temperament and more suited to his talents, was to reason with reasonable men who were concerned about Kansas but also deeply disturbed by Southern mutterings of secession. Lincoln attempted to persuade such listeners that the only remedy for Kansas lay in the election of Frémont and that his election would not jeopardize the perpetuity of the Union.

The results of the 1856 election, disappointing in some ways, proved that Lincoln had at least one of the qualifications of the able politician—the ear-to-the-ground quality that gives him a sense of how things are going. On August 4, Lincoln predicted that unless the Whigs could be won over from Fillmore, Buchanan would carry the state. The following table compares Lincoln's prediction with the actual result:[29]

	Buchanan	Frémont	Fillmore
Lincoln's estimate	85,000	78,000	21,000
Lincoln's estimate plus 20,000	105,000	98,000	41,000
Actual vote	105,348	96,189	37,444

That Lincoln underestimated the total vote is an interesting comment on the extremely rapid growth of population in the state. Lincoln had allowed for an almost 19 percent increase in the electorate in four years whereas it turned out to be nearly 53 percent.

Although the Republicans won the state offices, Lincoln's attempt to win the reluctant Whigs to the Republican party on national issues must be adjudged a failure, for the central Illinois Whigs divided almost evenly in the election, the proportion varying almost directly in proportion to latitude. In Henderson, Warren, McLean, and Fulton counties, for example, a three to one majority of ex-Whigs supported Frémont. In Tazewell, Coles, Hancock, and Logan counties, a little farther south, the split was more nearly even, but in Sangamon, Jersey, Macon, and Madison, a majority of former Whigs stayed with the Fillmore ticket. The Fillmore electors carried Bond, Edwards, Madison, and Piatt counties and were second in 41 other central and southern Illinois counties, in each case having received more votes than the Republican electors.[30] In the northern part of the state fusion was so substantially achieved that few old Whigs voted for Fillmore—in 13 counties of the northern part, 50 or fewer Fillmore votes were recorded. In southern Illinois, on the other hand, Frémont received fewer than 50 votes in each of 16 counties.

The more conservative Whigs threw away their votes in the presidential contest rather than commit themselves to either of two distasteful choices. Over a third of these, however, voted effectively, as was their habit, against the Democratic state candidates. Thus, although Richardson, the Democratic candidate for governor, ran ahead of Buchanan in the state, he lost to Bissell by nearly 5,000 votes. In Sangamon County, for example, 1,612 Fillmore ballots were cast to 1,174 for Frémont, but B. S. Morris, the American party's gubernatorial aspirant, received but 390 to Bissell's 2,252. The Republicans thus won all of the state offices but failed to win the legislature. A solid Democratic delegation represented Illinois south of a line from Hancock County to Edgar County, with the exception of one Republican from St. Clair and five American party candidates who represented Madison, Sangamon, Wabash and White.[31] The Republicans swept everything north of the line. Thus, the new party had its greatest strength in the newer, northern portion of the state, but had little support in the earlier settled, southern portion. Like the nation, Illinois was dividing into a Republican North and Democratic South. In the center lay the bulk of the undecided voters.

1. *Transactions of the McLean County Historical Society,* III (1900), 177–9.
2. Trumbull MSS, Belleville, Jan. 24, 1856, Thos. Quick; Yates MSS, Jacksonville, Feb. 14, 1856, Paul Selby.
3. *Papers in Illinois History and Transactions for the Year 1942* (Springfield: Illinois State Historical Society 1944), p. 41; Paul Selby, "Editorial Convention, February 22, 1856," *Transactions of the McLean County Historical Society,* III (1900), 34–7.
4. State of Illinois, *Senate Journal,* 19th Gen. Ass., pp. 5, 6; *House Journal,* p. 5; *Collected Works,* III, 505, Springfield, Dec. 9, 1859, Normal B. Judd.
5. *Quincy Whig,* Mar. 18, 1856.
6. *Chicago Daily Democrat,* Mar. 29, 1856.
7. Selby, "Editorial Convention," pp. 36–7; RTL no. 643; Trumbull MSS, Chicago, Mar. 21, 1856, C. H. Ray.
8. Selby, "Editorial Convention," pp. 37–40.
9. See Trumbull MSS, Mar. 29, 1856, Geo. T. Brown for a report of a local meeting of leaders engaged in this enterprise; *Illinois Journal,* May 28, 1856. The admission of Kansas as a free state was proposed by the Sangamon County convention as an alternative to the restoration of the Compromise restrictions; Trumbull MSS, May 5, 1856, W. H. Bissell.
10. *Chicago Democratic Press,* May 21, 1856, quoted in *Transactions of the McLean County Historical Society,* III (1900), 172–7.
11. *Illinois Journal,* May 30, 1856.
12. Yates MSS, June 9, 1856, J. M. Knox; also informal note-manuscript. The punctuation is mine.
13. *Chicago Democratic Press,* May 31, 1856, quoted in *Transactions of the McLean County Historical Society,* III (1900), 174.
14. Albert J. Beveridge, *Abraham Lincoln 1809–1858* (Boston: Houghton-Mifflin Co., 1928), II, 293.
15. Trumbull MSS, Atlanta (Illinois), Feb. 26, 1856, Jeff L. Dugger.
16. Salmon P. Chase MSS (Library of Congress), Chicago, June 10, 1856, I. Codding; Wallace-Dickey MSS, Chicago, July 29, 1856, T. L. Dickey to John J. Dickey; Bloomington, July 18, 1856, David Davis to T. L. Dickey.
17. Yates MSS, Washington, Mar. 17, 1856, J. M. Knox; *Collected Works,* II, 342–3, Springfield, June 7, 1856, Lyman Trumbull; Trumbull MSS, Chicago, June 10, 1856, E. Peck.
18. *Collected Works,* II, 342–3.
19. *National Era,* June 26, 1856.
20. *Illinois State Journal,* Mar. 5, 1856.

21. Trumbull MSS, Albion, June 6, 1856, Wm. Pickering.

22. *Ibid.*, Springfield, July 24, 1856, B. S. Edwards. He joined the Democrats, as did Webb, and as a prize exhibit, presided over the first meeting Douglas addressed at Springfield in the 1858 campaign.

23. *Illinois State Journal,* Aug. 19, 1856. County candidates were nominated by a county "Anti-Nebraska" convention; see also Oct. 15, 1856; *Collected Works, II,* 347–8, Springfield, July 10, 1856, James Berdan; Douglas MSS, Springfield, Aug. 8, 1856, Daniel McCook.

24. *Collected Works,* II, 344–5. It is possibly authentic in spite of the hostile source for the general theme was already established among Lincoln's private convictions in August, 1855, as is indicated by his letter of that date to George Robertson of Lexington, Kentucky, see pp. 317–8. Also, Lincoln speaks of having used the "House Divided" theme a year before in the manuscript, see pp. 448–54, which I date between Dec. 10, 1857 and Feb. 18, 1858. It is not too unreasonable to assume that the politician's year could be a synonym for a campaign rather than a calendar year.

25. *Ibid.*, p. 352 ff., 374.

26. Angle, *Lincoln 1854–1861,* pp. 128–48. Subsequent dates on Lincoln's campaign travels are derived from the same source.

27. *Chicago Democratic Press,* May 27, 1856, July 8, 1856; Wallace-Dickey MSS, Bloomington, July 18, 1856, Davis to T. L. Dickey; Trumbull MSS, Salem, June 2, 1856, O. Whittlesey.

28. *Peoria Press,* Sept. 24, 1856. The *Press* was Democratic, the judge, the Republican candidate for Congress.

29. *Collected Works,* II, 358 (Lincoln's estimate); *A Political Text-Book for 1860,* p. 221 (actual vote).

30. The official vote was given in the *Quincy Whig,* Nov. 29, 1856.

31. State of Illinois, *House Journal,* 20th Gen. Ass., pp. 3–5.

The Great Debate

As Republicans viewed the results of the election of 1856, they found many reasons for self-congratulation. They had won control of the executive branch of the state government of Illinois away from the Democrats for the first time since there had been a distinctly Jacksonian party. This gave them their first patronage, and if it was nothing comparable to the federal offices, it was still something. Their gains had been most striking in the area of the state that was growing the most rapidly.

CHAPTER 6

The Fillmore vote "ought" to be Republican: it was opposed to the wicked Democratic administration and, more to the point, to Douglas.

Until the summer of 1856, it had been supposed that the Republican amalgam would consist of the long time minority party, the Whigs, plus certain other fragments—a part of the German vote, the dissident Democrats, and the abolitionists. The Whig portion of the alliance was the base to which the others would be added by concessions of policy and of offices. Whigs had yearned for this possibility since the vote for Van Buren in 1848 had impressed them with its logic. This had been Lincoln's thought until the unexpected support for Fillmore manifested itself in mid-summer.[1] It has been pointed out that the failure of the central Illinois Whigs to rally to Frémont threw the electoral vote of the state to Buchanan. This turned out to have been of no importance since Buchanan would have won without the Illinois electors.

What did change the whole aspect of the internal relations of the Republican party of the state was that the Whigs, hitherto the group that could be counted on and that must make the sacrifice of position and place to woo the doubtful groups, had now become the doubtful group to which the concessions must be made. Not only in Illinois but in New Jersey, Indiana, Pennsylvania, and New York the former followers of Clay had come to represent the balance of power between the Republican and Democratic parties. This circumstance strengthened Lincoln's position with the coalition. He had become essential.

If the Fillmore vote of 1856 was more than half of the vote for "Fuss and Feathers" Scott, the Whig standard bearer of 1852, it is obvious that the Republicans had obtained a vast support unaccounted for by the kind of reckoning discussed above. The plurality of over 30,500 votes won in the northern 23 counties of the state could not be explained in terms of the conversion of Democrats to Republicanism. As a matter of fact more people in these counties voted Democratic in 1856 than in 1852. In Cook County, for example, a Democratic plurality of 1,700 votes in 1852 was changed to a Republican majority of 3,300 in 1856 while the Democratic total increased 1,900 votes over the same period. The answer lay in the new immigration into the state, some German, some Scandinavian, but in the main, native Americans from the East. Why the new citizens—aside from the Germans—should have been so overwhelmingly Republican is impossible to determine with certainty. That many of them came from areas in upstate New York and the lake region of Ohio where a similar swing was taking place is true. Perhaps, in addition, the new settler found it as easy to cast off his old party connections as to turn his back on the old home farm and the graves of his parents. To the new man, the Democratic party may have seemed to represent the hold of the slower-moving old settlers and the power of the earlier settled part of the state. Newcomers to the West may have felt more than the usual empathy for the recent immigrants into Kansas from the free states. Another possible factor was that the new settler believed that he was lining up with the more progressive element which, in the state legislature, was more concerned with schools and banks and, in the national congress, favored internal improvements along the route which he had travelled to Illinois and over which the wheat from his fields must pass to market.

The politicians, if aware of this (and there is little contemporary evidence that they were), had no reason to know that these people, their children, and their children's children in northern Illinois and southern Wisconsin and in the areas of Indiana, Michigan, Iowa, and Minnesota (all settled about the same time) would be Republicans until death or depression. At the time, these relative newcomers to the West added an uncertain and ill-understood building block to the known and predictable ones out of which the Republican amalgam was formed. They had no leaders of their own to be tempted by office. It is comparatively safe to assume that the northern Illinois people, whose understanding of the South had been acquired from *Uncle Tom's Cabin,* were something of an enigma to Whig politicians of Southern origin and connections such as Lincoln and his circle of friends.[2]

On ideological grounds the Republicans were less well off than most of them supposed. In 1854 the great Anti-Nebraska wave of feeling that produced a successful working arrangement had been based in the more conservative areas on a rationale that was wholly defensive in character. The vast western territories, committed to freedom by the Missouri Compromise for over a generation, were opened to slavery by an act that seemed purely aggressive. The Anti-Nebraska people had demanded no new restrictions on slavery: they had been defending what they understood to be theirs. No constitutional guarantee as then understood, no compromise reached by the revered forefathers was to be touched.

Even set in the wider context of the problem—the difficulty

of dealing with a moral issue that divided the country geographically in a political system in which the Constitution was fixed and the powers of government divided between the states and the nation—the Anti-Nebraska forces in 1854 and the Republicans of 1856 had been in the fortunate position of having their cake and eating it, too. The restoration of the territories to the position they had been in before the Kansas-Nebraska Bill required no amendment to the Constitution and no reversal of any compromise. Indeed, the precedents of the Northwest Ordinance and the Missouri Compromise were comforting to those most tender on the subject of the Constitution. What their consciences demanded of them, their lawyers thought they could do and do constitutionally.

The Bloomington convention had found the one issue upon which the *"strange, discordant* and even, *hostile* elements" of the Republican party could agree—opposition to the extension of slavery into the territories.[3] The public appeal of this issue had been strengthened in its concrete application to Kansas. Here people were dying, shooting and being shot, burning and being burned out, and, of course, voting and abstaining from voting. The fraudulent elections, the incursions of Border Ruffians (this term began to replace Loco Foco as the ultimate term of abuse for Democrats in 1856), the pillage of Lawrence, the turning back of Illinoisans bound for Kansas through Missouri, these events crowding in upon each other, compelled an identification of the principle with its application in Kansas. Kansas was not *a* trial case: it was *the* trial case testing whether slavery could be extended to the territory into which the Kansas-Nebraska Bill permitted it to flow. If freedom won in Kansas, bordered as it was by slave Missouri, how could areas more distant from slavery stand in the slightest doubt? The very timeliness of the commitment of the Republican cause to saving Kansas, had proved extremely useful in the campaign of 1856. Again, the Republican policy was defensive and conservative.

What would happen in Kansas was vital to the Republican future. There were a variety of views about it. Congressman

James Knox wrote that "if for a time the settlers can be let alone, *I* think they will work out their own salvation." Trumbull was convinced that Kansas would in the end remain free. Lincoln, on the other hand, assumed that the Kansas-Nebraska Bill had been passed to make Kansas slave and that the administration of the act was merely carrying into effect this intent. The Anti-Nebraska majority in the lower house of Congress was not anxious to close out a most effective partisan argument. The failure of the Toombs Bill, intended to bring the controversy in Kansas to a close, was charged to this partisan viewpoint. The House did not fail to take advantage of the situation by appointing a committee to investigate the vote frauds nor did the Republicans fail to make use of its findings. Judge David Davis joined an appreciation of the short duration of the Kansas question with a prediction of the effect of its solution on the Republican party. He thought "that the elements now uniting in electing Col. Frémont & Col. Bissell can't coalesce long. They will have one feeling in common, but antipodes in everything else. If Kansas gets admitted as a free state, the party is *ipso facto* dissolved. . . ."[4]

Between the election of 1856 and the senatorial election of 1858, the Republican position on slavery in the territories received two sledgehammer blows. The first of these was the Dred Scott decision for which they could blame themselves, the case having been pushed by certain party leaders and part of the costs assessed on the Republican members of Congress although this was not widely known at the time.[5] The pertinent part of the decision, so far as Republican doctrine was concerned, was that portion which denied the power of Congress to exclude slavery from the territories. The Missouri Compromise restriction, the repeal of which had called the Republican party into existence, was unconstitutional. If accepted as the final word, the Dred Scott decision would have had a devastating effect on the Republican party for it left no important way that slavery could be the subject of legislation at the federal level. The issue would have been removed from the halls of Congress and therefore from national politics. Indeed, there are strong indications that it was intended to do just that.

If the Republican party in Illinois and in the nation had been in a majority, the decision would not have been so upsetting. Strong Republicans simply refused to accept this as settled law and hoped that the Supreme Court, preferably a Republican one, would reverse the decision if the problem should ever again come before the court. As it was, the Republicans were hoping to win in 1860 by the accession of old line Whig votes in the key states. This put quite a different aspect on the matter for the Whigs tended to be more sensitive to the constitutional and legal proprieties than to the need for reform. The Democrats, just as aware as the Republicans of the balance of power position of the Fillmore vote, pressed the advantage the decision gave them. Douglas, in a Springfield speech, warned that

> Whoever resists the final decision of the highest judicial tribunal, aims a deadly blow to our whole Republican system of government—a blow, which if successful would place all our rights and liberties at the mercy of passion, anarchy and violence. I repeat, therefore, that if resistance to the decisions of the Supreme Court of the United States . . . shall be forced upon the country as a political issue, it will become a distinct and naked issue between the friends and enemies of the Constitution—the friends and enemies of the supremacy of the laws.[6]

The second blow was Kansas. In spite of Lincoln's dire prediction, the Kansas situation began to play itself out through 1857. The Democrats, and especially Douglas, recognized that the chaotic situation was playing into Republican hands and made a restoration of peace there the first order of business of the Buchanan administration. Robert J. Walker, several cuts above the usual caliber of territorial governors, was persuaded to undertake the task of getting the Kansas problem solved. It was agreed by all hands that the prospective constitution for Kansas must be submitted to the voters of Kansas and that Walker must succeed in bringing both sides into one election.

The situation Walker stepped into was chaotic. Kansas had,

in effect, two governments. The legitimate territorial government, which he would head, was dominated by Missourians as a result of gross and obvious frauds in voting. The Free-Staters, Northern settlers who wished to see slavery excluded from Kansas, earned that name by calling a convention at Topeka where they had framed a state constitution barring slavery. Although it had been submitted to Congress, it had no legal basis, for the Democratic Senate was sure to reject it. In the autumn of 1857 the famous or infamous Lecompton constitutional convention met quite according to law but representing only a minority of the people of Kansas because the Free-Staters had boycotted the election of delegates. The somewhat pro-slavery document it produced—the Lecompton Constitution—was submitted to President Buchanan. In spite of the fact that only the slavery clauses were submitted for acceptance or rejection by the voters and that the negligible existing slavery in Kansas was protected, President Buchanan submitted the constitution to Congress for its approval, thus violating his understanding with Douglas and Governor Walker. The Lecompton Constitution was not acceptable to Douglas who had been informed that the people of Kansas were "eight to one for making a free state."[7] Whatever his motives, Douglas led a fight against the Lecompton Constitution that continued through most of the session (1857–8), with the outcome that the constitution was to be submitted to the people of Kansas for ratification. If the Lecompton instrument were rejected, statehood was to be postponed until the population had more than doubled. This result, coupled with the assurance that the Free-Staters would vote in the balloting on the constitution, led to a general assumption that the passage of the English Bill (embodying the compromise described above) would guarantee eventual freedom for Kansas.

Two consequences of importance to the politics of Illinois derived from these stirring events. One was that Stephen A. Douglas, who had boasted that he could have travelled from Washington to Chicago by the light of his own burning effigies in 1854 after the passage of the Kansas-Nebraska Act, emerged as the anti-slavery hero of the North. On the eve of the senatorial contest which presumably would pit Lincoln against Douglas, the latter had become the darling of the abolitionists. The other consequence was that Douglas broke with Buchanan and a new 1854 appeared in the making. A fairly sizeable group of Northern and especially Northwestern Democrats followed Douglas's leadership into opposition to the administration. Whether they would leave the Democratic party or remain and attempt to win control of it was an open question.

The Republicans were compelled to seek a new basis for existence as an anti-slavery party as first the Dred Scott decision and then the assurance of freedom to Kansas undermined the old grounds for the party's being. Restoration of the Missouri Compromise was not only constitutionally impossible but of no practical consequence since Kansas, the test case, was becoming free. The Republican issues had evaporated. A party had to stand for something. It might put the slavery question in the background and coalesce with all others opposed to the unpopular Buchanan administration. This amalgam would include the remnants of the Whig-Americans who were still potent in the border states and far from ready to join the Democrats. As a matter of fact, this sort of proposition had been made from time to time. It described the kind of cooperation that still existed on the local level in the old Whig area in central Illinois. In Lincoln's home county, for example, the precinct caucuses for the county convention for the nomination of county officials in 1857 were called in the name of "all those who are opposed to the policy of the present National Administration." There is no indication that Lincoln yielded to this purely political policy's obvious attraction beyond local necessity and tradition. He certainly rejected it out of hand later.[8]

Such a fusion of the "outs" was impossible in Illinois because Douglas had become an "out." Few Illinois Republicans cared to

120

coalesce with him as we shall see. The alternative to a new fusion that would softpedal the slavery question was the development of a new creed, a fresh examination of the moral issue in politics. The right position on the slavery question was crucial for the Republican party, veteran of but one election when these problems came to a head. It seemed a fragile alliance of delicately balanced parts. Any mistake might lose the Germans, the former Democrats, or, at least, the hope of winning the Whigs who had supported Fillmore.

It is possible to trace Lincoln's search for a satisfactory alternative, that is, a new anti-slavery ground upon which the Republican party could stand. Indeed, the direction of this change was foreshadowed by Lincoln's conclusion that an anti-slavery party must be formed. This decision was not unique with Lincoln, of course. However, in his case, we have evidence from both his public life and private convictions marking the stages in the development of the new doctrine. His public pronouncements were monopolized by forms of the slavery question from 1854 onward.

A curious letter reaches into Lincoln's private thoughts in the early stages of this progression. In the depression and uncertainty of 1855, after his defeat for the Senate and before he had started the work of building the Republican party, Lincoln wrote to a stranger, an elderly Kentucky lawyer, who had taken an active part in the politics of his state at the time of the Missouri Compromise controversy. Lincoln wished to thank the lawyer for a book and to give his own response to it:[9]

> You are not a friend of slavery in the abstract. In that speech [in the book] you spoke of *"the peaceful extinction of slavery"* and used other expressions indicating your belief that the thing was, at some time to have an end. Since then we have had thirty six years of experience; and this experience has demonstrated, I think, that there is no peaceful extinction of slavery in prospect for us. The signal failure of Henry Clay, and other good and great men, in 1849, to effect any thing in favor of gradual emancipation in Kentucky, together with a thousand other signs, extinguishes that hope utterly. On the question of liberty, as a

principle, we are not what we have been. . . . The fourth of July has not quite dwindled away; it is still a great day—*for burning fire-crackers! ! !*

That spirit which desired the peaceful extinction of slavery, has itself become extinct, with the *occasion,* and the men of the Revolution.

Our political problem now is "Can we, as a nation, continue together *permanently—forever*—half slave, and half free?" The problem is too mighty for me. May God, in his mercy, superintend the solution.

The "House Divided," in spite of Herndon's recollection to the contrary, was yet in 1855 a question and not a positive conviction. As a question it implied uncertainty as to the outcome, but there was no uncertainty in Lincoln's mind that this was the ultimate question. The gloomy belief that the faith in the perfectability of man, the easy confidence in moral progress of the Revolutionary forefathers, had ebbed beyond recall, he would reverse. No democratic politician dare give up hope in human betterment. In fact, this very hope—a revival of the flagging spirit "which desired the peaceful extinction of slavery"—was to be a cornerstone of the new Republican faith, as Lincoln understood it.

So long as the belief that slavery and freedom were locked in a life and death struggle remained in the area of Lincoln's private convictions, it was without significance in the area of politics. In 1856 when, as we know, he was at least half convinced of the truth of this long-time abolition doctrine, he was still able to concentrate on a very limited political objective—Kansas. It was not a lack of sincerity or honesty that led Lincoln to advocate something far short of his personal convictions but, on the contrary, proof of his skill in the tactics of the democratic process. His job, as a politician, was to secure support for the most favorable fraction of what he thought right according to what his judgment of public opinion determined as possible. Lincoln was a master at playing the political game, at demanding no more than could command a public following significant enough to exert political leverage. The sense of timing is a reflex of as great importance to the politician and to the successful operation of the political process as the sixth sense of the shortstop that gets him off instantly in the right direction for a ball hit by the batter. In 1856 Lincoln might well have killed the Republican party in Illinois with the positions that he used to carry half of that state's voters with him in 1858. It is given to few to be prophets of political, social, and economic changes which fuse in politics. Most prophets have been outside politics or have been spokesmen of third (or fourth) parties in the American system. Politicians are required to bring the prophet's vision of the future to reality—a step at a time.

Step at a time, Lincoln's public commitments were creeping up on his personal beliefs. At a Republican banquet in Chicago, shortly after the 1856 campaign, Lincoln responded to a toast with the following words:

> All of us who did not vote for Mr. Buchanan, taken together, are a majority of four hundred thousand. But, in the late contest we were divided between Fremont and Fillmore. Can we not come together for the future? Let every one who really believes, and is resolved, that free society is not, and shall not be, a failure . . . join together. Let us reinaugurate the good old "central ideas" of the republic.[10]

Solving the problem of slavery by reinaugurating the attitudes of those who founded the Republic, might save it.

Douglas made a speech in Springfield in 1857 intended to lever the uncommitted Whigs into his camp by means of the Dred Scott decision. As had become a tradition, Lincoln answered that speech two weeks later. He attempted to reply to Douglas' rather diffuse speech and the reply had the flavor of debate rather than of a set speech. He pointed out that the Republicans were not resisting the Dred Scott decision. The direct effect of the decision involved only the Scott family and the law was taking its course in regard to them. But, he pointed out, the Republicans opposed it as a precedent and promised to do what they could to get it overruled as such.[11] Lincoln attacked Taney's history and especially his interpretation of the Declaration of Independence which Lincoln called "a standard maxim for a free society" and something to be "constantly labored for." In spite of the decision, the "Republicans inculcate, with whatever ability they can, that the negro is a man; that his bondage is cruelly wrong, and that the field of his oppression ought not to be enlarged."

Some time earlier Lincoln had given an address in connection with the Chicago city election that reflected another slight shift of ideas. Here he introduced a word that may have been intended to test the ideas toward which he was groping. Here, where the atmosphere was more radical than in Springfield, he stated that "upon those men who are, in sentiment, opposed to the spread and nationalization of slavery, rests the task of preventing it. The Republican organization is the embodiment of that sentiment. . . ."[12] The progression of Lincoln's ideas is seen more clearly if the three stages are juxtaposed. In 1854, the simplified statement would have been: The Anti-Nebraska fusion wants Congress to restore the Missouri Compromise. In 1856, the statement would have been: The Republican organization wants to prevent the spread of slavery in the territories, particularly Kansas. In 1857: The Republican organization is the embodiment of anti-slavery sentiment. The key word, of course, is "sentiment," divorced from any concrete legislative program. The remarkable thing about this progression toward a broader anti-slavery attitude is that the outcome of the Dred Scott case was not known until a few days later.

Sometime in mid-winter of 1857–58 another long step was taken in the translation of Lincoln's private conviction that the slavery question would dominate American politics until settled one way or the other into Republican dogma. The evidence is found in some notes in the Lincoln papers.[13] At this time, the Lecompton issue was roiling the political waters and the channels which would define their flow were obscured by the variety of alternatives. Squatter Sovereignty might become an attractive doctrine if Douglas were to bring enough help to the Republicans in Congress to prevent the adoption of the Lecompton Constitution. Lincoln's right to run for the Senate was threatened by the possibility that Douglas might become a Republican.

Lincoln's mind was grasping for a distinction between the crucial work being done by Douglas for freedom in Kansas and the long term mission of the Republican party. Lincoln believed that, in the defensive sense, there still was a need for a Republican party because the Democrats would "filibuster indefinitely for additional slave territory—to carry slavery into all the States as well as Territories, under the Dred Scott decision, construed and enlarged from time to time, according to the demands of the regular slave Democracy,—and to assist in reviving the African Slave trade. . . ."[14] In all this Douglas would join—after the Republican organization had been broken down by following him on Lecompton. Lincoln went on:

> His [Douglas] whole effort is devoted to clearing the ring, and giving slavery and freedom a fair fight. With one who considers slavery just as good as freedom, this is perfectly natural and consistent.

> They [Republicans] think slavery is wrong; and that, like every other wrong which some men commit if left alone, it ought to be prohibited by law. They consider it not only morally wrong, but a "deadly poison" in a government like ours, professedly based on the equality of men. Upon this radical difference of opinion with Judge Douglas, the Republican party was organized. There is all the difference between him and them now than there ever was.

> I am glad Judge Douglas has, at last, distinctly told us that he cares not whether slavery be voted down or voted up. Not so much that this is any news to me nor yet that it may be slightly new to some of that class of his friends who delight to say that they "are as much opposed to slavery as any body."

The notes contain a passage which was to be nearly duplicated in the "House Divided" portion of his Springfield speech of June 16, 1858, when he opened the campaign against Douglas. Other elements of that speech were also clearly foreshadowed: especially the charge that the Dred Scott decision was a step toward the nationalizing of slavery. The fight over this, Lincoln forecast, "will be a severe one: and it will be fought through by those who *do* care for the result, and not by those who do not care— by those who are *for,* and those who are against a legalized national slavery."

In this new, broader setting "Kansas is neither the whole nor a tithe of the real question." The "real question" was slavery *per se.* A basic shift had taken place since the Peoria speech of 1854, a shift away from the assumption that the question of slavery in the territories was the only legitimate basis for political activity on the slavery question. This had been enough to build a party on. The hard problem in 1858 was to find a form of the "real question" which would preserve that party and, preferably, win the Fillmore vote besides.

Solving the problem of finding a new platform for the Republican party of Illinois was difficult; no less difficult was the task of dealing with Stephen A. Douglas and his following. Douglas had made a clean break with the administration of President Buchanan, a fact which Illinois Republicans were very reluctant to admit. They were slow to believe because this was a most unpleasant fact to face. If Douglas were no longer a Democrat, should he be welcomed into the Republican fold? Eastern Republicans thought so. As Lincoln complained, the *New York Tribune,* the Bible of the radicals of northern Illinois, had been constantly "eulogizing, and admiring, and magnifying Douglas" throughout the Lecompton struggle. Everyone had known that Douglas was to be the Democratic candidate for the Senate, Lincoln the Republican. This praise of a Democrat by the Eastern Republicans seemed less than comradely to the Illinois Republicans. When Greeley went beyond praise to a recommendation that Republicans assist in the "reelection of every Democratic or American member of Congress who resists the

Lecompton fraud to the bitter end . . .," Illinois Republicans were frantic.[15]

The alarmed Republicans consulted each other frequently. There was a meeting at Springfield in January at which it was decided that there was nothing to do but await developments. Herndon, Lincoln's partner, announced the result of a second meeting to Washburne as a warning to that Congressman, who, it was feared, was friendly to those who would make a deal with Douglas. The meeting "somewhat disapproved" unnamed editors and members of Congress for "passing eulogies upon Harris & Douglas. Every such eulogy was at the expense of the warm, [undecipherable], & true blood of honest and manly Republicans."[16]

Apprehension that Easterners would make a deal with Douglas was real and widespread among the leaders of the fusion. Charles H. Ray, one of the Democratic bolters of 1854, feared "that we have got to deal with him in our camp." He felt it unfortunate that Eastern Republicans "can know nothing of the extent and depth of feeling here against the author of the repeal of the Missouri Compromise. . . ." Judd's impression was that the Republicans in Illinois were to be broken down by outsiders who would "chain us to the car of Douglas." It would be better to serve the administration than Douglas, he thought.[17]

There were proposals and counter-proposals but nothing came of them. The Republicans had a third informal meeting in April in which those present were unanimous for rejecting any offers from Douglas. The state auditor felt that "it is asking too much for human nature to bear to now surrender to Judge Douglas after having driven him by force of public opinion to do what he has done[,] to quietly let him step foremost in our ranks now and make us all take back seats." The Republicans were too near victory to take part in another fusion like that of 1854 and share the profits. Soon thereafter, however, Douglas surprised everyone by the ease with which his followers controlled the Democratic state convention and—to the immense relief of the

Republicans—the danger of a forced marriage with Douglas passed.[18]

For reasons that had nothing to do with national politics, the Illinois politicians had rejected a possibility that might very well have made the Republican party a certain victor in the national election of 1860. One very substantial reason for this decision was the fact that antipathy to Douglas among the *politiques* was one of the most efficient cements holding the Illinois party together. A second reason was the fact that the terms of the alliance among the leaders of the political factions had included, it is reasonable to assume, a division of the offices. The Democrats already had one U.S. Senator—Trumbull. In 1856, they had received the governorship in the person of Bissell. It was now the Whigs' turn, provided Lincoln could win the seat held by Douglas. It would have been too much to ask the Whigs to postpone their dividend indefinitely, especially since the Fillmore men of 1856 were the best prospects for the additional votes necessary to win in 1858.[19]

A third reason was to be found in the prospect of bitter internecine warfare among the Democrats. In February, Lyman Trumbull, the Republican Senator from Illinois received an appeal to help replace a Douglas postmaster with another Democrat. Heads had begun to roll among the postmasters and other federal appointees and the cleavage between the two branches of the Democracy—the followers of Douglas and the supporters of Buchanan—seemed very wide indeed. The Republican state chairman, N. B. Judd, predicted that a third of the Democrats would go to the administration party.[20] Such a split would have guaranteed Lincoln's election. Altogether, the incident was another evidence that American parties, regardless of national doctrine or national party interest, were in practice very sensitive to the states' rights of political parties.

Lincoln's concern for the effect of the reasoning of the *New York Tribune* on the Republicans of northern Illinois was not without basis. Below (or above) the stratum of politicians was a class of earnest anti-slavery people who called themselves

Republican but who felt as Greeley did. W. B. Ogden, one of Chicago's richest men and a prominent Free Soiler in 1848, indicated that among the old Free Soil Democracy others besides himself favored a new fusion.[21] The Douglas papers contain letters from all sorts of people applauding his stand on the Lecompton issue, including some from long-time political opponents. One of the most interesting was from a radical, abolitionist professor whose views and forceful statement of them had imposed on O. H. Browning, one of the Knox College trustees, the burden of straightening things out on the campus. Professor Jonathan Blanchard assured Douglas that if he would continue to support freedom as he had indicated that he would, he, Blanchard, would favor Douglas' return to the Senate and his election to the presidency.[22]

Lincoln did not read Douglas' mail. From other sources, however, came alarms that the abolitionists of the North (recall the 30,500 majority the Republicans had won in this region in 1856) were attracted to Douglas. Lincoln wrote about this to Washburne whose district lay along the Wisconsin line. The inquiry was prompted by a letter from Medill of the *Chicago Tribune* "showing the writer to be in great alarm at the prospect North of Republicans going over to Douglas. . . ." A few days later a letter from Washburne's district arrived, saying that all was well in the first district but that the Republicans of the second district (crossing the state from Rock Island to Chicago) "were more of them Democrats in origin and that their tendency is considerably toward Douglas." Ward Lamon, Lincoln's old friend and law associate, sent alarming news from Joliet. "I find," said he, "very many of the old Republicans who express themselves freely on the subject of Douglas's course—and some of them say he is good enough Republican for them. . . ."[23]

On the eve of the Republican state convention where Lincoln, as principal speaker, would face delegations from all over the state, Lincoln was compelled to bracket the least known and least understood portion of his party—the radicals of the new northern section—with the Fillmore people of the center as the uncertain elements in the coming election. There was no room for the Republican party in the middle—between the man who had just saved Kansas for freedom on the one hand, and the administration on the other. It must find a place to the left, to the more radically anti-slavery side of Douglas if it were to have a reason to exist as a party. Douglas, it must be remembered, had not yet spoken. Lincoln elected the course which would hold the party together, rather than the line which might win him the Senate seat, as every fact of his past promised that he would. It was time for a long step in party doctrine.

On June 16, 1858 in Springfield, Lincoln opened his campaign with a memorable address before the assembled Republicans of the state. In the short opening section which gave the speech its title, Lincoln stated:[24]

> If we could first know *where* we are, and *whither* we are tending, we could then better judge *what* to do and *how* to do it.
>
> We are now far into the *fifth* year, since a policy was initiated with the *avowed* object, and *confident* promise, of putting an end to slavery agitation.
>
> Under the operation of that policy, that agitation has not only, *not ceased,* but has *constantly augmented.*
>
> In *my* opinion, it *will* not cease, until a *crisis* shall have been reached, and passed.
>
> "A house divided against itself cannot stand."
>
> I believe this government cannot endure, permanently half *slave* and half *free.*
>
> I do not expect the Union to be *dissolved*—I do not expect the house to *fall*—but I *do* expect it will cease to be divided.
>
> It will become *all* one thing, or *all* the other.
>
> Either the *opponents* of slavery, will arrest the further spread of it, and place it where the public mind shall rest in the belief that it is in course of ultimate extinction; or its *advocates* will push it forward, till it shall become alike lawful in *all* the states, *old* as well as *new*—North as well as South.

This was Lincoln's appeal to the radicals. It was in their language, paraphrasing the stock argument of the abolitionists about the "eternal conflict between right and wrong." It warned that the Lecompton struggle had been but a skirmish in a war which would continue until slavery either triumphed or was downed. Until one or the other of these points was reached there was work and a noble work for the Republican party to do. It was not the party of any isolated or temporary political aspect of the moral issue but the party of the moral issue itself.

The impact of these words, and of the step in the more radical direction on the scale of anti-slavery which they implied, was great enough (as Herndon recalled) for Lincoln to provoke "a million of curses," from his conservative colleagues. Even from radical Chicago came complaints. A year later, answering Lincoln's protest that the Ohio Republican convention might injure Republicans elsewhere by its radical plank on the Fugitive Slave Law, Salmon P. Chase deftly turned the point against Lincoln citing the "House Divided" speech as evidence "that this avoidance of extremes however is not at all inconsistent with the boldest[,] manliest avowal of our great principles & aims your own example in that noble speech of yours at Springfield which opened the campaign last year in Illinois makes evident enough."[25] The time had come when Lincoln's private belief had become politically useful, or so Lincoln thought.

The second theme of his Springfield speech was a charge that the Dred Scott case was but part of a vast conspiracy involving Douglas, Pierce, Buchanan, and Taney to make slavery national. This was the new aggression, a substitute for the Nebraska Bill of 1854 and bleeding Kansas in 1856. If this should prove convincing, it would unite the same forces that had stood together victoriously to repel the previous attempts to extend slavery. It reverted to the tried and true, defensive, conservative stance of the earlier years. It was the concrete threat against which the Republican party was needed to guard in 1858 and the future. It proved a rather ineffective argument because the purpose alleged was beyond proof and, indeed, beyond the suspicions of most reasonable men. Too, the Kansas-Nebraska Bill was a vital link in Lincoln's chain of circumstantial evidence and Douglas' stand against the Lecompton Constitution apparently exonerated its author. If the "House Divided" was for the radicals, the house that Stephen, Franklin, Roger, and James were alleged to have built was for the old line Whigs.

Thus in the very opening gambit of the campaign, Lincoln had committed himself and his party to a broader stand on the slavery question beyond any possibility of retreat, although his speech at Charleston savored of some backing up.[26] This reducing of the slavery question to general terms, to an "irrepressible conflict," rather than an application to a particular territory like the Mexican Cession, Nebraska, or Kansas, was a return to the older, pre-Wilmot mode of arguing the question. Formerly only abolitionists had so argued. It was a measure of how great a distance the anti-slavery movement had travelled since 1846. Lincoln contributed very greatly to the broadening of the focus on the political level.

Lincoln's moderation in speech and manner has obscured one fact: Lincoln was almost a monomaniac on the question of slavery in politics from 1854 forward. For example, the Republican party in the convention at which Lincoln used the figure of the "House Divided" passed a fairly comprehensive platform, touching on internal improvements, homestead laws, and other current economic problems.[27] Nowhere did Lincoln defend the economic side of this program, at no time did he argue for those positions which were outside the ring of the slavery argument. He had slowly progressed to a notion of the role of the Republican party concerned only with the slavery question, the broad foundations of which he unveiled in this campaign. This very concentration on the slavery question, hitherto associated with abolitionists, made Lincoln appear more radical than did any substantive propositions that he advanced.

Whether the "House Divided" approach was necessary as a gesture to the Republicans of northern Illinois depended on how Douglas intended to campaign. It turned out that he conceded the radicals of the northern Illinois to the Republicans and campaigned from the very first to win the undecided vote of the Whigs of the central part of the state. Was this decision dictated by the nature of Lincoln's Springfield speech? Probably not, for Douglas had not given up his presidential ambitions and probably would have remained as "national" as he could in order to retain the chance to become President.

In his perceptive *Prelude to Greatness,* Don E. Fehrenbacher sums up Lincoln's aims for the "House Divided" address in the statement that "Lincoln was defending his own candidacy for the Senate and trying to save his party from disintegration."[28] Primacy belongs to the second of the two phrases. Lincoln was a party-before-self politician. He had been inching toward the new, more generalized anti-slavery stance enunciated at the state convention since before the Dred Scott decision. The settlement of the Kansas question, one way or the other, was in the offing when the "House Divided" fragment was composed in December or January. The turn of events between then and June 16, 1858, resolved the question in favor of freedom (or so it was quite generally and correctly believed). This made the completion of this transition in doctrine essential for the campaign of 1858 whether or not Lincoln's candidacy had been threatened. The new doctrine was a party need, not for Illinois only but for Republicans everywhere: its timeliness and serviceability to the party provided much of Lincoln's impact beyond Illinois.

Lincoln did justify his candidacy for the unseen audience in northern Illinois and in the East where Douglas support had been suspected. He continued to justify it long afterwards. But he did not need to sway the convention to win its support, for his nomination by that body had been made as sure as anything in politics could be rendered certain. Indeed, it had been for that purpose that it had been arranged. It was merely politic to reassure the delegates that they had done the right thing for the party, not just for Abraham Lincoln.

Now that the bands have stopped playing, the flickerings of the noisy torch-light parades have been extinguished, and hum of insect and human voices in the groves stilled, the shouts of excited partisans silenced, and the timbre of voice and manner of gesture of the orators reduced to memories entombed in print, the great debate of 1858 seems somehow less great. In cold print, the words prompt the question, what was the shouting all about? Extraneous matters intrude, such as wonder that orators could have made themselves heard to 10,000 people without the aid of a public address system and in the open air at that. Or that audiences could stand so long or that voices could wear so well (Douglas' didn't: he was very hoarse in the last debates). Even Albert J. Beveridge, no mean orator himself and less removed from the rural quality and 19th century pace of life than we, found the debates repetitious and less exciting than he had anticipated.[29]

Historians have not only not agreed on who won the debates but there is no unanimity on which of the contestants entered the contest as the underdog. It is true that Douglas was the great nationally known statesman, that he was challenging a national administration for the control of his party, that his name had been before two national conventions as a candidate for the presidential nomination and that, if he won, he would be a leading candidate again. He came home to Illinois with fresh laurels won in the Lecompton fight. Lincoln, on the other hand, while not unknown beyond his state, was at best one of the leaders of a new and vigorous party in Illinois who had served one not especially distinguished term in Congress. Lincoln encouraged the view that he was an innocent David challenging a Goliath, albeit a "little" Goliath.

The contest has been seen in another light. The "Little Giant" was fighting for his political life not just against the Republicans but against the national administration of President Buchanan. Very important to Douglas was the loss of patronage which would have provided the troops of party workers, the post offices from which party literature would be distributed, the political plums which would keep political editors fed when paid subscribers were few. Trumbull acted in liaison with the administration after initial contacts with Isaac Cook, R. B. Carpenter, and Charles Leib, Democratic officeholders who were in charge of organizing a Democratic opposition to Douglas. From Springfield, Douglas was informed that Republicans sat with the Danites (Anti-Douglas Democrats) in their convention "to prevent their numbers from appearing too ridiculously meager. . . ." Republican papers magnified the numbers and importance of the Danite movement. The administration men promised to, and in some cases did, bring out National (Anti-Douglas) Democratic candidates for the legislature in the vital central part of the state. In the main, the cooperation between the Republicans and the administration Democrats was managed for the former by old Democrats, Trumbull in Washington, and George T. Browne, secretary of the state committee and Alton editor, in Illinois. Lincoln probably spoke the truth as he knew it when he denied that a deal with the Danites (Buchanan Democrats so named because the inner circle of Mormon faithful was well remembered in Illinois) such as had been hinted at and condemned by Greeley in the *New York Tribune,* existed.[30] However, the campaign of 1858, among other things, was a two-against-one fight, with Lincoln the beneficiary of important aid by a Democratic administration.

The result was not decided wholly by the oratory. The candidate must not only persuade the electorate but he must also have the right candidates for both houses of the state legislature since the United States Senator was chosen by joint ballot of the two houses. Now voters did not vote for a man for representative in the state legislature solely because he was committed to vote for Lincoln or for Douglas for Senator. The legislative candidate might be unpopular with his party, might lose votes because he was of the wrong religion or because he was for the construction of the wrong railroad. If he were a Republican and were defeated because of such extraneous reasons—extraneous so far as the national issues which Lincoln and Douglas were talking about—Lincoln's chances of election would be diminished by one vote. So organization, getting the right candidates selected, and ironing out difficulties in the districts were part of the campaign on both sides. Both Lincoln and Douglas, as has been noticed, were strong proponents of thorough organization. The loss of patronage and his long absence from the central part of the state (not so long that people were not impressed with his ability to call by his first name almost every person who came to shake his hand) were handicaps to Douglas in this respect. Problems or just information concerning the Chicago city slate, legislative district slates, and the congressional district candidates crowd his files for 1858. The desperateness of the battle was shown by the willingness to give high places on the ticket to former Whigs.[31]

Lincoln had a lively correspondence, in some of which he took the initiative, getting personal friends to secure suitable nominations. Republicans were willing to nominate Fillmore men to bring about a reunion of the old Whig vote. The prospects of such a reunion differed in different counties. In Madison, it was feared that half of the American party vote would go to Douglas, but the same correspondent thought that the Americans of Bond and St. Clair were safe.[32]

The Tazewell County situation provoked a very lively correspondence between Judge Davis and Lincoln. The Democrats had gained the county by capturing a good many Whig votes in 1856 and were running an ex-Whig for the legislature. The outcome was that Shelby Cullom, a Sangamon County American who was supporting Lincoln, at Lincoln's request persuaded his father to run in Tazewell. At Monmouth, the competition for the votes of the former Know-Nothings was not quite so strong: both parties gave the coroner spot on the county ticket to different former American party members. The White-Wabash district looked favorable to the Republicans because the White County Democrats had usurped the turn of the Wabash Democrats for the legislative post.[33]

Lincoln prepared an elaborate chart for the districts that he considered to be in doubt. He combined the Frémont and Fillmore vote of 1856 in each district, and where the total was reasonably close to the Buchanan vote, the district was considered worth fighting for. These districts spread from the Indiana line to the Mississippi River across the center of the state and coincided with the area of greatest Whig strength before 1854.[34] The detail, the leg-work of politics and the careful doing of it weighed in the balance of this election as much or more, perhaps, than the question that elicited the Freeport doctrine—the notion that by not passing a slave code a territorial legislature could keep slavery outside its boundaries. Some historians, probably mistakenly, believe that wily Lincoln trapped Douglas into this pronouncement which cost him Southern support in his campaign for the Democratic nomination in 1860.

There were other problems. State officers Dubois and Miller toured the northern part of the state to secure harmony in the convention on resolutions. They argued that "the resolutions shall not be so strong as to drive off all who would otherwise gladly act with us from southern Illinois." Because of the importance of the former Whigs, Lincoln himself wrote Senator John J. Crittenden of Kentucky on whom the mantle of Clay had fallen to ask "hands off," for the Democrats were using a letter from the Kentuckian with telling effect among the old-line Whigs.[35]

The most important single line of argument of the campaign derived from the "House Divided" portion of Lincoln's opening address. Douglas challenged Lincoln's generalization in his first speech in Chicago and returned to the attack again and again, insisting that if these paragraphs meant anything, they meant that Lincoln was committed to the abolition of slavery in the states where it existed, a not unreasonable inference. Douglas proclaimed that:

Mr. Lincoln advocates boldly and clearly a war of sections, a war of the North against the South, of the free states against the

slave states—a war of extermination—to be continued relent-
lessly until one or the other shall be subdued and all the states
shall either become free or become slave.

Douglas opposed to this concept that the Union must be all slave
or all free a different mode of preserving it:

> I believe that the Union can only be preserved by maintaining
> inviolate the Constitution of the U.S. as our fathers have made
> it. That constitution guarantees to the people of every state the
> right to have slavery or not have it; to have negroes or not have
> them; to have Maine liquor laws or not have them; to have just
> such institutions as they choose, each state being left free to
> decide for itself.[36]

Douglas renewed the attack from a different angle in the first
debate. At Ottawa, in enemy territory, he brought up a radical
platform, actually the 1854 production of the fusion convention
of the second congressional district but which Douglas care-
lessly identified as the Republican state platform of 1854. Before
a strongly anti-slavery audience which cheered the planks as
read, Lincoln was asked to affirm or deny his support of such
propositions as the repeal of the Fugitive Slave Act and the
admission of no more slave states. The strategy was to commit
Lincoln to some more definite area of the spectrum of anti-
slavery. The radical and conservative wings of the Republican
party were to be wedged apart.[37] As a matter of fact, this tack
was less than successful since Lincoln's answers were on the
conservative side and the radicals had no alternative to Lincoln.

At Alton, Douglas asked the question that out-weighed in this
election the one that brought forth the Freeport doctrine, or the
question at Jonesboro that anticipated the slave code debate.
The question that had been implicit throughout the debates was,
"Let me ask him then how is he going to put slavery in the
course of ultimate extinction everywhere, if he does not intend
to interfere with it in the states where it exists?"[38] Why this sectional party, why this fuss and agitation, why this threat to the
Union, if it were not leading somewhere?

Lincoln's answer, like the question, took form through several debates. He contended that the line between the parties was not drawn upon legislative propositions then before the public, but between those who considered slavery a moral wrong and those who did not so consider it. Lincoln put it this way at Alton:

> The real issue in this controversy—the one pressing upon every mind—is the sentiment on the part of one class that looks upon the institution of slavery *as a wrong,* and of another class that *does not* look upon it as a wrong. The sentiment that contemplates the institution of slavery as a wrong is the sentiment of the Republican party. It is the sentiment around which all their actions—all their arguments circle—from which all their propositions radiate. They look upon it as being a moral, social and political wrong; and while they contemplate it as such, they nevertheless have due regard for its actual existence among us, and the difficulties of getting rid of it in any satisfactory way and to all the constitutional obligations thrown about it.[39]

This moral test was not a matter of conviction in the realm of personal behavior but, in the context of these debates, must have applied to the political process of which these debates were a part. Otherwise, it would have been more appropriate in a sermon. Hedged by conditions as it was, this test seems to have divided the sheep who regarded slavery as a proper subject for legislation when "the difficulties of getting rid of it in any satisfactory way" would be overcome, from the goats who were willing to leave slavery with murder and the "cranberry" laws (Douglas' favorite example of the minuteness to which federal control might go) in the hands of the states alone. Yet Lincoln denied emphatically and repeatedly that he proposed to interfere with slavery where it existed.

What exegesis of the text of the debates can save Lincoln from a seemingly glaring contradiction? Lincoln had removed the slavery question from the *cul de sac* of the Wilmot Proviso formula that had imprisoned the moral issue in the narrow confines of slavery in the territories. Yet, confronted with the next logical step—doing something about slavery where it existed—he merely joined the hope of ultimate extinction to the policy of restriction. At Springfield, he had said, "I do wish to see the spread of slavery arrested and to see it placed where the public mind shall rest in the belief that it is in the course of ultimate extinction." There was no closing of the gap between "arresting the spread" and "ultimate extinction." At Jonesboro, he restated it, "I have no doubt that it *would* become extinct, for all time to come, if we but readopted the policy of the fathers by restricting it to the limits it has already covered—restricting it from the new territories." Again at Charleston, "I do not suppose that in the most peaceful way ultimate extinction would occur in less than a hundred years at least; but that it will occur in the best way for both races in God's own good time, I have no doubt."[40]

Lincoln's last three speeches in the debate each contain some expression of this notion of a final conclusion to the slavery question. At Galesburg, he identified himself with those who looked "hopefully to the time when as a wrong it [slavery] may come to an end." At Quincy, among people divided in origin between East and South, and almost equally divided in political allegiance, Lincoln asserted, "I now say that whenever we can get . . . all these men who believe that slavery is in some of these respects wrong, to stand and act with us in treating it as a wrong—then, and not till then, I think we will in some way come to an end of this slavery agitation." At Alton, an old Whig stronghold, he stated that "Republicans desire a policy that looks to a peaceful end of slavery at sometime, as being wrong." In the same debate, he lashed out at Douglas and his neat formula of popular sovereignty by charging that *"he looks to no end of the institution of slavery.* That will help the people see where the struggle really is."[41] Popular sovereignty may have been good medicine for the disease of slavery in Kansas Territory but even its champion made no claims for it if it were agreed that slavery in Georgia ailed the body politic.

Lincoln set the problem on a time scale. Somewhere at the end of the scale was total abolition. Now there was nothing but a moral conviction. In between, somewhere in time and somehow in method, "the difficulties of getting rid of it" would be overcome. The moral test was no strait gate but, rather, a broad basis upon which the Republican party might stand ready to repel extension or nationalization of slavery or restrict it as opportunity presented itself. The moral imperative covered every degree of urgency from that which, reined in from considerations of peace and practicability, could see nothing to do at the present to that in which the higher law minimized the constitutional obstacles.

Lincoln's view was of a morally dynamic society. Time would bring not only growth, wealth, numbers, but also moral regeneration. The people of the South, once the growth of slavery was choked off, would return to the libertarian views of the Revolutionary generation. Popular sovereignty and strict observance of the rights of states, Douglas' platform, were static. These propositions accepted slavery as perpetual and of no concern to those outside the slave states. Progress was for everyone but slaves. Douglas was concerned with sectional peace and material progress. Lincoln was interested in moral change.

Somewhat of a pattern with other areas of the debates was a discussion of the place of the Negro in the American society. It arose out of the debate over the meaning of the Declaration of Independence. Douglas played on the popular fear that emancipation would bring droves of freedmen to Illinois and challenged the notion of Negro equality. In this matter, Lincoln conceded the substance, requiring the concession of no specific right to the black man save that of freedom, but held to the principle so that the door should not be closed to him for the long future.[42]

At Alton, he quoted himself in the passage which revealed most clearly his vision of a society that was morally dynamic:

> I think the authors of that notable instrument [the Declaration of Independence] . . . did not mean to assert the obvious untruth, that all were then actually enjoying that equality, nor yet, that they were about to confer it immediately upon them. . . . They meant simply to declare the *right* so that the *enforcement* of it might follow as fast as circumstances should permit.

141

> They meant to set up a standard maxim for free society which
> would be familiar to all: constantly looked to, constantly labored
> for, and even though never perfectly attained, constantly approxi-
> mated and thereby constantly spreading and deepening its influ-
> ence and augmenting the happiness and value of life to all
> people, of all colors, everywhere.[43]

Lincoln's ideas embraced two seemingly antagonistic fixed
points: The constitutional system which left slavery to the discre-
tion of the states and, on the other hand, the "ultimate extinction
of slavery." He was advocating a party committed to the latter
end but mindful of the constitutional system as an inflexible
barrier to direct action. He did not consider a constitutional
amendment. He and his generation had thought of the Constitution as fixed and unalterable. At one time in reference to
another question, he said of the Constitution:

> Better rather habituate ourselves to think of it as unalterable.
> It can scarcely be made better than it is. New provisions would
> introduce new difficulties, and thus create and increase appetite
> for still further change. No sir; let it stand as it is. New hands
> have never touched it. The men who made it have done their
> work, and have passed away. Who shall improve on what they
> did?[44]

A party so limited at the national level could do only two things
related to its ultimate purpose in any direct way: prevent the
farther spread of slavery and restrict it in the nationally owned
territory where it already existed as in the District of Columbia.

That Lincoln expected slavery to be abolished by the
states where it existed is an inescapable conclusion. The repeti-
tions of his disclaimers of intent to use the federal Congress for
this purpose and his reiterated belief that the federal government
lacked the power to do so were sincere. In 1861, when a word
from Lincoln would have killed the abortive Thirteenth Amendment which would have made explicit and perpetual the understood ban on federal legislation for this purpose, Lincoln
withheld his veto.[45]

He expected a resurgence of the ideals of the earlier age, it may be safely assumed, and necessarily in the South. This resurgence of the idealism, this revival of the humane spirit of Jefferson, he invariably associated with the policy of restriction. In the age of Jefferson, the policy of restriction had been the result, not the cause, of the spirit of the age. How did Lincoln expect a reversal of cause and effect to be made?

The march of King Cotton, in Lincoln's own lifetime, had changed the sentiment of the South from one of toleration of an admittedly immoral institution to an active, aggressive, even boastful defense of the peculiar institution. Cotton wedded to slavery had been the virile, expanding, aggressive motif of Southern life since 1830. Just within the year (1858) when depression had hit the North, Southerners had boasted that their civilization rested upon a firmer foundation than that of the North—on cotton and slavery.

Lincoln was familiar in a general way with the slave-surplus border states which the march of King Cotton had by-passed. He could remember well attempts of Virginia, Kentucky, and Missouri to enact plans of gradual emancipation, frustrated by the immense difficulties involved and by the growth of the aggressive pro-slavery spirit. Here slavery was not dynamic but a hampering relic of the past.

Should slavery be contained by the federal government, would not the institution of itself lose its virility, its support by the selfishness of men who expected to ascend the ladder of success by means of it? Would not the Cotton South at some day be another Virginia groaning under its burden of slavery? It must have no Cuba, no Sonora, no Nicaragua, as well as no West to prolong the march of slavery, to give time a chance to answer these questions. When restriction should deprive slavery of its confident support, of its liaison with cotton profits, of its psychological dominance and aggressiveness in Southern life, would not Southerners rejoin the march of moral progress?

Douglas included in nearly every speech an account of the battle against the Lecompton Constitution, an account from which emerged naturally enough a hero—Stephen A. Douglas.

In one sense, this was pure personal vindication for Kansas had become free as he had predicted in 1854 when he had suffered not only political defeat but personal abuse because he was not believed. In another, it was intended to cast a wider net, to prove not only that he had been right in 1854, but that the "great principle" had brought freedom, not slavery, to Kansas, the test case. The Republican amalgam had been formed on the shifting sand of error and, if defense against extension of slavery was still its one bond of union, then this dangerous sectional party should dissolve into its component parts.

The Republican answer to the rehabilitation of Douglas' character was provided by Trumbull who dug up an accusation that Douglas' self-proclaimed consistency was marred by his having removed a submission requirement from the Toombs Bill in 1856, a story too long for telling and too involved for establishing its validity. In effect, it purported to establish that in 1856 Douglas had not been favorable to the submission of a Kansas constitution to the voters. The charge seemed to administer a pinprick to the inflated account of Douglas' consistent support of the "great principle" and Lincoln took it up at Charleston.[47] The present day reader finds Lincoln's performance at Charleston the weakest of the seven debates largely because the Trumbull charges mar the structure of argument and seem inappropriate. Curiously enough, however, and in spite of forebodings by Republican friends, the eastern area was the one part of the old Whig area where there were any significant Republican gains. Whether telling argument or skillful politics in preparing nominations produced that result, Lincoln had had a hand in producing it.

The Republicans failed to capture the legislature and Lincoln lost the senatorship. The total legislative vote for Republican candidates was higher than the Democratic total by about the same few thousand votes captured by the National Democrats, but with the 1850 districts, the Democrats gained seats with this minority vote. The five American party candidates who had represented the old Whig districts of Sangamon, Madison, Wabash, and White, were replaced in the new legislature by Democrats, one of them a former Know-Nothing elector.[48] Tazewell and Logan, former Whig strongholds, also returned Democrats, but were offset by the recapture by the Republicans of two districts in the faster growing eastern region. The southern part of the state, with the exception of German St. Clair County, was Democratic; the northern was solidly Republican. The doubtful middle ground of central Illinois had been carried by the Democrats although by small majorities. The Republican majority in Chicago had been narrowed to about 1,500 votes.

Whig rank and file as well as Whig leaders such as T. L. Dickey, B. S. Morris, the American candidate for governor in 1856, and John Henry, Lincoln's predecessor in the House of Representatives, went over to the Douglas party. So many Whigs had transferred allegiance to the Democratic party in the Springfield district that a Democratic candidate for the congressional nomination complained of their power in the district—28 of 70 delegates in the district convention. Yet the actual number of former Whigs who had finally found a home with the Democrats was considerably less than a majority of the Fillmore vote, for the central counties vote was very close. Judge Davis thought it was Dickey's desertion and Crittenden's intervention for Douglas that had turned the tide.[49] No doubt, the two radical portions of Lincoln's speeches, the "House Divided" and the defense of the Declaration of Independence helped Douglas.

Cruelly disappointing to the Republicans was the showing of the Buchanan Democrats. According to one paper, "They have made no impression—have not left a trace of their efforts in the general result. . . . The polls show that Douglas is the party and Buchanan the bolter with whom the party will not affiliate." As a matter of fact, the senatorial district in which Peoria was located and the Marshall, Putnam, Woodford assembly district were both carried by the Republicans only because of the small group of Buchananites. In the latter case, the Danite voters of tiny Putnam exactly equaled the Republican majority.[50]

The Republican party, in losing the senatorship and the control of the legislature, had gained character as a party. The elements out of which the party was formed had cooperated in 1854 on a single, clearly defined, popular issue. In 1856, they had been formally organized and won a major success under the stern necessities of the Kansas crisis. They had won more popular votes than their opponents in 1858 without the compacting influence of a national crisis and without a live, immediate issue. In spite of losing the senatorship because of the out-of-date distribution of legislative seats which favored the older, more Democratic areas, Lincoln took comfort in the fact that "We have some hundred and twenty thousand clear Republican votes. That pile," he thought, "is worth keeping together." Lincoln must have esteemed one letter he received after the election above all the others. "I consider that your campaign permanently established the Republican party," wrote an old friend. Indeed, the Republican party was now no longer a bundle of factions, not, as Judge Davis had said, "a confederation," but what he had thought it was not, "a consolidated party."[51] Far from the bottom falling out of the thing, the party was as united in defeat as it had been in victory.

This did not mean that Whigs forgot that they had been Whigs. One of Lincoln's correspondents in 1858 had written that he was "still fiting [sic] in the old Whig ranks." His intimate, H. C. Whitney was suspicious of "little Caucusses" which had been held occasionally by old Democrats, Judd, Cook, Scripps, Bross, and Ray, "which I as an old Whig don't like." Soon after the election, Judge Davis entertained suspicions that campaign funds had been withheld for use in making Judd governor and Browne lieutenant governor in 1860. But the same gentleman could never forgive the "pharisaical old Whigs of the central counties" for letting Lincoln down.[52] The case of Judge Dickey, who, disgusted at the renomination of Lovejoy in the third district, bolted the party and supported Douglas, illustrates the change. There was no place to go for anyone who could no longer stomach the fusion except to cross the Rubicon and join the old enemy. No faction was itself whole any longer. Treason was possible but no secession.

The Republican party was firmly grounded on a deep-seated hostility to slavery and to the South. Four years of the poison of sectional bitterness had had its effect even among the Democrats. A partisan of Douglas wrote a strong letter against the Lecompton Constitution and added, "You may think by the way I write I am a Rep. I have never voted any ticket yet but the Democratic but cant [sic] vote for the South any more." Douglas' own lieutenants were affected by it. Harris noted in Washington "a more sullen hostility & bitterness than I ever saw before." After a visit to his home area of the Military Tract, General James W. Singleton wrote that "We are not in a condition to carry another ounce of Southern weight."[53] If leading Democrats were seething with anger at the South and the pro-slavery Southerner, imagine the depth of feeling of those who voted Republican, read Republican newspapers, and listened to Republican oratory!

If Lincoln's fine line of the moral issue as the basis for the Republican party had a logical and a political necessity, it has a sociological foundation as well. Lincoln had enunciated a truth of which Republicans, especially those of Whig origin, were keenly aware: that the Republicans were the better people. In 1854, a correspondent pointed out to Lincoln that the Democrats had an advantage, "they have the whiskey boys on their side who will go to the polls for a spree." In 1856, the Whig organ of western Illinois (by then, Republican) thought that the Republicans were the elect, if not the elected. It contrasted the parties:

> On the Republican side have stood shoulder to shoulder in the hard fought battle, not only all the skill, the enterprise, the intelligence of the community, but also the great moral and religious body of the people.

> It is a mournful fact, but nevertheless true that the supporters of
> the triumphant, proslavery democracy are the ignorant, the unin-
> formed, the slothful and the vicious.

In 1858, defeat was less bitter for one Vandalia Republican
because "Generally the more moral, religious, intellectual and
temperate portion of our village are naturally enough *Republicans.*" The report of the Ottawa debate quotes the chairman of
the Republican committee as breaking in to silence hecklers of
Douglas with these suggestive words, "The *masses* listened to
Mr. Lincoln attentively, and as *respectable men* we ought now
to hear Mr. Douglas, and without interruption."[54] If the moral
issue served to separate the sheep from the goats, the Republicans, as the Whigs before them, knew that they were sheep.

The party had a distinctly sectional basis in Illinois. A Chicago journal, in assessing the importance of the Buchananites in
the election, analyzed the result in Johnson County (southern
Illinois), "where Republicanism is a higher crime than horse-
stealing," and in northern Illinois counties "where Republicanism is a form of religion and the common faith of the people."
The people of the northern section, come recently from the East,
more prosperous, more advanced educationally, had a set of
attitudes and beliefs about the Negro which they had learned
from that section's partisan newspapers, its anti-slavery journals,
and its abolition preachers. The southern section, poor and
poorly schooled, largely Southern in ancestry and tradition, had
another set of assumptions that led to a hostile attitude toward
the Negro and a strong love of the Union. The Negro had represented a form of economic competition, slave or free, in Kentucky and even the scant Republican sentiment in the southern
portion of the state would scarcely have been recognized as
Republican in the northern portion. A call for a Republican
party meeting in Olney was addressed to "the Republican party
and all who are in favor of keeping the territories uncontam-
inated with the negro race. . . ."[55]

In 1852, the reasons one editor assigned for the Whig defeat
of that year was that the Democrats were the "well drilled reg-

ular soldiers" while the Whigs were "gallant but uncontrolled militia." Six years later, the Republicans were the "regular" soldiers and the Democrats had taken a back seat to them in organization. The Republicans, as noted, had succeeded in manipulating federal patronage to their own interests and in depriving Douglas of its benefits. They had perfected an efficient organization of their own. For this, Lincoln deserved some credit. The circulation of Republican newspapers in doubtful areas was stimulated at some cost to party leaders and office-holders. A veritable flood of campaign documents was directed into the central counties. Chicago had been in Republican hands for all but one year since the Anti-Nebraska forces had acted together. A machine existed there which the Republican state chairman believed "if exposed" would "damn us to everlasting infamy" but which effectively garnered in the votes.[56]

The notion of a party formed on the basis of a moral attitude had not seemed ridiculous to the voter. The Republican party was here to stay. That was the message of B. C. Lundy who ran up the names of Seward for President and Lincoln for Vice-President on the masthead of his paper at Hennepin.[57]

---

1. *Quincy Whig,* Oct. 14, 1851; *Collected Works,* II, 342–3.

2. I am thinking here of the reports of Ward Lamon and H. C. Whitney to Lincoln about third district politics in 1858 and the difficulties of Judge T. Lyle Dickey, ex-Whig, Kentuckian, and son of a mild abolitionist (in the Kentucky sense) preacher, in the same district.

3. The quoted phrase is from Lincoln's speech before the Republican State Convention of 1858 as found in Angle, *Created Equal,* p. 9.

4. Yates MSS, Washington, Mar. 17, 1856, James Knox; *Chicago Weekly Times,* Oct. 18, 1855; *Collected Works,* II, 320–3, Springfield, Aug. 24, 1855, Joshua Speed; *Congressional Globe,* 34th Congress, 1st Session, App., p. 844; Wallace-Dickey MSS, Bloomington, July 18, 1856, David Davis to T. L. Dickey.

5. Trumbull MSS, Washington, May 12, 1857, G. Bailey. Bailey, editor of the *National Era,* the Republican organ in Washington, in asking $2.00 from each Republican member of Congress, reminded them that Montgomery Blair and he had guaranteed the costs.

6. *Collected Works,* II, 401. Lincoln quoted from Douglas' speech of June 12, 1857.

7. For events in Kansas, see Roy Franklin Nichols, *The Disruption of American Democracy* (New York: The Macmillan Company, 1948), chapters 6, 7

and 9. The Douglas manuscripts have a number of interesting items showing that Douglas, through John Calhoun, the former Springfield Democratic politician and surveyor-general of Kansas, was attempting to influence events in Kansas toward a settlement; Douglas MSS, Paris (Illinois), Nov. 23, 1857, W. D. Latshaw.

8. *Collected Works,* II, 424. The name of Abraham Lincoln headed the list of those making the call; that of Shelby M. Cullom, an American, was second; *Collected Works,* III, 380, Springfield, May 17, 1859, Theodore Canisius.

9. *Collected Works,* II, 318, Springfield, Aug. 15, 1855, Judge George Robertson.

10. *Ibid.,* p. 385, Dec. 10, 1856.

11. *Ibid.,* pp. 398–410 (speech of June 26, 1857).

12. *Ibid.,* pp. 390–1 (Feb. 28, 1857).

13. *Ibid.,* pp. 448–54. The editors of the *Collected Works* date this document tentatively as having been delivered May 18, 1858, at Edwardsville. From internal evidence, i.e., reference to Douglas' bill for determining the fate of Kansas, the date can be narrowed to the span of time from December 10, 1857, and February 18, 1858. This is between the announcement that he would submit such a bill by Douglas (December 10) and the report of the Committee on Territories (February 18), which proposed the admission of Kansas under the Lecompton constitution. An interesting and provocative account of Lincoln's change of front, Don E. Fehrenbacher, "The Origins and Purpose of Lincoln's 'House Divided' Speech," *Mississippi Valley Historical Review,* XLVI, No. 4 (March, 1960), 637–641, concludes that it was written in the last ten days of December, 1857. One cannot be certain that all parts are of the same date.

14. *Ibid.*

15. *Ibid.,* p. 430, Springfield, Dec. 28, 1857, Lyman Trumbull; *New York Weekly Tribune,* Mar. 4, 1858.

16. Trumbull MSS, Springfield, Jan. 14, 1858, O. M. Hatch; Washburne, MSS, Springfield, Apr. 10, 1858, W. H. Herndon.

17. Trumbull MSS, Chicago, Mar. 9, 1858, C. H. Ray; Chicago, Mar. 7, 1858, N. B. Judd.

18. *Ibid.,* Springfield, Apr. 8, 1858, Jesse K. Dubois; Springfield, May 7, 1858, W. H. Herndon.

19. Palmer, "A Collection of Letters," pp. 38–40.

20. Trumbull MSS, Peoria, Feb. 28, 1858, C. Ballance; Chicago, Mar. 7, 1858.

21. Douglas MSS, New York, Apr. 12, 1858, Wm. B. Ogden. Among those whom he had been told were in favor of such a move was Judd whose letters prove Ogden to have been misled or Judd guilty of the greatest duplicity.

22. Douglas MSS, Galesburg, May 1, 1858. The heat of the following campaign changed all this, of course. In a campaign speech reported in the *Galesburg Democrat* (Republican), Sept. 4, 1858, Blanchard was reported to have replied to Douglas' ridicule of Negro equality by asserting that should Douglas become a widower again, Northerners would not object to his marrying one of his slave girls.

23. RTL No. 810 (a typed copy of a letter from Lincoln to Washburne dated May 27, 1858); Nos. 814–5, Belvidere, May 29, 1858, S. A. Hurlbut; Nos.

859–61, Jolliett [sic], June 9, 1858, Ward H. Lamon. "Old Republican" equates with "abolitionist" for it refers to the abortive Republican party of 1854.

24. Angle, *Created Equal,* pp. 1–2.

25. Emanuel Hertz, *The Hidden Lincoln* (New York: The Viking Press, 1938), pp. 97–8; RTL Nos. 907–10, Chicago, June 22, 1858, John L. Scripps; Nos. 1748–52, Columbus, Ohio, June 13, 1859, S. P. Chase.

26. RTL Nos. 1435–7, Naperville, Oct. 11, 1858, J. G. Wright. Wright was convinced that the copies of the Charleston debate being circulated in northern Illinois were forgeries and were hurting Lincoln.

27. Beveridge, *Abraham Lincoln,* II, 569–71.

28. Don E. Fehrenbacher, *Prelude to Greatness, Lincoln in the 1850's* (Stanford, Calif.: Stanford University Press, 1962), p. 94.

29. Beveridge, *Lincoln,* p. 635.

30. Trumbull MSS, Alton, Feb. 24, 1858, George T. Browne; Douglas MSS, Springfield, Apr. 22, 1858, James A. Barret; *Daily Whig and Republican* (Quincy), June 5, 1858; Trumbull MSS, Chicago, July 20, 1858, Charles Leib; *Collected Works,* II, 471–2, Springfield, June 23, 1858, Lyman Trumbull. The most obvious indication that Lincoln was not aware of all of the collusion between the Danites and his party is the fact that he made the denial to Trumbull who knew everything.

31. Douglas MSS, Ottawa, July 9, 1858, Wm. Reddick. Suggests Churchill Coffing, former Whig, for Congress.

32. *Collected Works,* II, 443, Urbana, Apr. 23, 1858, T. A. Marshall; RTL Nos. 981–3, Edwardsville, July 18, 1858, Joseph Gillespie. (Gillespie had been an American elector in 1856.)

33. RTL Nos. 1099–1100, Bloomington, July 30, 1858, David Davis; Nos. 1324–5, Monmouth, Aug. 20, 1858, Philo E. Reed; Nos. 1384–7, Greyville, Sept. 3, 1858, Sidney Spring.

34. *Collected Works,* II, 476–81.

35. Washburne MSS, Galena, May 16, 1858, William Cary; *Collected Works,* II, 483–4, Springfield, July 7, 1858, John J. Crittenden.

36. Angle, *Created Equal,* p. 18 (Douglas' Chicago speech); p. 54 (Douglas' Springfield speech).

37. *Ibid.,* pp. 105–6; RTL Nos. 1301–2, Chicago, Aug. 26, 1858, H. C. Whitney.

38. Angle, *Created Equal,* pp. 400–1.

39. *Ibid.,* p. 390.

40. *Ibid.,* pp. 76, 205, 270.

41. *Ibid.,* pp. 304, 335, 390, 393.

42. *Ibid.,* pp. 39–42, 235–6, 379–82.

43. *Ibid.,* p. 393.

44. *Congressional Globe,* 30th Congress, 1st Session, App., p. 710.

45. See below, p. 197.

46. Douglas MSS, Elgin, Jan. 12, 1858, E. Wilcox. His letter in part said, "Your position upon the Lecompton folly . . . enables us to triumphantly call the attention of black republicans to their infamous falsehoods against your

honesty of purpose in the inception of and engrafting upon the Kansas-Nebraska bills the fundamental principles of the people's sovereignty."

47.   Angle, *Created Equal,* pp. 235–75.

48.   State of Illinois, *House Journal,* 21st Gen. Ass., pp. 4–7.

49.   Douglas MSS, Jacksonville, Sept. 29, 1859, M. McConnel; RTL Nos. 1463–5, Danville, Nov. 7, 1858, David Davis.

50.   *Chicago Daily Press and Tribune,* Nov. 8, 1858; A. C. Cole, Notes on Elections (unpublished notes on file in the Illinois History Survey).

51.   RTL No. 1480, Springfield, Nov. 15, 1858, Lincoln to N. B. Judd; Nos. 1616–8, Vermont, Jan. 29, 1859, H. S. Thomas; No. 879, Bloomington, June 14, 1858, David Davis.

52.   *Ibid.,* No. 1445, Columbus, Oct. 25, 1858, J. R. Heman; Nos. 1411–4, Chicago, Sept. 23, 1858; Nos. 729–30, Bloomington, Jan. 1, 1859 (misdated 1858); Nos. 1463–5, Danville, Nov. 7, 1858.

53.   Douglas MSS, Utah (Illinois), Apr. 14, 1858; McClernand MSS, Washington, Feb. 16, 1858; Douglas MSS, Quincy, Feb. 20, 1859.

54.   RTL No. 664, Macomb, Dec. 28, 1854, W. H. Randolph; *Daily Whig* (Quincy), Nov. 14, 1856; Trumbull MSS, Vandalia, May 26, 1858, J. H. Wilkinson; Angle, *Created Equal,* p. 131. I have added the italics.

55.   *Chicago Daily Press and Tribune,* Nov. 8, 1858; RTL No. 804, *Olney Times,* May 21, 1858.

56.   *Alton Daily Telegraph,* Nov. 24, 1852; *Collected Works,* II, 410; Trumbull MSS, Springfield, Feb. 27, 1858, John O. Johnson; Springfield, Feb. 27, 1858, W. H. Herndon; Chicago, Dec. 26, 1858, N. B. Judd. There may be more than a trifle of exaggeration in this statement since Judd, like most of the political leaders, hated Mayor Wentworth passionately.

57.   RTL Nos. 1495–7, Magnolia, Nov. 22, 1858.

The Moral Issue and the Nation

The "House Divided" doctrine had evolved out of Lincoln's personal analysis of the moral issue in politics and had become dogma for the Illinois Republicans under the pressure of political necessities peculiar to the situation in the state. Under most circumstances, Lincoln's words and doctrine might have been consigned to that crowded section of the forgotten past reserved for defeated politicians and their ideas. The year 1858 was different.

CHAPTER 7

It is abundantly clear that Lincoln was vaulted into national prominence by the campaign against Douglas. The *New York Tribune,* which had a very wide circulation among the more radical Republicans all over the Great Lakes region, gave more attention to the Illinois race than to any other outside New York. It carried Lincoln's Chicago speech and the Ottawa debate in full. In each case the introductory and summary material as well as the verbatim reports were taken from the *Chicago Press and Tribune* and the comments were slanted very favorably to Lincoln. A Trumbull speech was printed in full on September 7, 1858. Several articles from correspondents left the thorough *Tribune* reader better informed on Illinois politics from a Republican viewpoint than on any contest other than the shorter New York campaign.[1] In spite of the fact that Greeley had wished Lincoln to step aside in favor of Douglas and was still of the same opinion after the election, Lincoln had no ground for complaint that the *Tribune* had not supported him loyally during the campaign.

When it was all over, Greeley paid a graceful compliment to Lincoln by quoting a highly laudatory article from the *Press and Tribune* which congratulated Lincoln on a "memorable and brilliant canvas." It spoke of Lincoln's "high moral qualities and the keen, comprehensive and sound intellectual gifts" which he possessed. He, in the writer's opinion, had "created for himself a national reputation."[2] To this Greeley added his own word of praise. "Mr. Lincoln's campaign speeches were of a very high order," he thought and the Springfield (House Divided) speech was "a model of compactness, lucidity, and logic." The great editor believed that Lincoln could have attacked Douglas more persistently on the weaknesses of popular sovereignty and furnished Lincoln with some *post mortem* examples of what he might have done.

Other Eastern papers used the stenographic reports of the speeches and debates. The *Boston Daily Advertiser* carried large extracts from the Ottawa debate. "The country is looking to the progress of the senatorial contest in Illinois with increasing and absorbing interest," was the judgment of the *Springfield* (Massachusetts) *Republican*. The editor of the *National Era,* in answer to a complaint from an angry Illinois reader, averred that "every careful reader of the *Era* knows that in this matter the *Era* dissented from the position of some Eastern Republican papers, and that we devoted more space to giving aid to our Republican friends in Illinois than to our friends in any other state."[3] In sum, Lincoln had a hearing throughout the North because, next to the local political contest, the fate of the "Little Giant" and his doctrine was of the most interest to Republicans everywhere.

In 1858, Illinois politics had required a rethinking of the Republican position on slavery. One reason for the urgent need to develop a new doctrine in the Prairie State was the candidacy of Douglas. The Republicans of Illinois could not stand aside and watch two wings of the Democratic party fight each other in their state as outsiders could, nor could Lincoln enter the lists without weapons of creed. The time element aside, however, the Dred Scott decision and the laying to rest of the Kansas issue had precisely the same effect on Republican doctrine elsewhere that it had had in Illinois—except that the lack of a Douglas running for the highest office dulled the sense of urgency for finding a new anti-slavery stand. Outside Illinois, it was a year of drift and improvisation for the Republicans. The year 1855 could have been described as the year of politicians looking for a party: 1858 was the year of a party looking for a principle.

Two courses other than that which Lincoln had adopted seemed open and each had its advocates. One possibility that appealed to some Republicans was that Douglas' squatter sovereignty, now that the Buchanan Democrats were against it, should be taken up as the new Republican theory. It had proved its effectiveness in bringing Kansas safely to the port of freedom. Some anti-Lecompton Democrats had been supported by the Republicans in 1858. The most sensational presentation of this viewpoint was made at the Massachusetts State Republican convention by Eli Thayer, well-known for his promotion of Northern emigration into Kansas:

> Now if it is a fact that we are able to do better and do more for freedom without a law [the congressional prohibition of slavery in the territories], then I say that, instead of its being the duty of Congress to legislate for the territories, it is the duty of Congress to take the best steps for the extension of freedom; and, in my opinion, the true ground for any party desiring to secure the freedom of the territories is to work for absolute nonintervention, either by Congress, by the Federal Executive, or by any other non-resident power whatever.[4]

The *Springfield* (Massachusetts) *Republican* waited until after the election to agree:

> As to the territories, there could be no reasonable question, with such fair play, not to say favor, as a change in the national gov-

ernment would ensure, that the substitution of this policy of popular sovereignty for that of congressional intervention would be equally serviceable to freedom, while more satisfactory to the country.[5]

Greeley's reaction to Thayer's bombshell was like a leaf from Lincoln's book:

Senator Douglas says he is for Non Intervention [the term Thayer suggested as a substitute for popular sovereignty], by which he means that he is utterly indifferent whether Slave Labor or Free shall prevail in any embryo State. . . . But, even *if* there had ever been a possibility of genuine Non-Intervention, we insist that the Dred Scott decision had demolished it.[6]

Thayer's proposal was ill-timed, either too late or too early. It might have increased the pressure on Illinois Republicans to accept Douglas if it had been proposed in March and been coupled with arrangements that would have taken care of Douglas and his following. To have accepted or better, appropriated Douglas' doctrine, even thinly disguised, without absorbing the Douglasites, would have been very risky, even fatal, should Douglas have won control of the Democratic party away from Buchanan. The proposal might have had some value in 1860 if Douglas either lost the nomination or appeared to be losing it before the convention assembled.

The other alternative that attracted a great many Republican partisans was produced by the general political outlook in 1858 and 1859. The Buchanan administration was extremely unpopular. It was blamed for the depression of 1857 and was also accused of corruption. Its dealings with the Mormons had been characterized by weakness and vacillation. After the 1858 elections, in which gains had been made by the opposition nearly everywhere, it was apparent that the only way the national Democratic party could win in 1860 was by the continued division of its enemies. In many of the Eastern states, large remnants of the American party had remained unassimilated by the older parties. The American party was the chief opposition party in the border states, battling the Democrats in state, congressional, and local elections on somewhat even terms. Deprived of any chance of success as an independent party in a national election, the Americans' one hope of success was to be taken into some sort of fusion of the opposition. Their hope of influencing the course of events in national affairs lay in the terms which they might require for their adhesion to such a combination.[7] The character which they wished to impress upon any possible fusion was in the direction of moderation on the slavery question. The strong possibility of victory in 1860 with fusion, the weakness of the Americans without combination, and the seeming disappearance of the issue of slavery in the territories, which had created the Republican party in the first place, united to create a great pressure for a merger.

Such notions were in the air in several states, particularly those in which the Fillmore vote had been heavy enough in 1856 to have been decisive. In Pennsylvania, the fusion was effected in 1858 and easily swept the October elections of that year. It was a "Peoples" victory won by the fact that "Republicans, Americans, democrats, whigs and others . . . united heartily. . . ." In southern Ohio, the Ross County Republicans instructed their delegates to the district convention at Portsmouth to try to "get a candidate for Congress who will conciliate all the various interests opposed to the present administration [of] the General Government; and all the pledge that shall be required from said candidate be that he shall be opposed to the general policy of the administration of James Buchanan." In Massachusetts and in New York, there was serious talk of union which led to a fused ticket in the latter but to nothing of consequence in the former. Greeley was not entirely happy with the fusion in New York for he thought that Republicans could not "for the sake of augmenting our numbers, or winning a triumph, adjure our principles or desert our friends."[8]

This threat to the kind of Republicanism that Lincoln was seeking was discerned by Salmon P. Chase of Ohio. He wrote that

The rise of the Know Nothing Party had a pernicious influence upon the growth of a true Antislavery Spirit. You remember that one of its aims was to be national; and to be national it must ignore the slavery question, or in other words become indifferent as to the progress of slavery in the north while the south tolerated no indifference. Some yielded to this under the idea that the south, or rather the slave oligarchy of the south, would adopt the policy of indifferentism as well as the north. . . . When the American Party became republicanized as in Ohio & some other states, a number of its members refused to vote republican tickets because they believed the antislavery principle represented. Often these men held the balance of power in their particular states, districts or counties. Under these circumstances politicians soon began to think of conciliating them, and this disposition has induced a number of republican leaders to urge an abatement or modification of our Antislavery creed so as to make conciliation [illegible]. . . . In Ohio, my maxim has been "conciliate, but no abandonment of principle;" and I am happy to say that we have succeeded very thoroughly.[9]

He went on to say that fusion in Ohio had taken place on the Republican articles of faith but with a fused ticket. It was New York and Pennsylvania that he was most concerned about because in these states "there seems to be a disposition to fuse upon simple opposition to the Administration, often without any & generally with little regard to Anti-slavery principles." He feared that the same tendency was appearing in Massachusetts.

The *Albany Argus* analyzed the campaign and the election of 1858 as follows:

In truth, except in the State of Illinois, where the Republicans have just been defeated, the recent elections have not been conducted on Republican issues. . . . Temporary and ephemeral issues have been substituted. [The] recent triumphs of the Opposition are not victories achieved by a regular, well organized, homogeneous party, having a definite understood purpose and a common aim and policy reaching into the future.[10]

Lincoln was in demand as a political speaker, not only because of the notoriety gained by having stood up to Douglas in Illinois, but because in the State of Illinois "the recent elections" had been "conducted on Republican issues." His Illinois speeches were recognized as pronouncing doctrine that might supply the want of "a definite understood purpose and common aim and policy reaching into the future." His major addresses, with the possible or partial exception of the Cooper Union speech, were aimed at Republican ears to help Republicans clarify their doctrine. He was invited because perplexed, divided, and uncertain Republicans wanted to hear someone who would tell them that their party's existence was justified and needed. Lincoln was not invited to Columbus to parade himself as a Republican candidate for the presidency nor did New Englanders invite him there solely to provide a platform for a possible rival for Governor Seward, although a study of the balloting in the 1860 convention shows that Lincoln was more than just another favorite son—largely because of his travels.[11] He had a message most Republicans desperately wanted to hear.

Lincoln spoke at Council Bluffs, Iowa without prearrangement while on a business trip. Even this extempore speech was described by the Democratic paper as "in the character of an exhortation to the Republican party." He was invited to help the Republicans of Ohio in their autumn campaign. Perhaps the knowledge that Douglas was assisting the Democrats made the request more urgent and natural and acceptance by Lincoln the easier. He spoke at Columbus, Dayton, Hamilton (briefly), and Cincinnati and on the way home stopped off for a speech at Indianapolis.[12]

On the last day of September, 1859, he delivered a non-political address to the Wisconsin State Agricultural Society at Milwaukee and followed this by two political addresses in southern Wisconsin. December 1, 1859, found Lincoln in Kansas, coaxed there by Mark Delahay who had assisted Lincoln in 1858. Here Lincoln made three or four speeches.

Certainly only rivaled in importance by the Columbus and

Cincinnati speeches was the address delivered at New York's Cooper Union before an impressive audience on February 27, 1860. This was followed by a swing through New England. "The difficulty," Lincoln wrote Mrs. Lincoln, "was to make nine other [speeches] before reading audiences who had already seen all my ideas in print."[13]

These speeches to an ever widening audience of Republicans were devoted to expounding notions of Republican doctrine which had been developed over the years but which had appeared near whole for the first time in the Illinois campaign. The set speech permitted more logical organization and fuller development of themes and rough ideas were polished and sharpened. More apt illustrations drove points home more effectively. They reveal that Lincoln had three purposes. The first and foremost was to demolish the popular sovereignty threat from within the party. The second was to secure the new, broader anti-slavery basis of the party on the moral issue and thus to dispose of the threat of the fusion of the opposition proposition with its meeting of the anti-slavery theme. The third was to give as conservative a cast to this program as was possible.

It was the first point—combatting the Thayer heresy that nonintervention was as good or better than congressional prohibition of slavery in the territories—that gave some of his addresses the appearance of being a continuation of the debates with Douglas. At Cincinnati, most of his speech was framed in a droll fashion, as an explanation to pro-slavery Kentuckians across the river that Douglas was their best candidate because his popular sovereignty doctrine was preparing the way for nationalizing slavery.[14] His largely Republican audience got the point. It was here on the banks of the Ohio which separated free from slave territory that Lincoln countered Douglas' claim that popular sovereignty, not the Northwest Ordinance, that nature, not law, had made the states of Ohio, Indiana, and Illinois free. He recalled that the earliest Hoosiers had wanted to admit slavery into Indiana and had been refused on the basis of the Northwest Ordinance. Illinois and Missouri, lying side by side geographically, became free and slave respectively because the former was covered by the Ordinance.

Douglas not only had spoken recently at Columbus but had written a magazine article which traced popular sovereignty back to the time of the founding fathers and beyond. "That insidious Douglas Popular Sovereignty," Lincoln warned in direct answer, "is the miner and sapper . . . preparing us for the onslaught and charge of those ultimate enemies"—revival of the slave trade and the nationalization of slavery. He pointed out that Douglas' support of both the Dred Scott decision and the Freeport doctrine was logically indefensible. The latter meant "when all the trash, the words, the collateral matter was cleared away from it, all the chaff was fanned out of it, it was a bare absurdity—no less than [that] a thing may be lawfully driven away from where it has a lawful right to be."[15]

In the Cooper Union address, the historical justification for popular sovereignty was attacked in a particularly skillful and effective way because it enabled Lincoln to use historical material that drove home three Republican points: that popular sovereignty—local self-rule—had not covered slavery, that the Dred Scott decision had perverted the intent of the writers of the Constitution, and the generation of the founders had thought slavery on its way to "ultimate extinction." In a thorough review of the subsequent careers of the signers of the Constitution, Lincoln established that a majority had at one or more times voted to sustain a congressional prohibition of slavery in the territories. It was a demonstration of Lincoln's analytic powers that did him no harm before a highly literate audience. He was able to climax this section with an impressive peroration:[16]

> But enough! *Let all who believe that "our fathers, who framed the Government under which we live, understood this question just as well, and even better, than we do now,"* [the quotation was from Douglas' *Harper's* article] *speak as they spoke, and act as they acted upon it. This is all Republicans ask—all Republicans desire—in relation to slavery. As those fathers marked it,*

so let it be again marked, as an evil not to be extended, but to be tolerated and protected only because of and so far as its actual presence among us makes that toleration and protection a necessity. Let all the guarantees those fathers gave it, be not grudgingly, but fully and fairly maintained. For this Republicans contend, and with this, so far as I know or believe, they will be content.

In a speech at Chicago, March 1, 1859, the occasion being the celebration by Republicans of a victory in the municipal elections, Lincoln stated very concisely the heart of the second point that he was making in these crucial months. In one paragraph he was able to restate his conviction of what the central Republican principle was and to couple with that statement a warning against fusion devoid of principles:

> The Republican principle, the profound central truth that slavery is wrong and ought to be dealt with as a wrong, though we are always to remember the fact of its actual existence amongst us and faithfully observe all the constitutional guarantees—the unalterable principle never for a moment to be lost sight of that it is a wrong and ought to be dealt with as such, cannot advance at all upon Judge Douglas' ground—that there is a portion of the country in which slavery must always exist; that he does not care whether it is voted up or down, as it is simply a question of dollars and cents. Whenever, in any compromise or arrangement or combination that may promise some temporary advantage, we are led upon that ground, then and there the great living principle upon which we have organized as a party is surrendered. The proposition now in our minds that this thing is wrong being once driven out and surrendered, then the institution of slavery necessarily becomes national.[17]

At Columbus, this was not quite so baldly stated. Here he said,

> The Republican party, as I understand its principles and policy, believes that there is great danger of the institution of slavery being spread out and extended. . . . This chief and real purpose of the Republican party . . . proposes nothing save and except to restore this government to its original tone in regard to this element of slavery, and there to maintain it, looking for no further change, in reference to it, than that which the original framers of the government themselves expected and looked forward to.[18]

He spoke more plainly the very next night at Cincinnati:

> I am what they call, as I understand it, a "Black Republican."
> I think that Slavery is wrong, morally, and politically. I desire
> that it should be no further spread in these United States and I
> should not object if it should gradually terminate in the whole
> Union.[19]

In notes that were prepared for an earlier occasion but which
also furnished much of the basis for the speeches on the Ohio
tour, we find one additional pregnant thought which he had
apparently mulled over some more:[20]

> We want, and must have, a national policy, as to slavery, which
> deals with it as being a wrong. Whoever would prevent slavery
> becoming national and perpetual, yields all when he yields to a
> policy which treats it either as being *right,* or as being a matter
> of indifference.

> We admit that the U.S. general government is not charged with
> the duty of redressing, or preventing all the wrongs in the world.
> But that government rightfully may, and, subject to the consti-
> tution, ought to, redress and prevent, all wrongs, which are
> wrongs to the nation itself. It is expressly charged with the duty
> of providing for the general welfare. We think slavery impairs,
> and endangers the general welfare.

Was this a tentative link across the hitherto unbridged chasm
between restriction of slavery and placing it on the way to ultimate extinction? Was it suppressed because it was premature,
this hint of a basis for federal expenditure for gradual emancipation by the states?

In the same document Lincoln attacked the problem of fusion
in two ways. In the first place, he insisted that there could be no
letting down of principles for "with such letting down, the republican organization itself would go to pieces. . . . No ingenuity
of political trading could possibly hold it together." In the second
place, "as a matter of mere partizan [sic] policy," fusion with
the Southern opposition would not produce any Southern electoral votes and would lose Northern electoral votes. This section
was probably the basis for similar remarks in the Cincinnati
speech.[21]

Allusion to this matter was more subtle in New York. Here, he asked Republicans to

> be diverted by none of those sophistical contrivances wherewith we are so industriously plied and belabored—contrivances such as groping for some middle ground between the right and the wrong, vain as the search for a man who should be neither a living man nor a dead man—such as a policy of "don't care" on a question about which all true men do care—such as Union appeals beseeching true Union men to yield to Disunionists, reversing the divine rule, and calling, not the sinners, but the righteous to repentance—[22]

Lincoln was aware that many thought that now that the substantive and immediate issues in regard to slavery were settled, the country should return to the normal party situation of two great national parties, each of which would tend to minimize the sectional conflict. A rising secession clamor in the South made this an especially attractive step as something which would avoid the calamity of a head-on sectional collision. Lincoln's reaction to this feeling was that it was seeking to avoid the inevitable. It would be merely a matter of delay for "the principles around which we have rallied and organized that party [Republicans] would live. . . . They would reproduce another party in the future." In the notes referred to before, Lincoln cited the lesson of the attempt to force Douglas on the Republican party, "Our principles [would] still live, and ere long produce a party; but we should have lost all our past *labor,* and twenty years of *time,* by the folly" of dissolving the party by abandoning its anti-slavery principles. At Cooper Union, Lincoln pointed out that "there is a judgment and a feeling against slavery in this nation, which cast at least a million and a half of votes. You cannot destroy that judgment and feeling—that sentiment—by breaking up the political organization which rallies around it." Destroy this anti-slavery party and another would rise to take its place. If not, some less acceptable form of expression of that sentiment, such as new John Browns might control, would be produced.[23]

In spite of the fact that the chief purpose of Lincoln's talks was to assure the continuation of the Republican party on the one basis which he thought practicable—hostility to slavery, defense against its spread, and setting it on the road to ultimate extinction (a program then challenged from the conservative side in the main)—there was a tone of sweet reasonableness, a lack of bitterness and vindictiveness which gave his speech an overall effect that was more conservative than the implications of his main arguments warranted. There was none of the name calling, the irritating tone of moral superiority, the preaching quality of the abolitionists and many of the radical politicians. Indeed, much of the acceptance of Lincoln as a moderate was based not on logic, not on argument, not on doctrine but upon his unfailing good humor, his humility, and his unpretentiousness. The radical implications of his doctrine came dressed in sheep's clothing.

He labored to make his doctrine acceptable to conservatives and in this he had had much practice in Illinois. In the first place, he did not fail to bracket the moral issue with the condition that constitutional obligations to slavery must be observed. At a time when radicals in New Hampshire and in Ohio were obstructing or trying to obstruct the operation of the Fugitive Slave Law, this in itself was a recommendation to the more conservative.

In the second place, the *Harper's* article by Douglas gave Lincoln the opportunity to delve extensively into the history of the slavery question and present his case in terms of the attitudes of the founding generation. An abbreviated report of his speech at Beloit, Wisconsin, gave an instance:

> If twelve good sound democrats could be found in the county of Rock, he would put them on oath as a jury. He would bring his evidence in the form of depositions in a court, and wring from them the verdict that the Republicans hold to the same principles which Washington, Jefferson, Adams, Madison and their compeers held.[24]

While urging his Cooper Union audience to be firm in the opposition to the spread of slavery and to hold to the conviction of its moral wrongness, Lincoln made a moving appeal for the sort of attitude toward the South which had characterized his public expressions:

> *It is exceedingly desirable that all parts of this great Confederacy shall be at peace, and in harmony, one with another. Let us Republicans do our part to have it so. Even though much provoked, let us do nothing through passion and ill temper. Even though the southern people will not so much as listen to us, let us calmly consider their demands, and yield to them if, in our deliberate view of our duty, we possibly can.*[25]

Some of these speeches were printed in full, some reprinted and used as campaign material. But the most flattering use of such materials came to Lincoln's attention when the Ohio Republican gubernatorial candidate wrote to ask him for a copy of the debates in order that he might employ their arguments against his Democratic opponent. Yet another important figure, Frank Blair, Republican leader in Missouri, brother of the man who would be Lincoln's Postmaster General, and son of Jackson's editor, Francis Preston Blair, Sr., mentioned to Lincoln that a section of a speech he had made in Minnesota had been suggested by Lincoln's Columbus speech.[26] To what degree the temper of the Republican party was stiffened by Lincoln's influence cannot be determined precisely, but it is clear that Lincoln's stand made an impression. Other factors that contributed to hardening the Republican position were the martyrdom of John Brown; the exciting speakership contest in which the Helper book (an attack on slavery by a Carolinian) was used to pry the Americans of the border loose from the Republicans; and Northern reaction to Southern threats.

Lincoln worked to achieve national harmony among the Republicans not only by speech-making but also by correspondence with Republican leaders. There was to be no popular sovereignty concerning Republican doctrine: no state should produce doctrines that would embarrass Republicans in other states. Lincoln was particularly anxious about Ohio, where an Oberlin fugitive slave case erupted into great excitement, aiding the Ohio radicals in attacking a judge who had performed his constitutional duty and in voting a plank against the Fugitive Slave Law into the state platform. He wrote Chase to impress upon him the bad effect of this inclusion on conservative Republicans in other states. S. P. Chase, one of the most radical of the politically successful Republican leaders, and a man with an abundance of confidence in his own judgment, turned the point on Lincoln, arguing against the constitutionality of the Fugitive Slave Law and hoping that Illinois would support the demand for repeal. Lincoln exchanged letters with Schuyler Colfax of Indiana "to hedge against divisions in the Republican ranks generally, and particularly for the contest of 1860." The Massachusetts constitutional amendment extending the period of residence required for citizenship distressed Lincoln, who feared that the German voters, important to the Republicans of the Northwest, might be disaffected.[27]

The Republicans of Kansas were warned against yielding to the temptation "to lower the Republican standard in order to gather recruits." This would "open a gap through which more would pass *out* than pass *in*." Surrender on issues, "the organization goes to pieces," Mark Delahay was told. An old friend of long standing had arranged a correspondence with Nathan Sargent, an old Whig then active in attempting to promote a fusion of the opposition. Lincoln's forthright reply gave him no encouragement:

> The republican party is utterly pow[er]less everywhere, if it will, by any means, drive from it all those who came to it from the democracy for the sole object of preventing the spread, and nationalization of slavery. Whenever this object is waived by the organization, they will drop the organization; and the organization itself will dissolve into thin air.[28]

Thus Lincoln, on the one hand, sought to keep elements of the party from steering the Republican creed too near the shoals beyond "all the constitutional obligations which have been thrown about" slavery and, on the other hand, tried to keep other elements of the party up to the mark of the "moral issue." All the while the whole crew had to be warned against the "Lorelei" of the union of the opposition on no platform save ouster of the Democrats from office. This was not campaigning for the presidency. It was the work of a recognized state party leader trying to attain party harmony among the states preparatory to a national campaign on the outcome of which all had high hopes. He was attempting also to shape the national party to meet the needs of the Illinois party as he understood them.

Positive as we may be that Lincoln sought, and to a degree succeeded, in giving the Republican party a more decidedly anti-slavery bent than otherwise might have been the case, we are on less sure ground in ascribing reasons and tracing the process of logic by which he arrived at the judgment that this was the best course both for the Republican party and the nation to take.

The absence of any broad issues involving slavery in any direct way before Congress was a fact which argued in many minds then and since that this period, 1858–60, was a time for allaying sectional fears in the South and the reduction of the tensions which were pulling the sections apart. There was no territory in which slavery was a real question. There was talk about but no serious demand for a slave code in the territories. A few strident voices called for reopening the slave trade but these were not supported by the Southern leadership. Any talk of "nationalizing" slavery was by Republican orators—including Lincoln—who used it to frighten voters into voting for an uncompromising anti-slavery party on a defensive basis. If there was any time after the fatal introduction of the Kansas-Nebraska Bill when, in the logic of the concrete political situation, a reversal of the trend toward a purely sectional orientation of politics might have taken place, it was in these months after matters in Kansas had been composed. Lincoln steadily, earnestly, and eloquently fought against the broadening of the base of the Republican party to include the border state "opposition" and against watering down the Republican concentration on the slavery question. If there was a real chance to save the Union in this period, then Lincoln followed the course best calculated to defeat that opportunity. Why?

Lincoln's experience as chief architect of the Republican party in Illinois, where all the skills of the consummate politician had been brought to bear to submerge all issues which divided politicians save the one question of slavery in the territories (and this the least anti-slavery stand possible), should have fitted Lincoln for the role of leader in a national fusion of the opposition, especially since the unassimilated portions of the opposition were of Whiggish ancestry. However, this was not the Lincoln who was known by the nation: the nationally known Lincoln was the Lincoln of the "House Divided," a bird of a feather with Mr. Seward's "Irrepressible Conflict."

There were some indications that Lincoln was justifying his and his friends' rejection of fusion with the Douglasites in Illinois before the Republicans of the nation. The repeated reference to Douglas, in no personal way to be sure, but over and over again, argues that Lincoln thought of himself as combatting Douglas and his doctrine on the wider stage of the nation as he had in Illinois. This may be accounted for on perfectly impersonal grounds. Douglas was the most likely and the most feared Democratic candidate for the presidency in 1860 so far as the Republicans of Illinois were concerned. They furnished money and helped to defeat Douglas at Charleston.[29] If Douglas were to be the candidate, national Republican strategy, as had been the case in Illinois, necessitated finding a place on the scale of anti-slavery to the more radical side of popular sovereignty. Fusion of the opposition would not work against the "Little Giant" for he too was of the opposition. The presidential race of 1860, Lincoln may have reasoned, would be the Illinois situation all over again, although it is very doubtful that he seriously thought of himself as the candidate of the Republicans until a few weeks before the convention.

As the Republican leader of Illinois, Lincoln was concerned with winning in 1860. There were both a governorship and a seat in the United States Senate at stake. The national party candidate and platform might make or break the Republicans of Illinois. In his judgment, Illinois would poll 50,000 fewer votes for a fusion ticket without an anti-slavery platform than the party had polled in 1858.[30] Lincoln's calculations may have been in terms of national victory in 1860 but his first duty was to the party of his home state. Very little of Lincoln's activity in 1859 and 1860 could be ruled out as inappropriate to the intelligent and dedicated performance of a state party leader doing his whole duty.

Three years before, Judge John D. Caton had written to Senator Trumbull:

> But you say he [the northern politician] can't . . . [reconcile the South] . . . without exciting the suspicion of his friends who will call him *doughface*[,] say he is sold to slavery or to the abolitionists as the case may be. Alas! that is too true, and therein the danger lies. Hence my fears. No one dares to pour on oil. To save his standing he must keep up the agony & lay on the passion.[31]

Was Lincoln keeping "up the agony" and laying "on the passion," making the sectional difficulties more difficult, helping make the Civil War certain, in order to win elections? Did he fail to take a view of the situation beyond "mere partisan policy?" Did he place a spoke in the wheel of the one movement at the one time the Union might yet have been saved? Was he the prisoner of the constricted views of the politician?

These questions are more easily asked than answered because Lincoln probably did not ask himself these questions and if he did, he left no answers for posterity. Lincoln did not believe the Union to be in danger. His remarks on this question at Cincinnati bordered on the flippant. Indeed, there was no indication that Lincoln, for all his Southern background and connections, believed that secession was more than mere bluster until the first states had actually seceded.[32]

We have seen that Lincoln had slowly progressed toward the notion that the mission of the Republican party was to work for a solution of the slavery question by defending the country against pro-slavery aggression and finally by putting slavery in the way of ultimate extinction. Any temporary adjustment of the question that called for the recognition of slavery as a permanent fixture in any part of the United States would have been doubly doubtful in Lincoln's eyes. In the first place, such an adjustment could be no more than a brief respite in the "durable struggle." The dynamic moral progress toward the realization of the promise of the Declaration of Independence would go on. It would go on because a million and a half voters were convinced that slavery was morally wrong and would not accept a truce that required the suppression of a strongly held sentiment against slavery.[33] The Republican party might be broken up by such a temporary accommodation but the feeling which created it would continue and would ultimately create a successor.

Assuming then that preserving the Republican party and its integrity on the slavery question was a fixed idea with Lincoln and his concept of the highest political duty, the probable effectiveness or appropriateness of a political party for the achievement of this or any other moral enterprise comes into question. No major party has ever, before or since in this country's history, been a party of a moral issue in the sense that slavery was a moral issue. Some few have had some years of life as third parties. But such success as came to the Prohibitionists came through the major parties, namely, by their voting for candidates of major parties committed to their views. The reason is obvious: a major party must either carry on or oppose the government over a wide area of subjects and interests. Suppose for the moment that the Republicans had won the election of 1860 and that the Southerners had had the restraint necessary to cooperate with the new administration rather than breaking up the Union because of it. Suppose farther that they had advanced no new claims for slavery because the territories were lost anyhow. Would not a governing party have been compelled to adopt positions in regard to the tariff, homesteads, the deficit, and a score of other matters of ordinary legislation on many of which it would find difficulty reaching agreement among its own members drawn together as they were on a moral issue? Would not the party, to remain anti-slavery in its bearing, be compelled to seek ways to secure the placing of slavery on the road to ultimate extinction within or without the framework of the Constitution? If the South did not supply a reason for the party's existence by new threats of expanding slavery would not the Republicans have had to become aggressive on the slavery question to have preserved their anti-slavery character and their existence as a party?

Apt instrument or not, Lincoln believed that the people of the North required a party committed to the moral issue until the question was settled one way or another. He had seen the Whig party broken down by the pressure of the anti-slavery minority. He was seeing the Democratic party riven and racked by the moral issue in one or another form. The moral issue might not be a satisfactory matter to be handled by the agency of a party, but parties which sought to evade it had not succeeded. With neither prospect good, the best escape was the lesser of two evils according to the politician's creed which he himself had once formulated:[34]

> The true rule, in determining to embrace or reject anything, is not whether it have any evil in it, but whether it have more of evil than of good. There are few things *wholly* evil or *wholly* good. Almost everything, especially of government policy, is an enseparable compound of the two; so that our best judgment of the preponderance between them is continually demanded.

The Republican party was justified, not because it was wholly right as an instrument of reform but because it was the best of the alternatives to achieve what was absolutely right—the containment and ending of slavery. Lincoln was neither wholly politician, devoid of deeply felt, substantive goals, nor wholly abolitionist, unconcerned about method and consensus, but rather, the politician of the moral issue.

The intensity and zeal of the abolitionists were twisting and torturing the moral issue to cover purely sectional and economic interests. The election of a speaker of the badly divided House of Representatives, though only remotely instrumental to the moral issue, aroused a great amount of feeling, not only in Congress but through the country. In Lincoln's Illinois, a small village fired a cannon in celebration of "the election of a Speaker upon the right side of the House."[35] The appearance of *The Impending Crisis,* a book sharply critical of slavery, written by a Southerner, created an enormous fuss. The Homestead Bill was argued in terms of the moral issue. Slavery was the issue "pressing upon every mind;" it was there to stay until solved. The party was the normal instrument by which a certain amount of discipline, a degree of consensus, a measure of agreement, all necessary to national political endeavor, was reached. Lincoln had been working within this concept of what a party was supposed to do. Within the framework of the moral issue and respecting the political rules—the Constitution—Lincoln spent his energies in 1859 and early 1860 attempting to head off those who would demand too much, notably repeal of the Fugitive Slave Law, and whip up the laggards who would be content with too little.

Lincoln's labors on the national scene did not protect him from onerous duties as the leader of the Illinois Republicans. Two factional fights among the Republicans swirled around Norman B. Judd, one of the leading Democrats in the fusion of 1856. Judd was state chairman of the party, had occupied this position during the Lincoln-Douglas campaign, and now sought the gubernatorial nomination. One of his difficulties was with John Wentworth, the contentious mayor of Chicago, a man whose political feuds were legion. Wentworth was at war with Judd and Ebenezer Peck, prior to 1854 an "old Hunker" Democrat, both of whom were accused of using their influence to promote railroads to the disadvantage of the city of Chicago. This issue among Republicans became more explosive and involved Lincoln when Wentworth published a claim that Judd had secured money for electioneering for Lincoln in 1858 and that it remained unaccounted for.[36] Judd sued Wentworth for $100,-000 damages.

This case was reaching a climax just as a city election campaign in which Wentworth was running for re-election got under way. The wily mayor suspected that Judd and Peck and the *Tribune* were going to oppose him. Lincoln was appealed to from all sides and by neutral persons concerned about the effect of the ruckus on the party in the state. One such outsider wrote Lincoln that "a truce or peace ought to be made and that you are the man to bring it about. You can command in the matter—as the acknowledged, indisputable leader of the party you can enforce the peace."[37]

Wentworth, fearful for his $100,000 or for his mayoralty, or both, approached Judge Davis and the latter acted as his intermediary with Lincoln. Peace was restored, on the surface at least, when Wentworth signed a disclaimer which Lincoln wrote and Judd promised to suppress the Republican opposition to Wentworth's re-election.[38]

Some old Whigs around Chicago and Herndon in Springfield took up the charge of the misuse of funds as a means of furthering the candidacy of Leonard Swett or of Richard B. Yates, ex-Whigs, who were Judd's rivals for the gubernatorial nomination. Lincoln was required to vouch for Judd's services in the election of 1858, a very risky business for a man who was being considered as presidential or vice-presidential timber, for he ran the risk of giving the appearance of taking sides among candidates none of whom he wished or could afford to offend. This was especially embarrassing to Lincoln for it involved relations with Trumbull which, in spite of Lincoln's keen disappointment at his own defeat in 1855, had been kept on excellent terms by Lincoln's exertions. Both Trumbull and Judd placed considerable pressure on Lincoln to throw his weight into the balance in favor of Judd's nomination on the ground that the Republicans of Democratic origin deserved the top spot on the ticket.[39]

Finally, Yates, who was to be the successful candidate, demanded a statement from Lincoln testifying that Yates had not lagged in his support of Lincoln in 1858 as had been alleged by friends of other candidates.[40] It was a tribute to Lincoln's well-established character for honesty and fairness that through all of this awkward business there was no charge of favoritism or bias on the part of Lincoln and that his own candidacy in the state convention, which followed close on the heels of the last of these exchanges, suffered nothing from his conduct.

A breath of scandal threatened the Republican state administration as it had scorched the previous Democratic administration. Out of the financial mire of the early 1840's, some New York speculators secured some state obligations for a few cents on the dollar, the validity of which was questionable, to say the least. The Republican governor had been persuaded to issue new bonds in their stead at face value, apparently by mistake. Lincoln, S. T. Logan, and Ozias Hatch warned the state treasurer not to honor the bonds. The latter was under pressure or inducement to pay off the bonds and sought to perform this act and resign. Wind of the deal reached Bloomington where Ward Lamon appealed to Lincoln to prevent James Miller, the treasurer, from resigning, whether under the impression that Miller would exchange or pay off the bonds and then resign or that the blame would fall on the governor who was then a very sick man.[41] In any case, there was a ripple of discord and a hint of scandal in the first Republican administration of the state. Moral crusaders were held to a stricter accountability than those who made no pretentions to moral superiority.

Such matters as the state ticket, getting the right man to run for Congress in the Springfield district, keeping an eye on the Mechanicsburg precinct of Sangamon County, getting a Republican appointed state's attorney of Wayne County to fill a vacancy, and seeing the Danites to get a Republican appointed to take the census in Jasper County because all of the Democrats there were Douglas men—these lesser things rounded out Lincoln's political activity and reminded him that if some thought of him as presidential timber, others considered him as the state political leader who owed his position to tending to just this sort of business.[42]

In the Lincoln-Douglas campaign of 1858, remarkable among other things for its wit, Lincoln's greatest hit, still likely to provoke a smile from any politician with a sense of humor, had been his second Springfield speech. He was setting forth the disadvantages under which he labored in the campaign as compared to Douglas, the nationally known statesman—the Goliath—and among them were these:[43]

> All the anxious politicians of his party, or who have been of his party for years past, have been looking upon him as certainly, at no distant day, to be the President of the United States. They have seen in his round, jolly, fruitful face, post offices, land-offices, marshalships, and cabinet appointments, chargeships and foreign missions, bursting and sprouting out in wonderful exuberance ready to be laid hold of by their greedy hands. [Great laughter. . . .] On the contrary nobody has ever expected me to be President. In my poor, lank face, nobody has ever seen that any cabbages were sprouting out.

One year and eleven days later, an acquaintance of New Salem days wrote to remind Lincoln of their past friendship and to tell him that he was promoting his old friend for Vice-President. The only favor the correspondent would require was the position of chargé to Denmark. The next day, a total stranger wrote to say that he was for Lincoln for President. The only thing he sought was pensions for orphans of soldiers of the Revolutionary War. Something worth cultivation, if not cabbages, had been found on Lincoln's lank face. By October, there was enough of substance to the prospects of Lincoln as a presidential or vice-presidential candidate that an imperious demand came out of the center of one of the most tangled political webs in the country. "Send Abraham Lincoln to Albany immediately," Thurlow Weed, New York's astute political wire puller and manager of Governor Seward, wired Judd.[44] Lincoln did not go.

Simeon Francis, former editor of the Whig and Republican paper in Springfield and about to remove to Oregon, wrote to Lincoln (now so busy with law and politics that Springfield friends had to write to him to get a hearing) to say that Lincoln should take himself seriously as a candidate for the presidency and urged him to begin to work at it. A New York man wrote to say that Republican success required Lincoln as the standard bearer of the party because he was the most available candidate.[45]

Delegates were being chosen for the convention as early as February. While the Iowa delegates were not pledged to Lincoln, Hawkins Taylor promised to attend the convention with the hope that he might influence them in Lincoln's favor. News from Indiana was better. While Chase had won the at-large delegates in Ohio, anti-Chase forces wanted to form Lincoln Clubs to work to secure district delegates, a movement which Lincoln discouraged.[46] Lincoln believed that his opportunity lay in being the second choice of many rather than the first choice of few.

In the meantime, the question of the Illinois delegation was growing in importance. Some of Lincoln's friends had not been impressed by his chances and some, like Orville H. Browning, had committed themselves pretty far with other candidates before Lincoln's candidacy had been seriously considered. Wentworth at first was for Simeon Cameron, the Pennsylvanian, whose entry into the cabinet caused Lincoln his most painful patronage problem, then at the last minute switched to Seward after some sort of deal with Weed. He was telling Judge Davis, who told Lincoln, then engaged in pulling Wentworth's chestnuts out of the fire over the Judd lawsuit, that he was for Lincoln *sub rosa*. As the Illinois convention neared, Trumbull wrote Lincoln a long letter canvassing the situation. While he wished "to be distinctly understood as first & foremost" for Lincoln, he didn't think that Lincoln had much chance. Lincoln was bracketed with Seward as a radical in the minds of those with whom Trumbull had talked. Of the candidates discussed, Trumbull seemed most favorably disposed toward McLean. Above all, he was for success. Lincoln reminded Trumbull that his own re-election to the Senate depended on control of the legislature which would be hard to obtain if Seward were the nominee.[47]

To a letter of inquiry about his prospects, Lincoln felt "disqualified to speak" of himself for "when not a very great man begins to be mentioned for a very great position, his head is very likely to be a little turned. . . ." Nevertheless, modesty did not prevent Lincoln from supplying the inquirer with a list of friends who would discuss nomination matters with him. To another he wrote, "as to the Presidential nomination, claiming no greater exemption from selfishness than is common, I still feel that my whole aspiration should be, and therefore must be, to be placed anywhere, or nowhere, as may appear most likely to advance the cause." While admitting to Trumbull that "the taste *is* in my mouth a little," he still put party considerations first. "You may confidently rely, however, that by no advice or consent of mine, shall my pretensions be pressed to the point of endangering our common cause." As late as May 2, Lincoln thought that Illinois would be the only unanimous delegation for him, a matter which the Illinois Republican convention decided.[48]

So rapidly did things move in the direction of the man whose first thought was the party's welfare that even he must have been surprised to learn that he had been second high on the first ballot at Chicago. On May 18, he was nominated. The platform proclaimed to the nation that Lincoln had been preaching to the Republicans, "that the history of the nation, during the last four years, has fully established the propriety and necessity of the organization and perpetuation of the Republican party, and that the causes which called it into existence are permanent in their nature. . . ." Homesteads for Westerners, tariffs for the East, and reform of a corrupt administration for everyone were included in the party's promises.

Lincoln's role in the campaign of 1860 followed the tradition of passivity established by earlier major party candidates but interrupted for the first time by Douglas. Others did the work, with a hint here and there by Lincoln. With the nomination, the record of the nominee was closed. The voter had the party platforms, the printed speeches of the candidates made before the campaign opened, and what might be found in the public record of the candidate. In the case of Lincoln, that record was very brief and not very illuminating, having been closed in 1849. This situation gave orators and editors a wide scope for interpretation suitable to the locale. Thus Lincoln could be "nothing more than an old line Whig of the Henry Clay school," in Springfield, while in Chicago the "mission of the Republican party" could be described as "the work of making the States all free."[49]

It was an ideal way for the Republicans to fight the campaign. The Democratic party had split at Charleston and offered two tickets. The administration was supporting the Breckinridge ticket which was the weaker of the two in the North. The Union-saving of Douglas had competition from the old Whigs who presented a ticket. It was obvious from the first that the successful conservation of Republican strength would win the election. Lincoln, writing confidentially to an anxious but distant friend in early August, had to admit that "it really appears now, as if the success of the Republican ticket is inevitable." A month before the reliable indicators of the October elections, Cameron sent word that Lincoln "may as well be getting [his] inaugeral [sic] address ready. . . ." Characteristically Lincoln's one intervention in the state canvass was to help in a situation in which Trumbull, not Lincoln, might have been the loser.[50]

The campaign of 1860 was exciting, not so much for the uncertainty of the result, as for a new high in organization and pageantry. In both departments, the Republicans excelled, for they were thoroughly organized when the Democrats were just beginning to prepare for the campaign. Moreover, this time the Republicans had plenty of money for campaign expenses unlike 1858 when they had ended up with a deficit.[51]

The campaign turned on "Union saving" by the Douglas and Bell parties versus the "moral issue" espoused by the Republicans. The threats of secession in the South, heard in 1850, in 1856, and more frequently since 1858, swelled to a chorus. The conservative appeal (and the political appeal) to compromise, to settle the sectional strife, led to the growing tendency of the Republicans to minimize or even deny the threat. Secession "talk frightened some old ladies in pantaloons, four years ago, but will not be likely to terrify the North this year," was a central Illinois comment. Another mid-state paper shrugged off the danger with:

> Our Southern brethren as every body knows, fret and fume at every Presidential election, and play horrid airs on the disunion harp.—They make less noise this year than usual, yet quite enough. . . . The North is not so easily frightened as it once was.[52]

Late in 1859, the *Chicago Press and Tribune* took notice of the rumbling in the South and warned men of that region that if they were serious, they would "meet the fate which all traitors richly deserve." The North was ready for "hanging of a few score fireeaters" if secession were to be the consequence of the election of a Republican President. But the editor didn't really think it a serious matter for he begged "the Quattlebums of the South . . . to remember . . . that their threats—intended to operate on the fears of timid minds and the nerves of old women,—the played out also."[53]

As has been noted, the campaign of 1860 did not demand that the radical side of the Republican party program be unveiled or its long term hopes and objectives emphasized. The Republicans played it safe. The doubtful vote was the conservative vote, so the orators and editorial writers turned their attention to the sort of argument which would appeal to the former Whigs and the remainder of the Know-Nothings. The application of the military principle of employing the minimum force necessary to win an objective, a maxim having equal validity in politics, presented the most conservative facet of the Republican party to the public. Although it seemed to embrace the whole range of the slavery question in 1860 and but a fraction in 1856 (Kansas), the party created an illusion of having been more conservative in 1860 than in the earlier year.

Beneath the deceptive surface of the party's offering to the public were deep-running and contrary currents that contradicted the superficial image created by the politicians. These forces were less subject to the management of the politician, less concerned with the objectives of the politicians—success, office, and power. They were the more elemental forces of hate—sectional hate and hate of sin and sinners—and intense moral concern over slavery. For example, and without expressing a choice as to which of the two forces were applicable in this case, the unpredictable Wentworth scorned the soft-pedal technique of the bulk of the Republican editors and stridently proclaimed that

> All there is in the [Republican] party to us is its radicalism on the subject of slavery. When Mr. Lincoln and Mr. Seward announced the doctrine of the irrepressible conflict, they drew the dividing line between radicalism and conservatism on the subject of slavery. . . . The moment you make the Republican party a conservative one on the subject of slavery, that moment you destroy it. Its radicalism is its strength, its power, its might, its hold on the masses, its most glorious, and, in fact, its most distinctive feature.[54]

This was but an echo of what Lincoln had been telling Republicans except that, as a politician attempting to persuade the largest possible support of his policy, Lincoln linked what Wentworth described as radical to historical precedent and endowed it with a conservative aura. Both agreed that its stand on slavery was the distinctive characteristic of the Republican party.

When the same newspaper went on to make fairly explicit what it meant by Republican radicalism a vast difference appeared. To Mr. Wentworth it meant that the Republican party would not remain on the defensive on the slavery question but should attack slavery where it existed. All federal support for slavery and legal recognition of the peculiar institution by the federal government should be withdrawn. Submission to this program was assured, in the opinion of the editor, because of a dilemma which lay threateningly before the South:

> Such must be the work of making the States all free, which is the mission of the Republican party. Such it must be, if the Union is preserved, for the dissolution of the Union is only another name for slave insurrection, which must result not only in the shedding of rivers of blood, but in the destruction of millions of property, and the disruption of the slave system by violence. In fact, the South has to choose between these two alternatives—either a constitutional, legal and equitable emancipation, the work of years and of patience; or an emancipation, sudden, horrid, stained with blood and illuminated by the conflagration of Southern homes.[55]

This was not the official party theory—far from it—but the editor who advanced this program was not an apolitical abolitionist or a withdrawn Garrisonite, but the mayor of the city of Chicago and a power in Illinois politics.

Another straw in the same wind appeared after the election and after secession had begun to jar Republican complacency. A suggestion was made and found its endorsers that the federal government appropriate a billion dollars for the purchase and manumission of all the slaves, thus settling the sectional difficulties forever.[56] This was seriously regarded as a tender of compromise and the responsibility for rejecting such a fair offer would rest with the "traitors."

For one other indication of this undercurrent of impatience within Republicanism, it is necessary to go back in time about a year to the raid by John Brown and his followers on Harper's Ferry. The reaction to the Harper's Ferry incident was indicative of the depth of feeling and the growth of an insensitivity to the political and legal framework in which the politician was accustomed to work. Brown, an extreme abolitionist and an activist in the movement in Kansas, formed a plot to liberate the slaves of the region of Harper's Ferry, Virginia, arm them, and establish a military republic of freedmen in the mountainous country, an area selected with a view to defense and to the recruitment of Negroes who would have had this enclave of freedom constantly inviting them to seek their liberty. Brown was the perfect case of the intense conviction of the evil of slavery unleavened by common sense, unfettered by facts, and unbalanced by other considerations. It was a crazy scheme which failed absurdly. Brown was eventually hanged by the state of Virginia for treason committed against it. Here was the irrepressible conflict in action.

Naturally enough, the politicians were very apprehensive about the effect of the incident on politics. C. H. Ray, the Republican editor and politician, wrote Lincoln:

> We are damnably exercised here [Chicago] about the effect of Old Browns wretched *fiasco* in Virginia, upon the moral health of the Republican party! The old idiot—the quicker they hang and get him out of the way the better.[57]

The real question was, would the voters believe that this violence was the natural outcome of Republican doctrine? "Moral health," freely translated, meant something quite concrete—the vote.

There were other views. A northern Illinois man wrote his congressman that "I wish they might have an 'old Brown' (he was a brave fellow) to go into one of the slave states every other month, just often enough to *keep em* in a *stew,* only I wouldn't want to have him caught. . . ."[58]

Another wrote that

> Old Brown is hung and the event is working with a mighty influence among the people here, at the North. . . . We believe, we hope, that the speedy dissolution of King Cotton is at hand. . . . Slavery has commenced the battle—the "irrepressible conflict" is already begun—and it will end only with the utter overthrow of the domineering Slave Power.[59]

Even some of the newspapers of the northern part of the state, usually so circumspect about political appropriateness, melted after the first weeks of passing the blame to the Democrats and began the process of creating an authentic American martyr. The *Bureau Republican* exceeded them all, however, with this perfervid bit:

> John Brown is a Thought. He is the actual embodiment of a winged Truth. From the long and moonless night that has hov-

ered over the fairest portion of our land, made doubly dreary by the ominous clouds, and the occasional revelation of the red lightning, this presence has shot across the darkness like a meteor. . . .

John Brown proper, is but the medium, the earthen vessel, from which is evolved a current, with ten million times more electrical power, than all the combined batteries in the world; its circuit is through the chain of human life that is linked together all over the continent, and the great Moving Principle is the great Central Truth that moves alike the souls of men to liberty, and the heart of the sparrow.[60]

A Chicago preacher voiced the optimism of the radical spirit in the Republican party in his Thanksgiving sermon:

But the sceptre of power has passed into the hands of the North. Already it has a majority in the Senate and in the House of Representatives and will soon have a majority in the United States Supreme Court, and will ere long surround slavery with such influences, hemming it in by free States and preventing its extension, so that it must die out.[61]

There was confidence that, at long last, the very citadel of slavery was ready to be assaulted. No hundred years would satisfy these people! The time was soon!

The discrepancy between this undertow of radical opinion and the public and official figure of the party was summarized by William Perkins, a lawyer turned Presbyterian clergyman and Republican:

The religious sentiment of the north runs somewhat deeper & faster than the mere political sentiment of the Republicans southward. In the march of our great party there seems to be a danger of a serious gap. . . . Having studied the Constitutions & Laws of our Country—appreciating the legal embarrassments in your way & at the same time sympathizing with the Christian sentiments against the whole wrong. . . .[62]

Here, neatly put, was the rub—a large segment of the Republican party existed in which the delicate balance between the moral imperative and the constitutional and legal obstacles to reform had been destroyed. To people who could justify a career such as Brown's, the constitutional and legal barriers to reform were just that—barriers, not as with Lincoln, binding guides to action which were just as important as the moral issue. They did not face up to what their concentration on reform was doing to their perspective of the constitutional system. They tended to rationalize away the limitations which Lincoln took so seriously. The Garrison abolitionists were more honest with themselves. They recognized the conflict and made their choice. In their 1859 platform they proclaimed again that

> *Resolved,* That in advocating the Dissolution of the Union the Abolitionists are justified by every precept of the Gospel, by every principle of morality, by every claim of humanity; that such a Union is a "Covenant with Death," which ought to be annulled, and "an agreement with Hell," which a just God cannot permit to stand; and that it is the imperative and paramount duty of all who would keep their souls from blood-guiltiness, to deliver the oppressed out of the hand of the spoiler, and usher in the day of Jubilee; to seek its immediate overthrow by all righteous instrumentalities.[63]

The Garrisonians did not participate in politics for this would involve them in duties which implied a recognition of slavery. They were few in numbers but for every Garrisonian who viewed the Constitution as above, there must have been hundreds of men of anti-slavery principles who chafed at the political system behind which the evil of slavery seemed to rest, secure and impregnable.

How important were these people in the politics of 1860? In numbers, they were a minority. Even in the Republican party, they were a minority, probably in every state. But they were the minority that the Republican party was formed to cater to. It was anti-slavery, it emphasized the moral issue, from a political viewpoint, to keep the sentiment of these people from returning to a separate political organization. Lincoln had estimated that the Republicans of Illinois, should they abandon an anti-slavery posture which would hold these people to their organization, would lose 50,000 votes.[64] However cohesive and strong the

Republican party had seemed in 1858 and in 1860, it was still a sectional and a minority party with one important segment attached only by hope and confidence that the Republican party would prove an apt instrument for attacking slavery where it was.

1. July 12 and 15, Aug. 26, 1858; July 12 (two articles), 13; Aug. 17; Oct. 8, 23, 1858.

2. *New York Tribune,* Nov. 17, 1858.

3. Aug. 28, 1858; Oct. 6, 1858; Dec. 2, 1858. The *National Era* was a Republican paper published in Washington, D.C.

4. *National Intelligencer* (Washington), Sept. 16, 1858.

5. Nov. 13, 1858.

6. *New York Tribune,* Oct. 19, 1858.

7. *National Intelligencer* and *Philadelphia North American,* July-December, 1858, *passim.*

8. *Philadelphia North American and United States Gazette,* Oct. 13, 1858; *Scioto Gazette* (Chillicothe, Ohio), Aug. 10, 1858; *New York Tribune,* Aug. 16, 1858.

9. *Annual Report of the American Historical Association,* II (1902) 278–9, Columbus, Ohio, July 16, 1858, Salmon P. Chase to Charles Sumner.

10. Quoted in the *National Intelligencer,* Nov. 9, 1858.

11. *A Political Textbook for 1860* (New York: Tribune Press, 1860), p. 27. On the first ballot, Lincoln received 19 New England votes to Seward's 32 but Lincoln passed him on the second ballot. His other first ballot votes came from states in which he had made speeches in 1859 and 1860 except for 4 from Pennsylvania and those of Kentucky, Virginia, and 1 from Nebraska territory.

12. *Collected Works,* III, 396; Angle, *Lincoln 1854–1861,* pp. 270–328, *passim.* This covers the period from his Chicago speech of March 1, 1859, to his last political speech made at Bloomington, Illinois, Apr. 10, 1860.

13. *Collected Works,* III, 555 [Exeter, N. H., Mar. 4, 1860.]

14. *Ibid.,* pp. 438–62.

15. *Ibid.,* pp. 400–25.

16. *Ibid.,* p. 535.

17. *Ibid.,* p. 368.

18. *Ibid.,* p. 404.

19. *Ibid.,* p. 440.

20. *Ibid.,* p. 435.

21. *Ibid.,* pp. 433, 461–2.

22. *Ibid.,* p. 550.

23. *Ibid.,* pp. 367, 434, 541–2.

24. *Ibid.,* p. 484.

25. *Ibid.,* p. 547.

26. RTL Nos. 1782, 1975–8.

27. *Collected Works,* III, 384, 386 (See the footnote accompanying the letter), 390–1, 376.

28. *Ibid.,* pp. 378–9, 387–8.

29. Douglas MSS, Chicago, Apr. 12, 1860, J. P. Campbell.

30. *Collected Works,* III, 387.

31. Trumbull MSS, Ottawa, July 3, 1856, J. D. Caton.

32. *Collected Works,* III, 454; see below, pp. 191–192.

33. *Collected Works,* III, 541–2.

34. *Congressional Globe,* 30th Congress, 1st Session, App., p. 710, June 20, 1848.

35. Trumbull MSS, Lena (Stephenson County), Feb. 6, 1860, Daniel Bailey.

36. *Chicago Weekly Democrat,* Mar. 26, 1859, Nov. 12, 1859.

37. RTL Nos. 2154–5, Springfield, Dec. 16, 1859, N. Niles.

38. *Ibid.,* Nos. 2396–400, Bloomington, Feb. 21, 1860, David Davis.

39. *Collected Works,* III, 507–8; RTL Nos. 2530–2, 2625–7.

40. *Ibid.,* Nos. 2617–8.

41. *Collected Works,* III, 392; RTL Nos. 1836–8, 1840.

42. RTL Nos. 1793–5, 1796–8, 1863–4, 2042–3, 2084–6, 2566–7.

43. Angle, *Created Equal,* p. 68.

44. RTL Nos. 1806–8, Uniontown, Penna., July 28, 1859, Ethelbert P. Oliphant; Nos. 1809–10, Monon, Ind., July 29, 1859, Joseph Day; Nos. 1981, 1982–3.

45. *Ibid.,* Nos. 1994–5; Nos. 2057–60, Fleming, N. Y., Nov. 13, 1859, Miles Griswold.

46. *Ibid.,* 2440–2, Des Moines, Feb. 25, 1860; Nos. 2430–2; Nos. 2478–80.

47. Pease and Randall, *Diary of Browning,* I, 380–1; Washburne MSS, Chicago, May 1 and 15, 1860, H. Kreisman; RTL Nos. 2607–9, Urbana, Apr. 23, 1860, David Davis; Nos. 2612–6; *Collected Works,* IV, 46, Springfield, Apr. 29, 1860.

48. *Collected Works,* IV, 36, Springfield, Apr. 6, 1860, R. W. Corwine; 43, Springfield, Apr. 14, 1860, Jas. F. Babcock; 45; 47–48, Springfield, May 2, 1860, R. M. Corwine.

49. *Illinois State Journal,* Nov. 1, 1860, and *Chicago Daily Democrat,* Aug. 15, 1860.

50. *Collected Works,* IV, 90, Springfield, Aug. 4, 1860, Simeon Francis; 110–111, Springfield, Sept. 4, 1860, Lincoln to Joseph Medill; 95, Springfield, Aug. 15, 1860, William Fithian.

51. Trumbull MSS, Moro, Apr. 1, 1860, W. C. Flagg; Chicago, Oct. 15, 1860, N. B. Judd.

52. *Illinois State Journal,* Aug. 18, 1860; *Quincy Whig,* Oct. 9, 1860.

53. Oct. 11, 1859.

54. *Chicago Daily Democrat,* July 2, 1860.

55. *Ibid.,* Aug. 15, 1860.

56. *Galesburg Democrat,* Dec. 14, 1860.

57. RTL Nos. 1996–7, Chicago, Oct. 31, 1859, C. H. Ray.

58. Washburne MSS, Richmond (Illinois), Dec. 19, 1859, G. C. Cutting.
59. *Ibid.*, Carey Station, Dec. 14, 1859, Ed. S. Hayden.
60. *Galesburg Democrat, Galena Gazette, Chicago Press and Tribune,* Oct. 19 to Dec. 30, 1859, *passim;* Dec. 1, 1859.
61. *Chicago Democrat,* Dec. 3, 1859.
62. RTL Nos. 2003–5, Lewistown, Nov. 1, 1859, Wm. Perkins.
63. *Political Textbook for 1860,* p. 173.
64. *Collected Works,* III, 387–8.

Persuasively but in Vain

Lincoln was faced with difficulties such as no President-elect had ever faced or is likely to be confronted with again. He was plagued with the difficulties which success had brought him— office-seekers, slate-makers, and advice-givers. With an extremely limited personal acquaintanceship among the outstanding leaders of his party, he had to construct a cabinet which would administer the departments effi- **CHAPTER 8** ciently, please all of the major elements and regions of the party, and take care of pledges made on his behalf at Chicago. Above all, the conservative and radical elements of the party had to be balanced.

Such would have been the overriding preoccupation of any new President. In Lincoln's case, however, this cabinet building was going on amid signs that the government which he had been elected to head was dissolving. The Gulf states set about seces- sion with such unseemly haste that the earlier blithe confidence of Lincoln and most of his party had been dissipated by the time Congress assembled in December. A shocked and worried public looked to a lame-duck and truncated Congress—Senators and Representatives from the seceding states began to withdraw soon after it opened—for some genuine "Union-saving," not the cam- paign variety.

The President-elect's party faced a problem which it had assured the Northern electorate did not exist. It had convinced itself, from top to bottom of the party, that there would be no secession, that secession threats were a sort of blackmail used to influence the election.[1] The party thus conditioned to regard the secession movement that was progressing like a whirlwind across the lower South naturally was without a program to meet this crisis. Others might take the lead in making proposals but no suggestion was worth serious consideration if the Republicans, who had elected the President, did not concur.

This failure to comprehend what had been and what was going on in the Southern tier of states was a natural fruit of the absence of a national Republican electorate. As politicians, the Republicans understood their constituencies perhaps as well as any others and certainly as well as the Fire-Eaters, who were dissolving the Union, understood theirs. No Republican, unfortunately for meeting this problem, had considered his constituency as extending below the Mason-Dixon line. Breckinridge, Bell, and Douglas had planned on possible votes and attempted to win voters from states in each of the sections. Not so Lincoln. Confident as his party had been of victory, no calculation of the most optimistic had included the electoral vote of any slave-holding state as part of the winning number of electors. The Republican constituency was the North.

Suddenly, the Republican party, a decided minority in the nation, was faced with the responsibility of governing the wider constituency of the nation. The most urgent political disorder on the whole national scene was forming like the outbreak of a new virus in that part of the nation in which not a single vote had been cast for Lincoln electors. In these Gulf states there was no Republican organization to stand as intermediary between Southern wants and the incoming administration and vice versa. No representatives of this region had participated in the selection of Lincoln as a candidate or in framing the Republican platform. No correspondence which talked of prospects and of the mood of the voters and which weighed the response to appeals and issues had flowed between Republican leaders and Southerners. Republican orators had not stumped these states and had not gripped the hands of these people. The intricacies of Pennsylvania politics were opened to Lincoln but the Lincoln correspondence growing out of and illuminating Lincoln's mind concerning the crucial secession struggle in Georgia consisted of an exchange of letters with Alexander H. Stephens.[2] This should not be understood to be a criticism of Lincoln or of Republicans. It was the natural outcome of the formation of a sectional party. It handicapped able politicians, for the raw materials of their trade was withheld from them—the confidential friends, the awareness of the personal qualities of leaders, the interests and the prejudices of the constituency. That great reservoir of power—the patronage—was lamed and useless without the advantages of which the Republicans were deprived.

The sectional nature of the Republican party had eliminated one of the essential steps of the political process in the two-party system. Our great issues normally pass through two compromising processes. The first takes place within each party before the program of the party relative to that issue is formed. A contemporary example is the quadrennial struggle over the civil rights issue in the Democratic party convention. The second stage for compromise is the halls of Congress. 1860 saw this typical process break down at two vital points. The Republicans as representative of the North compromised this issue only within the necessities imposed by their Northern constituency. The broader Democratic constituency failed to arrive at a compromise satisfactory to both sections; secession at the party level began at the Charleston convention. The South, in seceding, was refusing to play the game under the simplified rule of the one-step compromise.

Too, the sudden deflating of the confidence that secession was only a threat left the party in Congress and the President-elect unsure of themselves. There was a still lingering doubt that the South was in earnest, a doubt fostered by the fact that some of the secessionists had argued to Southerners that withdrawal would produce a better bargaining position than to remain in the Union. Most of the Southern politicians who corresponded with Lincoln were Union men, unfavorable to secession, and gave the President-elect a somewhat one-sided picture of what was transpiring. Presumably this was the case with other Republican leaders.

In the late summer, fortified by a letter from John Minor Botts, a Virginia Unionist and former Whig, Lincoln wrote that this communication "contains one of the many assurances I receive from the South that in no probable event will there be any very formidable effort to break up the Union." In January, Lincoln wrote Seward that, "Now we are told in advance, the government shall be broken up, unless we surrender to those we have beaten, before we take the offices. In this they are either attempting to play upon us, or they are in dead earnest." On the day that letter was written the seven, original Confederate states had elected conventions and the last seceded on the 28th of the same month. On July 4, 1861, after Ft. Sumter had been fired upon, after the lower border states had seceded, and after the Confederate capital had been moved to Richmond, Lincoln stated in his message to Congress that "It may well be questioned whether there is, to-day, a majority of the legally qualified voters of any State, except perhaps South Carolina, in favor of disunion."[3]

Thus Lincoln faced decision-making lacking the kind of facts and the kind of understanding upon which political decisions are made in ordinary circumstances. He lacked an essential means for harmonizing differences—party machinery extending to the disaffected region. Furthermore, his constituents who would be asked to give up the most in any compromise, the radicals, were even less well informed and even more than Lincoln the prisoners of fantastic misreadings of Southern intentions and Southern probabilities. The notion that secession would be self-defeating, that separation would leave the South helpless before slave insurrection was widespread among the more radical Northerners. Stephen A. Hurlbut, who should have known better, having been born in South Carolina and having for that reason acted as Lincoln's confidential agent at Charleston before Sumter was fired upon, wrote that:

> All parties in this State are rapidly merging into a strong [,] declared [,] energetic sentiment of resistance to the bitter end of the dogma of secession & separate Government and nothing but the baptism of blood through servile insurrection with which the seceding States are about to pass will restore any sympathy to North & South. Concession or the pretence of concession is simply folly.

A northern Illinois newspaper ingeniously blended two ways in which secession would defeat itself:

> The New York Herald estimates that it will cost each white citizen of South Carolina about $16 to commence an independent government, and hence bankruptcy would immediately follow secession. This would not be all: the slaves would rise up and assert their independence, and the complete annihilation of the whites in that State would be the result of their folly.

For some, the moral issue had so monopolized center stage that the Constitution and the Union had been shoved out of the limelight. They were willing to see the "erring sisters depart in peace."[4]

Any compromise which would have had any chance of bringing the departing states back into the Union (if such a chance existed at all) would have dissolved the Republican party. The suggestions for compromise, which were legion, all assumed that slavery would be permanent in the South. All yielded something in the matter of slavery in the territories, either a surrender to popular sovereignty at the least or to a geographic division of the territories. These proposals did not contemplate chopping off some peripheral or secondary part of Republican doctrine but aimed at its jugular vein. General Scott prepared a letter of advice for the incoming administration which outlined the four options from which he believed the administration had to choose.[5] These in abbreviated form were:

(1) To form a Union party and compromise.
(2) To blockade the South.

(3) To conquer the seceded states.

(4) To allow the seceded states to withdraw in peace.

Scott understood, as Lincoln understood, that compromise involved the end of the Republican party. The only concessions demanded (not by the secessionists but by the compromisers) related to the one distinctive characteristic of the Republican party—its anti-slavery character. The party of the moral issue was asked to bury the moral issue forever. This was to be the price of Union.

To William Kellogg, congressman from the Peoria district, member of the House Committee of Thirty-Three, and suspected of "caving," Lincoln wrote that "The instant you do [compromise on the extension of slavery], they have us under again; all our labor is lost, and sooner or later must be done over. . . . The tug has to come & better now than later." To his wavering, ex-Whig friend, Lincoln had condensed what he himself had said to a gathering of Republicans in Chicago on March 1, 1859:

> If we, the Republicans of this State, had made Judge Douglas our candidate for the Senate of the United States last year and had elected him, there would today be no Republican party in this Union. I believed that the principles around which we have rallied and organized that party would live; they will live under all circumstances, while we will die. They would reproduce another party in the future. But in the meantime all the labor that has been done to build up the present Republican party would be entirely lost, and perhaps twenty years of time, before we would again have formed around that principle. . . .[6]

Assuming that some of the context of the earlier and fuller statement remained unrepeated but understood in the terse communication to Kellogg, Lincoln's position was that concession to the South meant abandonment of principle and of party. If concessions should be made, it would not prevent clash on the slavery question: clash was inevitable. He had already thought out the implications of compromise in the situation within the party in 1858 and 1859 and applied the conclusions to the secession threat of 1860. The moral issue was permanent. It could not be disregarded safely. It would operate through a political party of necessity, if not in 1860, later. If the Republican party were destroyed, as Lincoln had said at the Cooper Union, it would reappear and at the end of the full circle, the country would be back at a crisis again. "The tug has to come. . . ."

In a sense, this was Lincoln's greatest moment. Unprepared by experience, uncertain of a large section of his country, and unsympathetic to the impatience of his followers whose inflexibility on the moral issue restricted his politicianship, Lincoln recognized the choice which confronted him at this juncture as between peace in his time or meeting the issue in his term of office. By taking the road of compromise, he could have sought the quiet term of a Fillmore after the Compromise of 1850 and a personal administration like that of Tyler in 1841–45. Instead, he chose to face the issue to some sort of conclusion. Not yet in office, he had been compelled to make one of the most important choices any President had ever made. No matter what "caving" took place among his cohorts—and a tendency to yield appeared among them—no compromise had any chance of acceptance in the face of his negative.[7] Lincoln elected to face the issue.

This begs the question of whether or not the Ultra men of the South would have compromised and returned to the Union had the Republicans accepted their party's destruction as the price of Union. It was irrelevant to Lincoln's decision for it is quite clear that he thought the South less rather than more intransigent and unyielding. There was no alternative of presenting a compromise for the political advantage of having the secessionists reject it, for Lincoln was not sure that they would reject it.

The tendency toward compromise was strongest among those whose inclinations had been to discount the slavery issue in 1858 and 1859. When Kansas had been saved, they had sought to dilute the slavery issue which lacked any urgent, concrete application. They had been fusionists or followers of popular sovereignty rather than favorable to the commitment of the party to the full moral issue of slavery. Unimportant because it was obscured by the onrush of events, it was nevertheless true that the fight to commit the party to the moral issue was won finally in the winter of 1860–61 when Lincoln's veto of compromise proposals killed them.

The length Lincoln himself had moved in appreciating the value of the moral issue in the equation—the Constitution and putting slavery in the course of ultimate extinction—was best understood by those who recalled that in 1854, Lincoln had said, "Much as I hate slavery, I would consent to the extension of it rather than see the Union dissolved, just as I would consent to any *great* evil, to avoid a *greater* one."[8] Of course, Lincoln could not have suspected that the "tug" would be so severe. Had its full implications in social upheaval, casualties, and tears been known to him, perhaps his choice might have been different. The word "tug" implied that his confidence in Union sentiment in the South gave him a very minimal notion of the nature of the "tug."

When choices on the slavery issue arose next, they were glossed over by the war, subordinated to the strategy of winning, and resolved more in terms of power than in terms of politics and persuasion. The moral issue would be submerged until some progress in solving the issue of the survival of the Union should be made. The plans for winning the war, the effort to hold the border states, the need for national unity would becloud and sometimes almost obscure the moral issue. But in December through February, as President-elect merely, Lincoln had faced a fairly clearly defined decision—to cling to or to abandon the moral issue in politics. Lincoln's answer was "I am inflexible."[9]

If the moral issue had been unimportant, if the continued, permanent existence of slavery in the South in an age when the Autocrat of All the Russians was liberating the serfs was acceptable, then the moral issue had no business in party politics and the Republican party should have settled for popular sovereignty or become a fusion of the opposition in 1858 and 1860, or, at the very brink of disaster in 1860–61, retrieved its mistakes (for which Lincoln must bear much responsibility) by compromise and adjustment. Then slavery would have become untouchable. As it was, Southern inflexibility, Southern last ditch defense of an institution adjudged immoral by most Americans and by world opinion met a hard inflexibility of moral purpose and confidence in moral progress, even if that moral purpose was imprecise and diluted in the hands of politicians who had "due regard for its actual existence . . . and the difficulties of getting rid of it in any satisfactory way and to all the constitutional obligations thrown about it."[10]

Lincoln's party, left in control of the expiring Thirty-Sixth Congress by the withdrawal of the representatives of the Confederate states, had been formally conciliatory. Three new territories had been created without any mention of slavery in the acts organizing these remote regions.[11] This retreat in the very area of Lincoln's firmness had been a safe concession since the Republicans would control the patronage in the newly created territories. They would be not only safe for freedom but also safe for the Republican party.

More reassuring to the South, yet less unitedly granted, was the proposed Thirteenth Amendment which spelled out and made perpetual the common understanding that the federal government might not interfere with slavery in the states where it existed. The amendment passed the Senate by a bare two-thirds majority with a dozen Republicans voting in opposition. The Republicans of the House were also divided. They rejected the amendment once but reconsidered and the amendment barely obtained the necessary majority. William P. Kellogg was the only Illinois Republican to support it. A reminder that it was Republican doctrine that Congress had no power to interfere with slavery in the states and that the Republican party had no disposition to do so was necessary to win enough votes to carry it. The words used were Lincoln's, both in the past and on the morrow in his inaugural address.[12] Grudging concession that this was, it was one that could be withheld by the Republican states (as it was, in fact) should the Union not be restored. The die-hard resistance to it by so many Republicans diluted its effect as a peace offering.

On March 4, Lincoln was duly inaugurated in spite of vague fears that Southerners would attempt to prevent his taking office. His inaugural address was intended to be firm on the maintenance of the Union and conciliatory on the matter of slavery. It proved not quite successful on either score. It was criticized by the most ardent peace men on the first count and by ardent antislavery people on the second count.

Lincoln and his cabinet, laboring often at cross-purposes, were handicapped in the secession crisis by the confusion unavoidable in a near complete change of government personnel usual at a time of thorough "to the victor belongs the spoils" philosophy. Self-appointed Union-savers both within and without official circles pursued varied and often contradictory plans. An overall policy of firmness against recognition of secession, tempered with a forebearance calculated to keep the border states within the Union, called for arresting the transfer of federal property into Confederate hands. The policy failed because the skeins of federal authority became tangled and because of the exuberant impatience of the South Carolinians.

The experiment of seeking a solution to the moral question of slavery through the normal channels of politics was brought to a sudden and final halt on April 12, when the new President had been in office barely five weeks. With the Confederate attack on Fort Sumter, the method became one of power—fire power, dollar power, horse power, man power and will power. It instantly dawned upon thoughtful people that this was so, that the moral issue would be solved somehow as part of the outcome of the war.

Orville H. Browning, to become a United States Senator after the tragic death of Douglas, wrote a beautiful letter of encouragement to his friend Lincoln immediately after Sumter in which he said:[13]

> I think I have a clear perception of the ultimate destruction of the cotton States. They have invited their doom. They can never

be again what they have once been. God is entering into judgment with them. He is dealing with *them* and will deal with the colored race also.

A thousand other patriots rushed to pen and paper to propose plans for saving the Union and administering chastisement to rebels. Hiram Sears, who described himself as a conservative hitherto, sent his neighbor, Senator Trumbull, one such plan. The second step of a detailed program called for the confiscation of all slave property held by rebels.[14] The South had brought onto itself the loss of what it most cherished by leaving the Union and attacking Fort Sumter. No outcome of the war would be satisfactory unless slavery, the cause of all the nation's tribulation, were ended. The North had no responsibility to protect slavery since the South had dissolved the constitutional bonds under which it had been sheltered. The necessity of using the political method of persuasion had passed; the possibility of using the method of power was dawning.

Thus, all of the political labor lavished by the war President on emancipation in the tedious four years to come was but postscript to the problem we have been considering. The supreme politician of the moral question had always labored under constraint of the Constitution and the necessity of obtaining consent. Now it was becoming merely a question of timing the exercise of power for maximum effectiveness. This was a matter of great political delicacy. But it was a different question from that which Lincoln had pondered deeply since 1854.

War, itself not notably moral, proved to be the essential instrument for the destruction of slavery. How early Lincoln was convinced that this was true is not known but in July of 1862, he told a delegation of border state congressmen that "If the war continue long, as it must, if the object be not sooner attained, the institution in your States will be extinguished by mere friction and abrasion—by the mere incidents of war."[15] Not only was the abrasion of war eroding slavery but the eagerness of political generals threatened to seize the initiative from the President in using the levers of power against it. Lincoln, although he reversed Generals Frémont and Hunter, was not opposed to emancipation. Quite the opposite was true. He sought to emancipate by persuading the border slave states to perform this necessary step in the one clearly constitutional way—by doing it themselves.

Lincoln's efforts along this line began in the fall of 1861 in Delaware.[16] In the face of rising sentiment for abolition by the exercise of congressional or presidential power, Lincoln asked Congress for a resolution committing it to support state emancipation with federal funds. He justified the measure as one which would deprive the South of hope of victory. Initiation of gradual emancipation by the border slave states would deprive the Confederacy of the hope that they would ever join it. The offer was not limited to the border states, however, and it is clear that Lincoln hoped that seceded states might find in this offer a way back into the Union once hope for independence was dead.[17]

He justified the constitutionality of the proposal on the basis that it did not interfere with the institution of slavery within the state. The states were free to decide for themselves. The federal government was merely extending an offer of assistance should they so decide. The expenditure of money was justified by the assumption that it would shorten the war.

Lincoln's suggested plan of emancipation involved compensation for owners, gradualism, and colonization, all of which had figured in his notions of what should be done about slavery from the time that he had proposed abolition in the District of Columbia when he had been a congressman. The process would be evolutionary rather than sudden. The plan contemplated permitting the time necessary so that "the two races could gradually live themselves out of their old relation to each other, and both come out better prepared for the new."[18] The change should take place with the least social and economic shock.

Lincoln's was a politician's plan. It combined the political best he could get accepted (or thought he could get accepted) with the moral "what was right." It would contribute to the winning of the war but it relied on satisfying the interests and desires of large blocks of voters. Emancipation would be actual and not prospective as in the Confiscation Act, thus satisfying (he hoped) the abolitionists. It would be gradual and compensated, making it palatable to the regions in which the plan would operate. Colonization would make it acceptable to Northern conservatives who feared an inundation of the North by newly emancipated Negroes.

Finally, emancipation would be produced by consent even if this were reluctantly given and obtained largely by the recognition of its necessity. As Lincoln's notions of the moral issue had been formed and hardened, they had always been equated with a respect for the law and the Constitution. The end he sought was moral; the method he would use political, based upon persuasion and the vote. He had never whittled down his understanding of the Constitution to fit the moral imperative. His plan fit the requirement which he had always demanded—the requirement of combining the moral end with the constitutional means. His plan, however, increasingly was thrown into competition with some method of emancipation which would rest upon a pure power basis—military, congressional or presidential exercise of the vague and elastic war power.

We know that the Emancipation Proclamation came as a result of the failure of the border states to make a timely response to this proposal. Lincoln, however, persisted. He submitted to the last session of the Thirty-Seventh Congress a proposal for three constitutional amendments by which emancipation would be compensated, extended in time up to 1900, loyal owners of slaves "who shall have enjoyed actual freedom by the chances of war" were to be paid for them, and colonization by Congress was authorized.[19]

The plan represented a return to consent as the basis for the most important national decision of generations. Lincoln, always the politician by preference, even in the midst of war and the most extensive employment of sheer power as a means of governance, longed to establish the new moral order on the firm basis of politics and consensus. The means should be worthy of a noble choice. It was much too late, however. The regulations and rules and traditions which hem in and surround those who govern in a government of law had been weakened and stretched and often suspended before the demands of necessity. Success had been glorified and failure execrated. Means had become unimportant. Lincoln's plan, accordingly, was weak, indirect, costly, and slow—all normal attributes of the political process. A large section of the public had no patience to wait for peacetime methods or any desire to obtain consent from rebels. The times were revolutionary, a vision grasped by the radicals but never fully understood by Lincoln.

1. David M. Potter, *Lincoln and His Party in the Secession Crisis* (New Haven: Yale University Press, 1942), pp. 9–12.

2. *Collected Works,* IV, 146, Springfield, Nov. 30, 1860; 160, Springfield, Dec. 22, 1860.

3. *Ibid.,* p. 95, Springfield, Aug. 15, 1860, John B. Fry; 172, Springfield, Jan. 11, 1861, W. H. Seward; Potter, *Secession Crisis,* p. 46; *Collected Works,* IV, 437.

4. Washburne MSS, Belvidere, Dec. 18, 1860, S. A. Hurlbut; *Bureau County Republican,* Nov. 15, 1860. One is reminded of the many times that the American public prior to 1939 was informed that Nazi Germany could not fight a war because it did not have the money; Dec. 6, 1860. For a comprehensive view of the same problem, see Potter, *Secession Crisis,* pp. 52–3.

5. Potter, *Secession Crisis,* pp. 92–111; RTL Nos. 7691–2, Washington, Mar. 3, 1861, Scott to Seward.

6. *Collected Works,* IV, 150, Springfield, Dec. 11, 1860; III, 367. Approximately the same statement appeared in notes used on Lincoln's Ohio tour of the same year. See p. 434.

7. Potter, *Secession Crisis,* pp. 69–72, 92–4.

8. *Collected Works,* II, 247–83.

9. *Ibid.,* IV, 183, Springfield, Feb. 1, 1861, W. H. Seward.

10. See above, p. 139.

11. *Congressional Globe,* 36th Congress, 2nd Session, Part 2, App., pp. 326–8, 337–8, 346–8.

12. *Ibid.,* p. 1403. Republicans who voted against the amendment were: Bingham, Chandler, Clark, Doolittle, Durkee, Foot, King, Sumner, Trumbull, Wade, Wilkinson, and Wilson; 1283–5.

13. RTL Nos. 9190–1, Quincy, Apr. 18, 1861, O. H. Browning.

14. Lyman Trumbull Photostats (Illinois History Survey), Elsah (Illinois), July 18, 1861, Hiram Sears.

15. *Collected Works,* V, 318 (July 12, 1862).

16. *Collected Works,* V, 29–30, dated tentatively as Nov. 26, 1861.

17. *Collected Works,* V, 144–6.

18. *Ibid.,* VI, 365.

19. Isaac N. Arnold, *The History of Abraham Lincoln and the Overthrow of Slavery* (Chicago: Clarke & Co., 1866), pp. 283–4; Roy P. Basler, editor, *Abraham Lincoln: His Speeches and Writings* (Cleveland: The World Publishing Company, 1946), pp. 679–80.

Bibliography

Public Documents

State of Illinois. *House Journal.* Fifteenth General Assembly.

State of Illinois. *House Journal.* Nineteenth General Assembly.

State of Illinois. *House Journal.* Twentieth General Assembly.

State of Illinois. *House Journal.* Twenty-first General Assembly.

U.S. Bureau of the Census. *Seventh Census of the United States.*

U.S. Bureau of the Census. *Eighth Census of the United States:* 1860. Population.

U.S. Bureau of the Census. *Eighth Census of the United States:* 1860. Preliminary Report.

U.S. *Congressional Globe.* Thirtieth Congress.

U.S. *Congressional Globe.* Thirty-fourth Congress.

Books

Angle, Paul M. *Created Equal? The Complete Lincoln-Douglas Debates of 1858.* Chicago: University of Chicago Press, 1958.

.... (ed.). *Herndon's Life of Lincoln.* New York: Albert and Charles Boni, 1936.

Annual Report of the American Historical Association, 1902. Vol. 2.

Arnold, Isaac N. *The History of Abraham Lincoln and the Overthrow of Slavery.* Chicago: Clarke & Co., 1866.

Basler, Roy P. (ed.). *Abraham Lincoln: His Speeches and Writings.* Cleveland: The World Publishing Company, 1946.

.... (ed.). *The Collected Works of Abraham Lincoln.* New Brunswick: Rutgers University Press, 1953.

Beveridge, Albert J. *Abraham Lincoln 1809–1858.* Boston: Houghton-Mifflin Co., 1928.

Bibliography

Current, Richard N. *The Lincoln Nobody Knows.* New York: McGraw Hill Book Company, Inc., 1958.

Fehrenbacher, Don E. *Prelude to Greatness, Lincoln in the 1850's.* Stanford: Stanford University Press, 1962.

Fergus, Robert (ed.). "Chicago River-and-Harbor Convention," *Chicago Historical Series,* VI, no. 18. Chicago: Fergus Printing Co., 1882.

Ford, Thomas. *A History of Illinois.* Chicago: S. C. Griggs & Co., 1854.

Gates, P. W. *The Illinois Central Railroad and Its Colonization Work.* Vol. XLII of the *Harvard Economic Series.* Cambridge: Harvard University Press, 1934.

Hertz, Emmanuel. *The Hidden Lincoln.* New York: Blue Ribbon Books, 1940.

Milton, George Fort. *Eve of Conflict: Stephen A. Douglas and the Needless War.* Boston: Houghton Mifflin Co., 1934.

Nichols, Roy Franklin. *The Disruption of American Democracy.* New York: The Macmillan Company, 1948.

Nicolay, J. G., and Hay, John (eds.). *Abraham Lincoln, Complete Works.* New York: The Century Company, 1894.

Papers in Illinois History and Transactions for the Year 1942. Springfield: Illinois State Historical Society, 1944.

Pease, T. C., and Randall, J. G. (eds.). *The Diary of Orville Hickman Browning.* Vol. XX of *Illinois Historical Collections.* Springfield: Ill. State Historical Library, 1925.

A Political Text-Book for 1860. New York: Tribune Press, 1860.

Potter, David M. *Lincoln and his Party in the Secession Crisis.* New Haven: Yale University Press, 1942.

Pratt, Harry E. (ed.). *Illinois as Lincoln Knew It. A Boston Reporter's Record of a Trip in 1847.* Springfield: Abraham Lincoln Association, 1938.

.... *Lincoln 1840–1846.* Springfield: Abraham Lincoln Association, 1939.

Quaife, Milo Milton (ed.). *The Diary of James K. Polk.* Chicago: A. C. McClurg & Co., 1910.

Riddle, Donald W. *Congressman Abraham Lincoln.* Urbana: University of Illinois Press, 1957.

Thomas, Benjamin P. *Abraham Lincoln, A Biography.* New York: Alfred A. Knopf, 1952.

.... *Lincoln 1847–1853.* Springfield: Abraham Lincoln Association, 1936.

McLean County Historical Society, Transactions of, Vol. III. Bloomington, Ill., 1899–.

Wiltse, Charles M. *John C. Calhoun: Sectionalist, 1840–1850.* Indianapolis: The Bobbs-Merrill Company, Inc., 1951.

Articles

Fehrenbacher, Don E. "The Origins and Purpose of Lincoln's 'House Divided' Speech," *Mississippi Valley Historical Review,* Vol. XLVI, No. 4 (March, 1960), 637–641.

Palmer, George Thomas. "A Collection of Letters from Lyman Trumbull to John M. Palmer," *Journal of the Illinois State Historical Society,* Vol. XVI (April-July, 1923).

Unpublished Material

James C. Allen MS. Privately held.
American Home Missionary Society MSS. Library of the Chicago Theological Seminary.
Mason Brayman MSS. Library of the Chicago Historical Society.
Sidney Breese MSS. Illinois State Historical Library.
John D. Caton MSS. Library of Congress.
Salmon P. Chase MSS. Library of Congress.
A. C. Cole. Unpublished Election Notes. Illinois History Survey.
Stephen A. Douglas MSS. University of Chicago Library.
Robert Todd Lincoln Papers. Microfilm of papers in Library of Congress.
John A. McClernand MSS. Illinois State Historical Library.
John M. Palmer MSS. Illinois State Historical Library.
Lyman Trumbull MSS. Library of Congress.
Lyman Trumbull Papers. Illinois State Historical Library.
Lyman Trumbull Photostats. Illinois History Survey.
Wallace-Dickey MSS. Illinois State Historical Library.
Elihu B. Washburne MSS. Library of Congress.
Richard Yates MSS. Illinois State Historical Library.

Newspapers

Alton Courier
Alton Telegraph and Review
Bureau County Republican
Chicago Daily Journal
Chicago Democrat
Chicago Democratic Press
Chicago Times
Free West (Chicago)
Galena Gazette
Galesburg Democrat
National Era (Washington, D.C.)
National Intelligencer
New York Tribune
Northwestern Gazette (Galena)

Bibliography

Olney Times
Peoria Press
Philadelphia North American
Quincy Whig
Rock Island Advertiser
Sangamo Journal (also *Illinois Journal,* Springfield)
Scioto Gazette (Ohio)
State Register (Springfield)
Watchman of the Prairies (Chicago)
Western Citizen (Chicago)

Index

Index

SPO, CARSON CITY, NEVADA, 1970